Language and Empiricism

Also by Siobhan Chapman

ACCENT IN CONTEXT

KEY IDEAS IN LINGUISTICS AND THE PHILOSOPHY OF LANGUAGE
(co-edited with Christopher Routledge)

KEY THINKERS IN LINGUISTICS AND THE PHILOSOPHY OF LANGUAGE
(co-edited with Christopher Routledge)

PAUL GRICE, Philosopher and Linguist

PHILOSOPHY FOR LINGUISTS

THINKING ABOUT LANGUAGE: Theories of English

Language and Empiricism
After the Vienna Circle

Siobhan Chapman
*Senior Lecturer in English Language,
University of Liverpool*

 Arts & Humanities Research Council

© Siobhan Chapman 2008

All rights reserved. No reproduction, copy or transmission of this publication may be made without written permission.

No paragraph of this publication may be reproduced, copied or transmitted save with written permission or in accordance with the provisions of the Copyright, Designs and Patents Act 1988, or under the terms of any licence permitting limited copying issued by the Copyright Licensing Agency, 90 Tottenham Court Road, London W1T 4LP.

Any person who does any unauthorised act in relation to this publication may be liable to criminal prosecution and civil claims for damages.

The author has asserted her right to be identified as the author of this work in accordance with the Copyright, Designs and Patents Act 1988.

First published 2008 by
PALGRAVE MACMILLAN
Houndmills, Basingstoke, Hampshire RG21 6XS and
175 Fifth Avenue, New York, N.Y. 10010
Companies and representatives throughout the world

PALGRAVE MACMILLAN is the global academic imprint of the Palgrave Macmillan division of St. Martin's Press, LLC and of Palgrave Macmillan Ltd. Macmillan® is a registered trademark in the United States, United Kingdom and other countries. Palgrave is a registered trademark in the European Union and other countries.

ISBN-13: 978–0–230–52476–7   hardback
ISBN-10: 0–230–52476–1   hardback

This book is printed on paper suitable for recycling and made from fully managed and sustained forest sources. Logging, pulping and manufacturing processes are expected to conform to the environmental regulations of the country of origin.

A catalogue record for this book is available from the British Library.

A catalog record for this book is available from the Library of Congress.

10 9 8 7 6 5 4 3 2 1
17 16 15 14 13 12 11 10 09 08

Printed and bound in Great Britain by
CPI Antony Rowe, Chippenham and Eastbourne

Contents

Introduction	1
1 The Vienna Circle	7
2 Falsification and Scientific Method	28
3 Holism	49
4 Ordinary Language Philosophy	68
5 Speech Acts and Implicatures	88
6 Oslo Philosophy	108
7 Interpretation and Preciseness	127
8 Empiricism in Linguistics	152
References	175
Index	186

Introduction

This book is about different attitudes to empiricism in the study of language. It is the product of two apparently unrelated ideas that I have held for some time, voiced on occasion, but had not until recently explored in much detail. The first is that the logical positivism of the Vienna Circle had an impact on the development of present-day linguistics that has not generally been fully recognized. I had a hunch that this impact came about largely indirectly, as a result of adverse reactions to the Vienna Circle from philosophers of language who were more or less contemporary with it. The second idea, and one that is perhaps more widely held, is that disagreements in recent linguistics over the role and nature of data are in many cases wrongly focussed and even unnecessary. Linguists from different traditions are not looking at a single phenomenon and choosing radically different types of data by which to investigate it; they are simply investigating different subjects.

These two ideas started to link together when I came across the work of the Norwegian philosopher Arne Naess. I was already familiar with J. L. Austin's reaction against logical positivism, and his advocacy of 'ordinary language philosophy', which proceeded from the painstaking analysis of the philosopher's own linguistic usage. But here was Naess, working at much the same time as Austin, similar in his dislike of the Vienna Circle's high-handed and dismissive attitude to ordinary language, yet pioneering the very different techniques of 'empirical semantics'. Austin worked in his armchair using contemplation and intuition. Naess worked on the streets of Oslo using clipboard and questionnaire. The similarities between Naess's now obscure work and mainstream, present-day disciplines such as sociolinguistics were too attractive to ignore. So too was the real-life debate that developed between Austin and Naess over methodology. Both ordinary language philosophy and the empirical semantics of the Oslo school of Philosophy developed, in part, as reactions to logical positivism. Each proposed a methodology for the empirical study of language, and each had striking resonances with the two sides in the debate about data in linguistics.

The different responses to the Vienna Circle from Austin and from Naess sent me back to the work of the Vienna Circle itself, and to some of the rest of the debate that it generated among its contemporaries. My main focus in this book, then, is not on present-day linguistics but on discussions of language that took place roughly during the half century from 1920 onwards. I am convinced that the story of these discussions should be of more than passing historical interest to linguists. Commenting in 1956 on what he saw as 'the revolution in philosophy' that had established analytic and linguistic methods as the dominant force, the British philosopher Gilbert Ryle wrote:

> The wise rambler occasionally, though not incessantly, looks back over his shoulder in order to link up the place he has got to with the country through which he has recently passed. It is equally wise for thinkers occasionally, though not incessantly, to try to fix in retrospect the courses that they have followed and the positions from which they have moved.
>
> (Ryle 1956: 1)

My aim in this book is to offer just such a retrospective view for those currently working in the various fields of present-day linguistics. The view is often obscured, in part at least, because some of the relevant courses run through the territory of philosophy. Work from philosophy has in many cases been highly influential on the development of linguistics, and in others can offer relevant insights and contributions to current debates in the subject, but is often not familiar, or not accessible, to linguists. There is no obvious reason why a linguist should decide to sit down with a copy of Russell and Whitehead's *Principia Mathematica*, for instance, or to hunt out some of the more arcane publications of a Norwegian ecologist who long ago visited Vienna. But these are just two examples of the unlikely sounding sources that have a lot to tell us about what people said about language during the twentieth century, and how they decided it should be studied. Austin is still widely known and read by linguists. But even in the case of Austin's work, there are aspects that are rarely discussed and a philosophical context that can shed a lot of light on what he was doing and why. Linguists know about speech acts. They do not necessarily know the story of how Austin pioneered a methodology that sparked something close to a national debate on the nature and the purpose of the study of language.

Austin's major impact on present-day linguistics has been felt and is acknowledged chiefly in pragmatics. Other branches, however, are more reticent on the subject of philosophical forebears, and here too Ryle's 50-year-old words prove relevant. In his overview of the revolution in philosophy, he outlined the reasons why attempts to trace the precedents of current thinking can be valuable. Switching metaphor, he suggested that: 'Like reports of Royal Commissions, they help the student to understand the contemporary scene – partly by disabusing him of fashionable misconceptions of what is going on' (ibid.). Ryle's analogy is undoubtedly grandiose, even self-aggrandizing, but the point he was making can nevertheless be carried over to the contemporary linguistic scene. Branches such as sociolinguistics and corpus linguistics rarely have much to say about early origins of the approaches they embody, other than in celebrating the contributions of individual pioneers of the disciplines themselves. Yet philosophers were saying remarkably similar things about the purpose and methodology of language study several decades before the acknowledged founding of these branches of linguistics. In drawing attention to possible philosophical precedents I do not intend to belittle the importance of these developments in linguistics, or to claim that what they are doing is in some way 'old hat'. Rather, my ambition is that identifying a philosophical pedigree for these approaches will afford them a position in the more general theoretical debate about language with which they have not always seemed fully to engage.

This book begins with a chapter on the intellectual context and the main doctrines of the Vienna Circle. This focusses on the notion of verification as a criterion for meaningfulness, and the implications of this for the Vienna Circle's views, both explicit and implicit, on language. These views were by no means the start of the philosophical link between language and empiricism. Discussions germane to the role of empiricism in language study can be traced back at least as far as the work of Aristotle, and were certainly prominent during the European Enlightenment. But the work of the Vienna Circle represents the highpoint of the revolution in philosophy that Ryle identified, a revolution that saw the analysis of concepts, and of the language in which those concepts are expressed, taking central philosophical place.

Perhaps as a result of the extremes to which it pushed the revolution, logical positivism generated enthusiasm and hostility in equal measure.

From the 1930s a lot was written about where the Vienna Circle was going wrong, and it is striking that these responses, almost all in one way or another, drew on the criticism that their ideas were unempirical. Chapter 2 begins the story of these reactions with the one that is probably best known in philosophy generally: Popper's rejection of verification and his account of scientific method based on falsification. For Popper, the inductive method of discovery on which verification was based could never afford certain knowledge, and therefore did not warrant the claims of empiricism that were made from it. Popper was not the first to identify problems of this type for induction; indeed by the middle of the 1930s such issues were already being addressed by members of the Vienna Circle themselves. But what Popper proposed was not a modification of induction to address these problems but a wholesale replacement of it by the deductive method. Scientific hypotheses need not be formed on the basis of empirical evidence but, however formed, must be amenable to successive testing against such evidence, always with the possibility that they might be falsified. Popper's rethinking of scientific method has been hugely influential in the natural sciences, where a version of falsificationism is now, more or less, canonical. By extension it has also been influential in those branches of linguistics that consider the study of language to be properly conducted as a natural science. Perhaps the most controversial of these has been Chomskyan linguistics. This has drawn, often implicitly, on Popperian notions of deduction and falsification. Popper's views have not been accepted with universal enthusiasm in the philosophy of science, however. They sparked a protracted debate in the middle of the twentieth century that revealed the contentious and possibly relative nature of terms such as 'scientific' and even 'empirical'.

Popper himself was outspokenly unconcerned with the philosophy of language. Others who raised objections to the work of the Vienna Circle concentrated more centrally on language, and proffered their own alternative ideas about how it should be studied and what philosophers should be saying about it. Chapter 3 is concerned with holistic approaches to language, associated particularly with W. V. O. Quine. Quine was convinced that, despite its claims to empiricism in other areas, the logical positivism of the Vienna Circle depended on sweeping, unempirical and unsustainable assumptions about language. Quine questioned the very existence of 'meaning' as a coherent autonomous concept, and hence the related notions of synonymity and analyticity on which verification depended. For Quine, the significance of the expressions of a language could only coherently be discussed and analysed as a whole, leading to his controversial principle of 'indeterminacy of translation'. Much of what Quine was saying about language was completely at odds with Noam Chomsky's emergent 'mentalist' approach. The lengthy written exchange between the two focussed on the nature of language itself and by extension the most appropriate means by which it should be studied and described.

The central part of this book, comprising Chapters 4, 5, 6 and 7, is concerned with the methods and some of the major works of Austin and of Naess, and with a comparison between the two thinkers. This comparison is striking for the similarities in their point of departure from the Vienna Circle, the extent to which their separate work converged on an insistence that philosophy should be informed by the empirical study of language, and the ferocity with which they disagreed about how such empirical study should be conducted. Austin's methodology was fundamentally introspective, subjective and analytic. Naess's was experimental and aspired to objectivity and scientific rigour.

The best-known results of Austin's methodology were the foundations he laid for the theory of speech acts. Together with Paul Grice's theory of conversational implicature, speech act theory has been hugely influential in linguistics, especially in the establishment of pragmatics as a discipline specifically concerned with meaning in use. Both theories have clearly identifiable roots in ordinary language philosophy but both also rely on some abstract and even questionably empirical concepts, particularly the distinction between 'literal' or 'core' and 'speaker' or 'contextual' meaning. Such concepts were highly controversial among contemporary philosophers of language, a controversy which has been inherited by present-day pragmaticists.

Naess, on the other hand, eschewed any notion of literal or context-independent meaning as unempirical. He insisted that descriptive linguistic categories, such as 'synonymity' and 'analyticity' must be motivated by what the researcher could find from objective investigations of language use and as a result that they could be applied only provisionally and relatively. They were always a matter of degree rather than absolutes, dependent on specifics of speaker, hearer and context. His sustained work on the twin concepts of interpretation and preciseness emerged against this background and developed into a practical, even prescriptive, account of the language appropriate for philosophical discussion, as well as of justifiable motivations and methods for studying language use.

The final chapter is concerned with attitudes to empiricism, and with a wide and surprisingly disparate range of claims to empirical credentials, in recent linguistics. It is far from being a comprehensive historical survey or an inclusive catalogue of current forms of linguistic research. Rather it focuses on a few branches of linguistics, principally sociolinguistics and corpus linguistics, which suggest particular resonances with the philosophical work reviewed in the rest of the book. Nowadays almost all linguists agree that their subject should be studied empirically, but they differ vehemently and sometimes vituperatively on the question of how this should be done. Linguistics is prey to the generic problems of empiricism; problems exemplified by just how many different ways of conceiving empiricism have developed even since the 1920s. But there are further problems that are perhaps peculiar to linguistics; it accommodates a wide range of contemporary opinions about what actually constitutes the subject matter and hence the appropriate data for empirical study. Language is variously, cogently and persuasively conceived in different branches of linguistics as a mental structure, as a means of social identification and interaction, and as a method of communication, among perhaps many other definitions.

The debate over the opposing merits of 'intuitive' and 'real life' data has been one of the most significant in linguistics in recent decades. It centres on the issue of whether data drawn from intuition are adequate and appropriate for linguistics, or whether data should be collected from sources external to the linguist. The terms of the debate are remarkably similar to those of the disagreement over method between Austin and Naess in the 1950s. But the differences between Austin and Naess over data should not overshadow their shared belief that the study of language must be based on evidence of how it is actually used; they each said things remarkably similar to what has been said recently in areas of linguistics that profess to be concerned with 'real life' language use. In particular, in this final chapter I will consider the case for Austin and Naess to be seen as philosophical forebears of corpus linguistics.

The present debate about intuitive as opposed to occurring data is sustained by the very different assumptions about the nature of language held by linguists. The mid-twentieth-century debate over scientific method, triggered by reactions to the Vienna Circle, demonstrated that what counts as empirical is relative to disciplines, historical periods and scientific subcultures. So, too, in linguistics, the definitions of language itself are open to various interpretations. Different types of linguists are concerned with different aspects of language, perhaps sometimes even with different subject matters. What counts as empirical in relation to these different forms of study is therefore bound to differ. The empirical in linguistics is not a given but a continually changing construction of its various subcultures. These subcultures need not be seen as symptomatic of a subject in disarray, but as a reflection of the complex and multifaceted nature of human language itself.

1
The Vienna Circle

Philosophers are not generally known for being team players. Philosophical ideas may sometimes be attributed jointly to two or more thinkers, but it often turns out that these people disagreed on fundamental issues, or that they worked in separate countries or even separate centuries. John Locke and George Berkeley are both regarded as influential 'British Empiricists', yet much of Berkeley's major published work was dedicated to arguing against Locke (Berkeley 1710). Gottlob Frege and P. F. Strawson are credited with introducing the logical account of presupposition that is sometimes referred to as the 'Frege-Strawson account'. But Frege worked and wrote in late nineteenth-century Jena, Strawson in mid-twentieth-century Oxford (Frege 1892, Strawson 1950). Even when philosophers manage to coincide and apparently to agree, they are generally reluctant to admit that they form an identifiable group or collective. The widespread use of the term 'ordinary language philosophy' would seem to suggest that a particular approach, or school, predominated in Oxford in the years after the Second World War. But those who worked in Oxford at this time, and to whom the label has been applied, have been keen to deny that any such school even existed (see, for instance, Grice 1986: 50).

The Vienna Circle was unusual. It consisted of a large but identifiable group of philosophers who met regularly, collaborated on work of mutual interest, and largely agreed on their conclusions. They even acknowledged their group identity by coining the term 'The Vienna Circle', or 'Der Wiener Kreis', in the title of a collaborative manifesto (Carnap et al. 1929). There were, of course, differences of interest, of emphasis and even of opinion. But commentaries on the work of the Circle, both from members and from outside observers, have repeatedly emphasized the cooperation, collaboration and consensus that it generally exhibited. A. J. Ayer commented that when he visited Vienna in the early 1930s he found that the tenets for which it is still best known 'were not considered by the members of the Circle as open to question' (Ayer 1987: 26).

Also unusually among philosophical movements, the work of the Vienna Circle had fairly clearly demarcated start and end dates. Philosophy had, of course, been practised in Vienna for centuries, and during the early years of the twentieth century various informal meetings and discussion groups with broadly empirical and scientific interests had been formed. But the defining event was the appointment of Moritz Schlick to the chair in philosophy of the inductive sciences at the University of Vienna in 1922. Although never interested in being seen as the leader of a philosophical movement, Schlick was enthusiastic and charismatic, and naturally attracted a group of like-minded students and colleagues. This group, numbering about 20, became known unofficially as the 'Schlick Circle' and then more officially as the 'Vienna Circle'. The end of the Circle was abrupt, and was driven by political rather than intellectual events. Increasingly mistrusted and persecuted by the occupying power because of its perceived socialist leanings, the Vienna Circle was broken up in 1938 and many of its members forced into exile. Writing in 1950, Circle member Victor Kraft reminded his readers that their work 'has not been finished but was suddenly disrupted' (Kraft 1953: vii).

The reasons for the unusually collaborative and consensual nature of the Vienna Circle are less clear-cut than those for its formation and dissolution. Nevertheless some plausible explanations, both historical and academic, have been suggested. When Schlick arrived in Vienna, the Austrian tradition was for intellectual activity to take place in public. Ideas were developed not in private houses or in university rooms, as was the tradition in, for instance, Britain, but in the context of discussion groups and societies. Barry Smith has linked what he calls this 'characteristically Austrian predilection' to 'the culture of the coffee house' (Smith 1987: 35), and indeed the first meetings of the Schlick Circle were informal gatherings in cafés. David Edmonds and John Eidinow have made a similar connection, drawing attention to the 'intersecting cultural, social and academic circles' that formed themselves around the numerous cafés in early twentieth-century Vienna (Edmonds and Eidinow 2001: 58).

The members of the Vienna Circle were not just inhabitants of an unusually gregarious city. They were also predominantly scientists by training. Schlick had come to philosophy via physics, having studied in

Berlin under Max Planck. He was instrumental in the appointment of Rudolf Carnap as instructor in philosophy at the University of Vienna in 1926. Carnap had also begun his academic career in physics. In his intellectual autobiography he described how as a young physicist he found that his interests were in the theoretical, rather than the experimental, aspect of the discipline. His initial idea for a doctoral dissertation was rejected by the head of physics at the University of Jena with a recommendation that Carnap try the philosophy department. Carnap's chosen tutor in philosophy then recommended that he submit the proposal to the head of physics. Carnap ended up a philosopher rather than a physicist almost by accident; he stuck with the same tutor but chose a more clearly philosophical doctoral topic (Carnap 1963: 11). Among other members of the Vienna Circle, Friedrich Waismann and Hans Hahn both had backgrounds in mathematics. Otto Neurath had studied many disciplines, including mathematics, economics and statistics, as well as his primary subject of sociology. Scientists are used to collaborating and to working in teams. It is not implausible that the members of the Vienna Circle brought these habits with them to their philosophical discussions.

Given the backgrounds of its members, it is perhaps not surprising that the work of the Vienna Circle has had a strong influence on subsequent discussions of the philosophy of science, and of scientific method. But it also had a huge impact on the ways in which the study of language developed in twentieth-century philosophy. One thesis of this book is that, as a result, its influence has also been felt in the development of present-day linguistics. This would appear to be a less likely legacy for a group of scientifically minded philosophers. A linguist looking for discussions of language among the work of the Vienna Circle would certainly find it. Carnap, for instance, took a keen interest in language, and went on to write books with such apparently promising titles as *Introduction to Semantics* (Carnap 1946). But in fact Carnap was unenthusiastic, even dismissive, about natural language as a subject of study, as opposed to artificially constructed languages used in the exposition of logic and of scientific theories. For instance, another book with a title that might seem appealing to linguists, *The Logical Syntax of Language*, included the comment that 'In consequence of the unsystematic and logically imperfect structure of the natural word-languages (such as German or Latin), the statement of their formal rules of formation and transformation would be so complicated that it would hardly be feasible in practice' (Carnap 1937b: 2). This statement would be anathema to the present-day linguist. In the decades that followed the publication of this book, linguistics proceeded as if in direct defiance of Carnap's warning.

The impact of the Vienna Circle on linguistics cannot be traced, then, to anything that its members had to say on the subject of language itself. Rather, it stems from a very specific and technical claim that they agreed on about the nature of scientific knowledge, and from the implications of the key terms of that claim. The 'principle of verification', as it has become known, is the tenet most closely associated with the Vienna Circle. It is primarily about the security of knowledge. It certainly touches on language, but only because knowledge finds expression in language, so a clarification of what can be known relies on a clarification of what can be said. It is surprisingly difficult to track down a concise statement of the principle of verification by a member of the Vienna Circle. They wrote around the subject and wrote about the different issues involved, but seem not to have felt the need to produce a specific slogan. This task fell to their self-appointed publicist A. J. Ayer, who published *Language, Truth and Logic* in 1936 in a deliberate and successful attempt to introduce the ideas of the Vienna Circle to a larger audience. In the second edition of this book he reflected from a greater distance on the ideas that had so enthused him a decade earlier. In doing so, he summarized the principle of verification as claiming that 'a sentence had literal meaning if and only if the proposition it expressed was either analytic or empirically verifiable' (Ayer 1946: 7). This is an extraordinarily succinct statement of a complex and sophisticated philosophical position. It is sparse and deceptively simple looking, yet contains the main precepts of a major philosophical movement. It also contains clues as to why the philosophy of the Vienna Circle has had such an impact on the subsequent study of language, and why that impact was largely driven by a reaction against what the Circle's critics found in its dogmas.

The reasons why the principle of verification took the form it did, why it was the cornerstone of a philosophical movement and why Carnap said such harsh things about natural language, can all be traced to the major philosophical allegiances of the members of the Vienna Circle. They were, first and foremost, empirical in their philosophical outlook. This is perhaps not surprising for a group from predominantly scientific backgrounds; empiricism had long been the touchstone of scientific method and description. But in philosophy, empiricism had been beset by problems and counter-examples that had at times threatened to overwhelm it. In maintaining an empirical philosophical line the members of the Vienna Circle were not simply accepting, or proposing to live with these problems; they thought they had found a way to solve them.

Early in the twentieth century the problems for empiricism were well established and to some philosophers seemed insurmountable. The basic claims of empiricism have an enduring commonsense appeal: that our knowledge of the world around us is built up from our experiences of it, and that our confidence in this knowledge derives from the immediacy of our own experience. Empiricism offers a reassuringly 'real world' measure for distinguishing those beliefs that stand up to rational scrutiny and discussion. It enjoyed a particular heyday during the Enlightenment. John Locke, for instance, proposed to demonstrate 'how men, barely by the use of their natural faculties, may attain to all the knowledge they have, without the help of any innate impressions, and may arrive at certainty without any such original notions or principles' (Locke 1690: Book I, Chapter II: 1). For philosophers like Locke, empiricism offered a check on irrational beliefs, superstitions and, crucially, the need to posit the existence of innate ideas.

The problems for empiricism were aired in some Enlightenment responses to Locke, perhaps most fully by Immanuel Kant. Kant did not take issue with experience as an important, indeed a necessary, source of knowledge. But he argued that it was not sufficient to explain the full range of what human beings know. There were many types of knowledge that could not be explained simply by establishing the existence of relevant data in the world. In identifying this weakness in empiricism, Kant drew attention to knowledge that is *a priori*, as opposed to *a posteriori*: that seems to precede any experience of the world rather than to follow from it. He noticed that not just analytic, but also some types of synthetic, statements must be *a priori*. An example such as 'All bodies are extended' is analytic because the predicate does not offer anything more than part of the definition of the subject. We do not draw on experience of the world but simply on acquaintance with the language for knowledge of the truth of this example. Part of knowing the meaning of 'all bodies' is to know that 'extended' applies to it. There would appear to be a clear distinction between this type of example and synthetic statements. 'All bodies are heavy' is not necessarily true just because of the words it contains. To determine its truth value it is necessary to look beyond the language and to consult the evidence available in the world; our knowledge of this example is *a posteriori*. But Kant argued that the distinction between analytic and synthetic did not follow neatly along the same border as that between *a priori* and *a posteriori*. There is some knowledge which is expressed in synthetic statements but is independent of any experience of the world. Empiricism fails.

Knowledge that is synthetic but *a priori* is knowledge that relies on some human system for making sense of the world: some system that is not itself found in experience. Mathematical knowledge is a central example. Kant drew attention to the impossibility of ever independently 'proving' the statements of mathematics, because their truth depends on the unempirical rules of mathematics themselves. 'The assertion that 7 + 5 is equal to 12 is not an analytic proposition. For neither in the representation of 7, nor in that of 5, do I think the number 12' (Kant 1781: A164). The link between subject and predicate depends not just on their meanings but on the system that determines how they are combined. It is not possible to consult the facts of the world in this case without doing so through the lens of the very mathematical system that has produced the proposition in question. '7 + 5 = 12' is a synthetic statement, but our knowledge of it is *a priori*. Mathematics apparently has no place in an empirical system of knowledge: the very sort of system that, because of its importance in the sciences, might most be expected to need mathematics.

Empiricism was rescued from this plight by developments in logic around the turn of the twentieth century. These made possible the work of the Vienna Circle, together with all its implications for the study of language. The developments in question took place over several years, involved a number of theoreticians, and are formidable in their complexity and technicality. But they can be summarized in two main points. Firstly, logic became much more formalized than it had previously been, with the development of a symbolic language fully to express logical formulas and relations. Secondly, and as a result of this development, symbolic logic was shown to be adequate to express the propositions of mathematics; in other words, mathematics was reduced to logic. It is difficult to establish exactly who deserves the credit for these two developments. It is clear, however, that two events were especially significant: Frege's breakthroughs in his work on logic and mathematics and the publication of Russell and Whitehead's *Principia Mathematica*.

Gottlob Frege is celebrated in language study today mainly for his distinction between 'sense' and 'reference', but his development of a system of symbolic logic is of at least equal importance. He established the systems of quantifiers and variables characteristic of modern logic, systems that allow for logical statements that generalize over many particular instances. 'France is a republic', 'The Thames has many tributaries' and 'The Earth revolves around the Sun' have many obvious differences, but they can all be analysed, and shown to have structural properties in common, by expressing them in the formula of predicate logic 'Fx'. They are all of simple subject-predicate form, 'F' being the usual symbol to stand in for any predicate and 'x' for any subject. Michael Dummett has explained that 'the discovery of the mechanism which enabled this analysis to be given, and the realization of its significance, are due to Frege' (Dummett 1973: xiv).

As a student between 1910 and 1914, Rudolph Carnap attended Frege's classes in Jena. Frege's teaching was formal and, even to a class of three, devoid of interaction, but Carnap was impressed by his ideas, and in particular his claim 'that the new logic to which he had introduced us, could serve for the construction of the whole of mathematics' (Carnap 1963: 5). It is not clear from Carnap's account whether Frege did in fact substantiate this claim. The first published attempt to reduce mathematics to logic came in 1910 in *Principia Mathematica*. Russell himself later credited Frege with showing 'in detail how arithmetic could be deduced from pure logic, without the need for any fresh ideas or axioms' (Russell 1924: 32). Certainly, Russell and Whitehead borrowed notation from Frege, as well as from the Italian mathematician Peano. Their explicitly stated aim was similar to Frege's insight; they planned to construct a logical notation 'with a view to the perfectly precise expression, in its symbols, of mathematical propositions' (Russell and Whitehead 1910: 1). Carnap saw their achievement as a fuller development of what had impressed him in Frege's programme, and an inspiration to think of philosophical concepts and propositions in terms of symbolic logic (Carnap 1963: 11).

As Frege had shown, an entirely formal system for describing logical relations generalizes over individual statements. It does not offer a full account, let alone a full semantic representation, of any individual expression. It is a closed system, explaining relations between terms, but having nothing to say about how those terms, or the formulas that result from combining those terms, relate to anything outside the system. Russell and Whitehead explained how in logical formulas truth can be derived simply by combining propositions of known truth value, without any recourse to empirical evidence outside the system. Logical formulas are not about the world and cannot be assessed against any data. They are, in effect, tautologies; what they express are necessary truths within the system. Russell and Whitehead's success in applying this same framework to mathematics was the breakthrough that made the Vienna Circle's new form of empiricism possible. The statements of mathematics were capable of being expressed in terms that made them necessary truths. Contrary to Kant's conclusion, mathematics did not produce synthetic statements of which human beings had *a priori* knowledge. Mathematical statements were analytic after all, so the fact that knowledge of them could not be independently justified was no challenge to empiricism. If Russell and Whitehead set the agenda for the next phase in empiricist philosophy, they also offered something like a manifesto for the rejection of ordinary language from philosophical consideration. Their introduction contained a numbered list of reasons why symbolic notation was to be preferred to natural language, including the inexact nature of word meaning, the many purposes, irrelevant to logic, that language was adapted to serve and the frequent mismatch between grammatical and logical structure. The structure of ordinary language 'does not represent uniquely the relations between the ideas involved. Thus, "a whale is big" and "one is a number" both look alike, so that the eye gives no help to the imagination' (Russell and Whitehead 1910: 2).

The reinvigorated form of empiricism developed by the Vienna Circle depended heavily on logic and has sometimes been described as 'logical empiricism'. This seems to have been the description most favoured by Schlick himself. But an article published in 1931 and aimed at introducing these ideas to an uninitiated audience chose 'logical positivism'. The authors of this article described the term as 'perhaps the best among many poor ones' (Blumberg and Feigl 1931: 281–2), and it has in general proved the most tenacious. It associates the work of the Vienna Circle with positivism, an empirical tradition of the nineteenth century that valued knowledge derived scientifically and deplored metaphysics and superstition. The term 'logical positivism' came to be used by some as a term of opprobrium, and as such almost inevitably was overextended to apply to anything that smacked of hard-nosed scientific analysis at the expense of speculation and synthesis. Writing in 1959, A. J. Ayer commented wryly that those who included, for instance, Russell, Wittgenstein and even Austin in their definition of logical positivism were doing so because 'they wish to tar all their adversaries with a single brush' (Ayer 1959: 3). Nevertheless it remains a convenient shorthand for a particular approach to the nature of scientific knowledge and to the language in which that knowledge is expressed, and more generally for the philosophical approach of the Vienna Circle.

That approach was based on the application of the radical and logical new version of empiricism to the business of philosophy itself: to questions of how it should be done and of what philosophers could and could not legitimately say. Ayer's summary of verification, quoted earlier, is again useful here: 'a sentence had literal meaning if and only if the proposition it expressed was either analytic or empirically verifiable'. Sentences expressing analytic propositions were exempt from the usual requirements of empiricism because they were necessarily true, and, therefore, not dependent on contingencies in the world. Logical and mathematical statements could now be included in this category. Verification was to handle everything else: the vast body of statements expressing synthetic propositions offering descriptions of the world. According to the Vienna Circle only a subset of those statements that purported to describe the world were actually meaningful and, therefore, appropriate to scientific and philosophical discussion.

The claim that meaningful statements are those that can be verified, or subjected to an identifiable process of testing against experience, suggests a debt to Wittgenstein. The question of how influential Wittgenstein's ideas of this period were on the Vienna Circle has puzzled many commentators, even those who were themselves members of the Circle. It is remarkably similar in type and in controversy to the question of the extent of the influence of Wittgenstein's later work, his 'meaning is use' phase, on the development of ordinary language philosophy in post-war Oxford. In response to both questions there are those who assume that the influence was direct and decisive and others who argue that it was, at most, circumstantial. Certainly Wittgenstein's *Tractatus Logico-Philosophicus* was read carefully and admired at early meetings of the Vienna Circle. Wittgenstein, a native of the city, was in Vienna between 1925 and 1929 and was invited to attend meetings of the Circle. He chose instead to meet with just Schlick, Carnap and Waismann, who then conveyed news of what they had heard back to the full Circle. But after a time Wittgenstein broke off even this restricted contact, and personal relations with the Circle became strained, particularly with Carnap, whom Wittgenstein accused of publishing ideas taken from him without acknowledgement.

Wittgenstein was undoubtedly impressed and influenced by the work on logic of his former teacher Russell. But he did not share Russell's interest in mathematics. Rather, he was concerned with using logic as a way of modelling language. However, at this stage in his career Wittgenstein shared Russell and Whitehead's disdain for natural language. As Russell points out in his 'Introduction' to the first English translation of the *Tractatus*, no actual natural language was to provide the basis for Wittgenstein's study because natural language was necessarily messy and imprecise. Rather, 'Mr Wittgenstein is concerned with the conditions for a logically perfect language ... [because] the whole function of language is to have meaning, and it only fulfils this function in proportion as it approaches to the ideal language which we postulate' (Russell 1922: x). A rigorous logical analysis was to determine what was sayable, or possible, in a logically perfect language, and, therefore, to highlight what in everyday language was illegitimate, or meaningless. Famously, Wittgenstein urged silence in those areas where logically legitimate language was not possible: areas that included metaphysics, aesthetics and ethics.

The terminology involved in Wittgenstein's account of logically justified language is notoriously tricky, not least because of the process of translation from his German, and because he was himself neither always clear nor always consistent in his usage. In effect, every meaningful statement must be either a simple, atomic proposition or must be shown to be derived from the combination of simple propositions. Simple propositions are meaningful because they give us a picture or a model of reality. They comprise names for objects in the world and tell us something about the properties or relations of those objects. More complex statements are built up from logically permitted operations over simple propositions and derive meaning and truth value from those simple propositions. Negation and conjunction are two examples of such operations. In common with many members of the Vienna Circle, Wittgenstein came to philosophy from a background in the more applied sciences. He had trained as an aeronautical engineer in Manchester before moving to Cambridge in order to study under Bertrand Russell. Susan Sterrett has suggested a direct link between Wittgenstein's technical training and the central conception of the *Tractatus*. Aeronautics depended crucially on the construction of scale models to predict accurately the effects of wind and speed, and Sterrett argues that 'foundational works on the methodology of engineering scale models ... figured in writing the *Tractatus*', where Wittgenstein conceived of propositions as models, or pictures, of reality (Sterrett 2006: xix).

There are, perhaps, three main points in Wittgenstein's vastly ambitious, obscure and enigmatic programme in the *Tractatus* that would seem to have had an effect on logical positivism. First, he claimed that to determine truth or falsity we need to compare a proposition with the world: 'A proposition can be true or false only in virtue of being a picture of reality' (Wittgenstein 1922: 4.06). Second, Wittgenstein drew out the implications of *Principia Mathematica* that logic, including mathematics, is ultimately a closed system that can express only tautologies: 'all the propositions of logic say the same thing, to wit nothing' and 'The propositions of logic are tautologies' (Wittgenstein 1922: 5.43 and 6.1). And third, he concluded that whatever cannot be resolved to simple propositions made up of simple names is just meaningless. The vast class of meaningless sentences include those used in much traditional philosophical discussion, such as metaphysics. The statements of metaphysics, therefore, have no place in serious philosophical discussion, and the problems they apparently pose are mere pseudo-problems, which have arisen because philosophers have not paid sufficiently close attention to logic. The only real way to do philosophy is 'to say nothing except what can be said, i.e. propositions of natural science – i.e. something that has nothing to do with philosophy – and then, whenever someone else wanted to say something metaphysical, to demonstrate to him that he had failed to give a meaning to certain signs in his propositions' (Wittgenstein 1922: 6.53).

The status of the simple propositions that for Wittgenstein were the touchstone of meaning remained somewhat obscure in the *Tractatus*. Wittgenstein did not commit himself as to whether the aspects of reality they pictured must be capable of being empirically observed. Russell seemed to think not. In his 'Introduction' he pointed out that the 'simples' that made up atomic facts were not necessarily available to inspection. Rather, a simple was 'a logical necessity demanded by theory, like an electron' (Russell 1922: xiii). When the ideas of the *Tractatus* were taken on board at meetings of the Vienna Circle, however, a much more clearly empirical interpretation was given to the notion of a simple, or elementary proposition. Jakko Hintikka has pointed out that 'The members of the Vienna Circle interpreted the elementary propositions (*Elementarsätze*) of the *Tractatus* as speaking of the content of one's immediate experience' (Hintikka 1993: 28). Appeals to immediate experience bring with them all the complications associated with the status of that experience, in other words of the relationship between the sense data that verify a proposition and the possibility of reality that is in itself inaccessible but that is the cause of those sense data. Logical positivism might appear to commit its adherents to realism, which itself has dangerously metaphysical leanings; if all we ever have access to are our own individual sense perceptions it is dubiously legitimate to claim definite knowledge that the physical world exists. Perhaps not surprisingly, logically minded philosophers of the time were generally reluctant to take a stand on the existence of the real world. Bertrand Russell declared himself agnostic in 1924 on the debate between realism and idealism, arguing that to him the distinction was of no real interest because 'I hold that logic is what is fundamental in philosophy, and that schools should be characterized rather by their logic than by their metaphysic' (Russell 1924: 31). Schlick seems to have taken much the same view: 'The denial of the existence of a transcendent external world would be just as much a metaphysical statement as its affirmation. Hence the consistent empiricist does not deny the transcendent world, but shows that both its denial and affirmation are meaningless' (Schlick 1932: 107).

The question of what logical analysis revealed to be meaningless, apparently posed by Wittgenstein, was a major theme for Carnap. He approached it by means of a rigorous analysis of language, and of what its rules determined to be sayable. The languages he was concerned with were, of course, artificially constructed languages, such as might be appropriate for logical exposition. The very fact that all natural languages allowed the expression of vague and unverifiable pseudo-propositions meant that such languages were not suitable for serious philosophical purposes. Statements were meaningless, that is they expressed pseudo-propositions, if their content could not be reduced to simple propositions. In every case, this would be because there was something wrong with the language in which the statement was expressed. Carnap summed up the types of problem that could arise with a statement. A language consisted of a set of words and a series of rules as to how these words could combine. In other words it comprised a vocabulary and a syntax. These two aspects of a language were sufficient to explain the two ways in which a statement could fail to have meaning. 'There are two kinds of pseudo-statements: either they contain a word that is erroneously believed to have meaning, or the constituent words are meaningful, yet are put together in a counter-syntactical way, so that they do not yield a meaningful statement' (Carnap 1932: 61).

The criteria of meaning outlined by Wittgenstein and given, more formally, syntactic and empirical expression by Carnap had far-reaching implications for philosophy. The Vienna Circle was not coy about these. In fact, they publicized their work as a new departure that would do away with many of the problems that had traditionally vexed philosophers by showing them to be expressed in meaningless statements and therefore not worthy of serious consideration. In 1929 Carnap, Hahn and Neurath published the pamphlet *Wissenschaftliche Weltauffassung. Der Wiener Kreis* ('The scientific conception of the world. The Vienna Circle') which both coined the name of the Vienna Circle and explicitly set out its philosophical manifesto. It defined the empiricism of the Vienna Circle: 'there is knowledge only from experience', and its methodology: 'scientific word-conception is marked by the application of a certain method, namely logical analysis' (Carnap et al. 1929: 331). It identified ordinary language as ambiguous and, therefore, as a source of logical mistakes that had made metaphysics possible. It also dismissed 'the notion that thinking can ... lead to knowledge out of its own resources without using any empirical material', that is the notion of synthetic *a priori* knowledge (Carnap et al. 1929: 330).

The 1929 manifesto dealt with cultural and political, as well as purely philosophical, dimensions of the work of the Vienna Circle. Indeed, the historical context of the Circle is an important part of its story. The development of logical positivism coincided with social upheavals in Europe. In Austria in general, and in Vienna in particular, there was a spirit of cultural rebuilding after the destruction of the First World War. There was more concrete rebuilding afoot too. Functional new housing was needed for Vienna's population, recently swelled by mass migrations from rural districts. The city's appearance changed dramatically as the old, very obviously, gave way to the new. The Vienna Circle seemed quite self-consciously to have linked their new way of thinking to these changes. Just as architecture was to be sparse and functional, eschewing earlier ornateness in favour of clean lines and undisguised structure, so philosophy was to deal in transparent and testable statements of observation rather than subjective speculation. In an article on this link, Peter Galison has commented on 'the Vienna Circle's often-repeated self-conception of being at one with the spirit of modernism' (Galison 1993: 76).

The prevailing political outlook among the members of the Vienna Circle was largely socialist and progressive but they differed from each other in the extent to which they expressed these views, and in the degree of their political involvement and activism. The 1929 manifesto linked philosophical with social reform: that group of people that 'faces modern times, rejects [metaphysics and theology] and takes its stand on the ground of empirical science' (Carnap et al. 1929: 339). But in his later account of the workings of the Vienna Circle, Carnap distanced himself from this stance:

> All of us in the Circle were strongly interested in social and political progress. Most of us, myself included, were socialists. But we liked to keep our philosophical work separated from our political aims. In our view, logic, including applied logic, and the theory of knowledge, the analysis of language, and the methodology of science, are, like science itself, neutral with respect to practical aims, whether they are moral aims for the individual, or political aims for a society.
>
> (Carnap 1963: 23)

The philosophical, if not the political, campaigning continued. In 1930 Carnap together with Hans Reichenbach, a professor of philosophy at the University of Berlin, took over the journal *Annalen der Philosophie* and relaunched it under the title *Erkenntnis* as a mouthpiece for the Vienna Circle. It continued until 1940 and published articles by many of the members of the Circle. The very first article to be published was by Schlick and was uncompromisingly entitled 'The turning point in philosophy'. True to his title, Schlick argued that awareness of the rules of logical syntax, together with rigorous empiricism, would show that many of the formulations of traditional philosophy were simply not genuine. In fact, eventually 'it will no longer be necessary to speak of "philosophical problems" for one will speak philosophically concerning all problems, that is: clearly and meaningfully' (Schlick 1930: 59).

As well as the manifesto, individual publications, and the annexing of *Erkenntnis*, the Vienna Circle publicized their ideas by arranging a series of congresses around Europe. Their 'Congresses on Unified Science' were held during the mid-1930s in Paris, Copenhagen, Cambridge and Massachusetts. These were particularly significant in disseminating the new philosophical ideas to a wider, and often an enthusiastic, audience. One member of that audience was the Polish logician Alfred Tarski, at the time a lecturer in mathematics and logic at the University of Warsaw. Tarski was working on formal logic and semantics, especially in relation to the notion of truth. His work in this area interested members of the Vienna Circle, particularly Carnap. In 1930 Tarski had been invited to give a series of visiting lectures in Vienna, and during that visit he also engaged in various informal discussions with members of the Circle. As a result of these discussions Carnap became convinced that a suitably formal theory of language was of the highest significance to the clarification of the philosophical problems then besetting the Vienna Circle, a conviction that resulted in his own development of the theory of logical syntax (Carnap 1963: 30).

Tarski's theory of truth had perhaps the greatest impact on the Vienna Circle of all his work. He presented this at the Paris congress in 1935, but he had already published a version of it in 1933 under the title, 'The concept of truth in formalized languages'. In 1944 he published a more accessible summary of this work under the title, 'The semantic conception of truth'. Tarski's explicit aim in these works was to 'construct – with reference to a given language – *a materially adequate and formally correct definition of the term "true sentence"*' (Tarski 1933: 152, original emphasis). His perceived success in this venture led to the enthusiastic adoption of his theory of truth by the Vienna Circle. It did no less than make the previously suspect term 'truth' acceptable in the vocabulary of logical positivism. The Circle's interest had been in the relationship between the expressions of a language and the world, certainly, but in terms of what made those expressions meaningful, and of what criteria established them as verifiable. On the subject of what actually made an expression true they had remained quiet. There was no satisfactorily rigorous definition of 'truth' that made it a term fit for logic. Indeed discussions of 'truth' were regarded as belonging more in metaphysics than in scientific philosophy. As Vann McGee has expressed it: 'Before Tarski's work, the notion of truth was regarded with grave suspicion, particularly by the logical positivists, who regarded the supposed connection between language and the world that makes true sentences true as the sort of quasi-mystical association that a scientific philosophy ought to eschew' (McGee 2006: 405–6). McGee even repeats the legend that Otto Neurath put 'truth' on a list of forbidden words.

As far as the Vienna Circle was concerned, Tarski rescued truth because he showed that it could be defined in syntactic and logical terms, instead of relying on a more or less vague semantic definition. In one sense, what Tarski was doing was anything but new. He was not attempting an entirely fresh account of truth, but was rather drawing on the 'correspondence' approach, dating back to Aristotle: the intuitively appealing explanation that a sentence is true if it corresponds to reality. The correspondence account had, of course, impeccable empirical credentials, referring as it did to the experiences of the world against which any expression must be judged. The problem was that it was irreparably vague. As it stood, it offered no account of what it might be for an expression to correspond to reality, or of how it might be possible to recognize that correspondence when it occurred. These issues had resurfaced in the vagueness of Wittgenstein's notion of the proposition as a 'picture' of reality, a problem that Wittgenstein had sidestepped by refraining from commenting on the status of elementary propositions.

Tarski's insight was that a successful account of truth must be modest in its ambitions. A rigorous account of truth in general was simply not possible, but what the logician could hope for was an account of what it was for a sentence belonging to a particular language to be true in that language. Tarski also noticed that in giving an account of truth it was necessary to distinguish between the language to which a certain sentence belonged and the language in which it was described. He defined the former as the 'object language' and the latter as the 'metalanguage'. The two must be kept strictly separate or discussion of the object language became impossible. Adapting Tarski's famous example, 'Snow is white is true if snow is white' is meaningless, but '"Snow is white" is true if snow is white' is a significant statement about the conditions for truth of a certain sentence. In this latter example the quotation marks indicate that it is the name of the sentence, not the sentence itself, that appears as the subject of a further, separate sentence in the metalanguage.

As well as the need for a metalanguage, Tarski specified that an account of truth could only be offered for a formal language. Natural language was not appropriate for such a treatment because it was unbounded: there were no principled limits to what it contained and what descriptions it could offer. It was also beset by vagueness and ambiguity. As he expressed it in his original article, '*The attempt to set up a structural definition of the term "true sentence" – applicable to colloquial language is confronted with insuperable difficulties*' (Tarski 1933: 164, original emphasis). Instead, the logician must resort to a formal language, by which Tarski meant an artificially constructed language in which the sense of every expression was unambiguously determined by its form. To the Vienna Circle, who had already rejected natural language as unfit for philosophical usage, this restriction on the applicability of Tarski's account of truth would not, of course, have proved at all troubling.

Tarski rephrased the form for an expression in the metalanguage using logical variables, and came up with a generalized form that he labeled (T): 'X is true if, and only if, p'. Here 'X' is the name of any sentence in the object language, and 'p' is a proposition. 'If' has become 'if, and only if' because only one proposition can offer the conditions of truth for any sentence. In a formal language, unlike in natural language, every sentence expresses exactly one proposition, and every proposition finds expression in only one sentence. Tarski's (T) form, therefore, shows the way to a re-expression in logical form of the old correspondence account of truth. It is not itself a definition of truth. Rather, it shows how truth may be defined for a given sentence in a given language. Every equivalence of the form (T) 'may be considered a partial definition of truth, which explains wherein the truth of this one individual sentence consists. The general definition has to be, in a certain sense, a logical conjunction of all these partial definitions' (Tarski 1944: 344). A full account of truth in any language would consist of a set of (T) forms, one for each sentence in that language. The result may sound unwieldy and indeed unworkable to the present-day semanticist, but for the logician it is capable of precise definition and avoids any reference to an intangible connection or correspondence between language and the world.

Tarski's formal definition allowed the Vienna Circle to use the term 'truth' without embarrassment and to talk about sentences as having the property 'true' or 'false'. The decision between the two was, of course, to be determined by verification. A true sentence expressed a proposition that could be demonstrated to be true with reference to empirically available evidence: a proposition that made predictions about what would be found in the world that were borne out by observation. A false sentence expressed a proposition that made predictions that turned out to be contrary to the available evidence. To say that a sentence was false was a significantly different thing from saying that it was meaningless. Even to be capable of being either true or false a sentence must first be established as meaningful; it must comprise meaningful words arranged in a syntactically justifiable manner. To say that a sentence was false was to say that it was meaningful but made predictions contrary to the available evidence. To say that it was meaningless was to say that it failed to make any predictions that could be empirically tested.

For the Vienna Circle, many of the traditional statements and problems of philosophy fell into this latter category. This was their source of distrust, even at times of outright ridicule, of anything that might be labeled 'metaphysics'. Leading members of the Circle repeatedly insisted that they were not interested in claiming that metaphysical statements were false, but rather than they did not even reach the criteria of meaningfulness necessary to be found false. For instance, in an early edition of *Erkenntnis* Schlick argued that the main reason for opposition to the work of the Vienna Circle was the failure to understand the distinction between saying something was false and saying it was meaningless. 'The empiricist does not say to the metaphysician "what you say is false", but, "what you say asserts nothing at all!" He does not contradict him, but says "I don't understand you"' (Schlick 1932: 107). In the previous edition of the journal, Carnap conceded that the claim that metaphysics, including all that had been said by eminent metaphysicians over the centuries, was meaningless would make many people uneasy. He suggested that although metaphysical statements did not offer descriptions of states of affairs, they did 'serve for the *expression of the general attitude of a person towards life*' (Carnap 1932: 78). And he went on to suggest that this sort of expression might more appropriately be achieved through poetry or even music.

The types of sentences that the Vienna Circle dismissed as meaningless included, inevitably, but perhaps most controversially of all, those connected with religious belief. 'God' was a prime example of a word that, according to Carnap's classification, was meaningless and would therefore render meaningless any sentence in which it occurred. Such sentences could, of course, be used to express general attitudes or emotional responses to life, but, in effect, adherence to logical positivism was incompatible with a personal religious faith. Carnap himself came from a religious background and grew up with a faith that he abandoned as a student. In his intellectual autobiography he was scathing about theology in general, arguing, as might be expected, that its statements are simply lacking in any real content. He displayed a more tolerant, if faintly patronizing attitude towards expressions of personal faith: 'At the present stage of development of our culture, many people still need religious mythological symbols and images. It seems to me wrong to try to deprive them of the support they obtain from these ideas, let alone to ridicule them' (Carnap 1963: 8).

Carnap insisted that a lack of religious faith in no way implied moral nihilism, in himself personally or in others. A logical positivist outlook was perfectly compatible with taking a stance on how life ought to be lived. Despite this, and despite the fact that pronouncements on religion and on ethics played a very minor part in the work of the Vienna Circle, negative contemporary reactions were dominated by an attitude to those who espoused logical positivism as moral nihilists bent on the overthrow of social and ethical codes. A. J. Ayer commented on logical positivism that 'it has even been asserted, without a shadow of empirical evidence, that its advocates were corrupters of youth' (Ayer 1959: 22). The view of logical positivism as radical and subversive seems to have predominated in Austria during the 1930s, and was instrumental in the downfall of the Vienna Circle.

Logical positivism had always been on the margins of Austrian philosophy, even in Vienna. The Circle met on university premises, but out of hours on Thursday evenings in an unprepossessing building housing the Institute of Physics and Mathematics, on the outskirts of the university precinct. This contrasted sharply with the philosophy department where Schlick and some of the other members of the Circle worked during the day, housed in the main university building on Vienna's prestigious Ringstrasse, complete with classical columns and sweeping marble staircases. The distance was intellectual as well as physical and cultural. Barry Smith has described how at the very time when the Vienna Circle was in its heyday, the mainstream teaching and writing on philosophy at the University of Vienna concentrated on a rather old-fashioned style of the history of philosophy. 'The circle around Schlick can be seen from this point of view to have consisted largely of philosophical outsiders or cranks, of individuals who would in fact be taken seriously only sometime later – and only without the boundaries of Austria herself' (Smith 1987: 47).

The more positive reactions that Smith describes, generally took place in the English- rather than the German-speaking philosophical world. From the early 1930s onwards, English language philosophy journals started taking note of this new approach to philosophy. Reactions were mixed, and remained so. Anthony Flew, writing in the early 1950s, commented of the Vienna Circle that 'at least in their published writings they often appeared narrow, dogmatic, philistine, uninterested in traditional philosophy, and militantly secular' (Flew 1953: 4). Many commentators, including Flew, dwelt on the Vienna Circle as a 'foreign' style of philosophy, and emphasized the difference between this and what was going on in Britain at the time. Gilbert Ryle looked back with the perspective of three decades on the 1920s and commented on the different attitudes to the relationship of traditional philosophy to science to be found in Vienna and in England:

> The contrast between philosophy and science was drawn in both places. In Vienna, where the autonomy of the sciences was actually challenged the object was to expose the pretensions of philosophy as a governess-science. Here, where, save for psychology, the autonomy of the sciences was not seriously challenged, it was drawn in order to extract the positive functions of logic and philosophy. Philosophy was regarded in Vienna as a blood-sucking parasite; in England as a medicinal leech.
>
> (Ryle 1951: 3)

Undoubtedly the single greatest stimulus to interest in logical positivism in England was the publication in 1936 of A. J. Ayer's *Language, Truth and Logic*. Ayer had travelled to Vienna a few years earlier; he had met with Schlick and had been invited to attend some meetings of the Circle. He was immensely impressed by what he heard, although his own limited grasp of German prevented him from taking a very active part in the discussion. On his return to England he set about writing a book that was to introduce the ideas of the Vienna Circle to a wider, that is to an English-speaking, world. The resulting radical and polemical interpretation of logical positivism caused quite a sensation. Reactions were both positive and negative, but together they brought logical positivism to the attention of many of those practising philosophy immediately before the Second World War. Ayer himself later commented that 'I wrote it in the conviction that I had discovered the proper path for philosophy to follow, without trying to disguise the fact that I owed the discovery to others, and this conviction, however ill-founded it may turn out to have been, does give the book an abiding force' (Ayer 1987: 24). Ayer's biographer Ben Rogers has commented that: 'Despite the mixed reviews and limited sales, *Language, Truth and Logic* quickly achieved cult status among students and young intellectuals' (Rogers 2000: 124). Many believed the claim that logical positivism would show the way towards solving, or at least dissolving, many of the traditional problems of philosophy, and opening the way to a new, more rigorous and strictly empirical method of inquiry.

However, Ayer was aware that by the time he had visited the Vienna Circle in 1933 the movement was already past its prime. Certainly by the time the majority of the English-speaking philosophical world became aware of the Vienna Circle through *Language, Truth and Logic*, they were already reading about a piece of philosophical history. Carnap had left Vienna for a chair in Prague in 1931. Gustav Bergmann recalled that after this, Wittgensteinian views became more dominant, there was less interest in the principle of verification, and 'leadership of the discussion shifted more and more to Waismann' (Bergmann 1938: 202). Hans Hahn died in 1934 while only in his mid-50s. But by far the most significant catalyst in the decline of the Vienna Circle was the death of Moritz Schlick, who was murdered in June 1936 on the stairs leading to the philosophy department of the University of Vienna. Schlick's death seems to have been the work of an individual acting alone; he was shot at point-blank range by a former doctoral student who was a paranoid schizophrenic and had become hostilely obsessed with him. But it was undoubtedly convenient for the Austrian authorities, who were becoming increasingly suspicious of the Vienna Circle, with its socialist and reforming tendencies. The chair in philosophy of the inductive sciences was abolished in favour of concentrating on the history of philosophy. Schlick's murderer was found guilty but treated leniently, and, indeed, commanded a certain amount of public and media sympathy. The Vienna Circle, several of whom were Jewish, were viewed with increasing suspicion, and many of them began to make plans to use their international philosophical contacts to flee Austria.

After the German occupation of Austria in 1938 the persecution of the Vienna Circle became more overt and triggered a philosophical diaspora. Waismann went to Cambridge. Neurath had already moved to Holland, sensing the trend of Austrian political developments, and later fled again, this time to England. Bergmann, assisted by Neurath, escaped to Holland and then to New York. All publications by the Vienna Circle were banned in Austria. Logical positivism was by no means over, and even the Vienna Circle had more to say. But after the German occupation the work was carried out by individual philosophers from their bases in new countries, particularly in the United States. There was another way in which the Vienna Circle continued to exert influence on philosophical developments. Philosophers who had not been members of the Circle, but who had learned of its work either first hand or through secondary sources were beginning to disseminate their responses. These responses, which were published largely in America, in England and in Scandinavia, are an essential part of the story of empiricism in the twentieth century. And they collectively represent the most significant impact of the work of the Vienna Circle on the study of language.

2
Falsification and Scientific Method

The Vienna Circle was disbanded by the end of the 1930s. It left behind a number of important philosophical writings outlining revolutionary and powerful doctrines. It had also acquired a firm hold over the imagination of certain groups of philosophers, who viewed it either as a paragon of unblinking scientific rigour or as a stultifying cult of literalness. The impact of both the writings and the reputation was felt in many branches of philosophy, including the study of language, for decades to come. The end of the Vienna Circle was brought about by outside events and pressures rather than by any natural completion or culmination of its work, but it had nevertheless already outlived its best-known doctrine. Partly through the efforts of its defenders and advocates such as A. J. Ayer, the logical positivism of the Vienna Circle was viewed by many as more or less synonymous with the principle of verification. But throughout the 1930s a number of problems for verification had been identified both by members of the Circle and by outside commentators on it. Individual members of the Circle were attempting to respond to, and perhaps to accommodate, these problems. As a result different factions were emerging in what had initially been a unified movement. But all were then beset by what is now often regarded as the final and most compelling challenge to verification: Popper's exposition of his criterion of falsifiability.

Despite problems and modifications, the criterion of falsifiability remains highly significant in the empirical sciences. In the study of language it has played a dominant role for some decades because it has been regarded by many as the touchstone of the appropriate type of linguistic theory. This view has of course been held by those who view linguistics as a science: who see language as a natural phenomenon that can be identified and studied in its own right. It is not universally held by linguists, so falsification has remained a controversial gage of the success of an account of language. Empiricism has been advanced on both sides of the argument. Those on the 'science' side of linguistics have argued that embracing falsification is the only way to advance truly empirical statements about language, because it allows only statements that are amenable to trial on the basis of the relevant data. Opponents of this idea have protested that it promotes speculative hypotheses, even metaphysical constructions, that take linguists away from the essential business of describing language, as it is manifest in the observable regularities of communication. These differences of opinion are explicable for exactly the same reason as they are unresolvable. They depend on very different views about what count as the subject matter, and therefore the appropriate data, of linguistics itself.

The radical logical positivism of the early days of the Vienna Circle was subject to a number of attacks and subsequent modifications during the 1930s, and to further attacks after the Circle had ceased to meet. The attacks were prompted by a range of different objections, but these can in effect all be seen as subdivisions of the general complaint that logical positivism was unempirical. There is an obvious irony in the spectacle of one of the most radically and avowedly empirical of philosophical doctrines crumbling under an onslaught of criticisms that it was unempirical. Nevertheless, the complaints were that while logical positivism claimed to take a strictly empirical approach to knowledge and truth, it depended on a series of assumptions and commitments that were themselves immune to the empirical test of evidence. If these were retained, logical positivism was supported on an aprioristic structure. If they were abandoned, it would collapse.

Some such criticisms focussed on the Vienna Circle's views on language: on the implicit suppositions about meaning that sustained their central doctrines. These criticisms, and the accounts of language that followed from them, will be the subject of the next five chapters. In general, these had little impact on the development of logical positivism during the lifetime of the Vienna Circle. Most of them were developed too late, in the decades following the Second World War, to have prompted a response from the Circle itself. And those that were published during the 1930s were either not recognized as a serious threat or were dismissed as wrong-headed. Some members of the Circle did pay more attention, however, to a challenge based on the analysis, not of language but, of mathematics. The system of mathematics, which they thought had been safely reduced to logic and was therefore exempt from the expectations of verification, was in danger of being cut loose from logic again and of reappearing as an indispensable but apparently unempirical component of the discourse of science.

In 1931 a young mathematician at the University of Vienna published a brief and densely technical paper on the status of mathematical propositions that had potentially devastating implications for logical positivism. Kurt Gödel was no stranger to the Vienna Circle, having attended meetings regularly since 1926 when he was introduced by Hans Hahn. He had been studying the system of logic and the notation used in Russell and Whitehead's *Principia Mathematica*. This was the book that had, in part, shown the way for the Vienna Circle to a new form of empiricism, by demonstrating that mathematical truths could be reduced to logic and could therefore be proved true within the system of logic itself. Gödel now argued that within Russell and Whitehead's system, indeed within any finite and formal set of arithmetic axioms, there would be certain arithmetical truths that could never be either proved or disproved. Using the abbreviation 'PM' for *Principia Mathematica*, Gödel introduced his intention to demonstrate how we 'obtain an undecidable proposition of the system PM, i.e. a proposition *A*, for which neither *A* nor *not-A* are provable' (Gödel 1931: 39).

If Gödel was right, and the mathematical world in general seemed ready to accept that he was, he had demonstrated the inherent 'incompleteness' of the mathematical system. There were mathematical facts that were necessarily accepted as truths, but accepted not on any mechanical or empirically justified grounds. They were accepted intuitively, aprioristically, almost as metaphysical beliefs. It was no longer possible to claim that all scientifically significant knowledge was either empirical or demonstrably true within its own system. Gödel may have attended meetings of the Vienna Circle but he had never been a full convert to logical positivism. In his eyes, the single-minded dedication to positivism caused the Vienna Circle, as Palle Yourgrau has put it, to 'underestimate the difficulty of rendering mathematics empirically acceptable by reconstructing it as a system for the formal manipulation of signs' (Yourgrau 2005: 40). His incompleteness theorem was undoubtedly an unwelcome and unpalatable discovery for the Vienna Circle, but it did not cause the immediate consternation and confusion that might have been expected. Carnap realized the force of what Gödel was suggesting, but he apparently found the mathematical technicalities of the proposal hard to follow.

Perhaps a more pressing concern for logical positivism at the time was not an unexpected assault such as Gödel's but a potential problem that had always existed within the approach itself, of which the Vienna

Circle had always been aware. The only questions were how long they could resist the pressure it exerted and in what other, separate directions it would eventually push them. The problem concerned the status of personal experience in the acquisition of knowledge. The principle of verification seemed to demand that the observable data required to verify a statement must be available, or available in principle, to the scrutiny of the individual researcher. The individual's personal experience was the ultimate arbitrator of what counted as true for that individual. This raised two questions. The first concerned the reliability of personal experience, which is surely subjective and arguably gives information about sense data rather than about any actual physical world. As discussed in the last chapter, members of the Vienna Circle tended to remain guardedly neutral on the question of realism, thereby declining fully to engage with this problem. The second question was whether and to what extent it is possible to extrapolate away from personal experience. The critic of logical positivism C. I. Lewis summed this up succinctly in an article published in 1934. He warned that if the principle of verification were followed to the extreme, 'knowledge would collapse into the useless echo of data directly given to the mind at the moment' (Lewis 1934: 131). Problems were beginning to show for the notion of 'protocol statements': the statements based on personal sensory experience that were apparently the basis of all empirical knowledge.

One member of the Vienna Circle to take on the problems of personal experience and protocol statements, and to propose an unflinchingly radical response to them, was Otto Neurath. He was a founding and central member of the Circle, but his background in sociology, rather than in the pure sciences, had always set him somewhat apart from the other members. His sociological interests were to come to the fore again in the ways in which he moved away from canonical logical positivism during the 1930s. Protocol statements were the basic units of truth, the building blocks of any scientific discourse. Neurath argued that it was unacceptable to define them as expressions of private sense experiences. To do so would be to go against everything that was expected of the public and intersubjective nature of science. Rather, protocol statements must be defined as those sentences accepted by a particular scientific community. They resulted from a series of observations made by a certain community in a certain space of time. Because they were relative to both a community and a time they were necessarily subject to future change and revision.

Neurath argued that in a rigorously scientific discourse personal experience should not be given an inappropriate character of reliability.

He even proposed that a truly scientific language would have no place for first-person statements of experience at all. 'I see a red circle', for instance, was to be replaced with 'Otto sees a red circle now' (Neurath 1932: 94). Such statements were not to be afforded any more privileged status than any other statements. People might in fact be more attached to statements based on their own experience than those based on others', but this was simply a fact of human psychology, not a matter of science; such statements must in fact be seen as just as tentative and amenable to revision as all other sentences. As Neurath put it, 'The fate of being discarded may befall even a protocol statement. There is no "*noli me tangere*" for any statement' (Neurath 1932: 95).

In Neurath's system, a statement was accepted as scientific by a process of comparing it with other statements, not with things. It was accepted if it fitted with the existing statements of science; otherwise it was rejected. Here Neurath's sociological interests were reasserting themselves; what he was proposing was in effect the sociological study of the community of scientists:

> When a new statement is presented to us we compare it with the system at our disposal and check whether the new statement is in contradiction with the system or not. If the new statement is in contradiction with the system, we can discard this statement as unusable (false), for example, the statement: 'In Africa lions sing only in major chords'; however, one can also 'accept' the statement and change the system accordingly so that it remains consistent if this statement is added. The statement may then be called 'true'.
>
> (Neurath 1932: 94–5)

Such a notion of truth and falsity was clearly very much at odds with that which had originally underpinned the work of the Vienna Circle. It suggested a holistic account of scientific truth whereby the whole system of scientific knowledge, rather than individual statements of fact, were subject to study and to decisions concerning validity and truth.

Few of Neurath's fellow members of the Vienna Circle followed him wholeheartedly down his path to holism. This may in part have been due to the extreme, almost eccentric nature of some of his views, such as his apparent belief that children could and should be taught from the start to speak only the scientifically rigorous language in which statements of personal experience were always replaced by third-person statements of the 'Otto sees ...' type. Nevertheless, his general approach did have an effect. By 1936 Carnap no longer believed that every descriptive sentence could be reduced or translated into a sentence about perception. He admitted that this belief had been expressed in the earlier works of the Vienna Circle, including his own, 'but I now think, that it is not entirely adequate' (Carnap 1936: 464). But Schlick was apparently unmoved and unimpressed by Neurath's ideas, seeing them as something of a betrayal of the principles of empiricism that had always been central to the Vienna Circle.

Perhaps the best-known set of difficulties facing logical positivism, which like the problem of personal experience had been lying in wait for it from the beginning, were the difficulties presented by the so-called 'problem of induction'. Logical positivism committed the Vienna Circle to the inductive scientific method. According to this, scientists make series of observations of the properties of the physical world on the basis of which they formulate the statements that constitute scientific knowledge. Such statements are in effect generalizations inspired and licensed by the available data. For the Vienna Circle, the principle of verification operated after the fact: stipulating that if such statements were to be accepted as meaningful it must be possible to identify the series of observations on which they were built and hence the type of observation that would now serve to verify them.

Induction is an intuitive appealing method of reaching apparently reliable, positive knowledge of the world around us. Indeed, it seems to follow, or to formalize, the methods that we all use in our everyday lives. We base our present decisions on past experience. We have accumulated a series of experiences in which the sight of black clouds has been quickly followed by the sensation of rain. Seeing black clouds overhead we pack an umbrella in the expectation of rain. In effect, we have acquired the inductive knowledge that 'black clouds are followed by rain'. Without an inductive approach to knowledge it would be impossible to live because we would not be able to form any expectations, make any plans, or take any precautions. However, for the philosopher and the scientist induction is beset with difficulties. The foundations of these difficulties had been known long before the Vienna Circle launched their positivist manifesto. Induction produced statements that could be described in terms only of degrees of probability, never of absolute certainty or truth. Related to this, since scientists must deal always in contingencies, the principle of induction itself remained unproved and unprovable; it was an unempirical assumption on which supposedly empirical science was based.

Philosophers at least as early as David Hume had pointed out that inductive methods lead to statements of probability, not to certain knowledge. A favourite philosophers' example is the belief expressed in the statement that 'the sun will rise tomorrow'. This certainly seems good enough in most usual contexts. Non-scientists would readily agree to the truth of the statement. But scientists must be more cautious. They must recognize that this is a prediction based on individual instances of past evidence. The evidence may be compelling, may appear overwhelmingly so, but remains indirect. Thousands and thousands of past instances of the sun rising in the morning do not preclude the possibility that the sun may not rise on any given morning in the future. The statement is highly probable, but cannot be said to be definitely true.

The same could be said of statements that appear to give a general account of some aspect of the physical world: statements such as 'oil floats on water'. Such statements are also in effect predictions. They predict the outcome of future experiments and observations, and as such are just as fallible as the prediction that the sun will rise tomorrow. The scientist may have observed many instances of oil floating on water and on this basis may be reasonably convinced that oil will float on water next time: in fact, that it will float on water in all future instances. But the record of past observations is not enough to make this conviction into a certainty or a truth. It is perfectly compatible with past experience, although it may of course be extremely unlikely, that at some future moment of observation oil will sink in water.

The problem of induction was acknowledged by the immediate predecessors of and influences on the Vienna Circle. In his *Tractatus*, Wittgenstein had pointed out that 'It is an hypothesis that the sun will rise tomorrow: and this means that we do not *know* whether it will rise' (Wittgenstein 1922: 6.36311, original emphasis). A decade earlier, Russell had presented it as one of *The Problems of Philosophy*. He pointed out that as soon as we make any judgments beyond immediate sensory experience we are relying on the principle of induction. In effect, the principle states that the more instances there are available where one phenomenon is associated with another the more probable it can be judged that those two phenomena will always be associated. A sufficient number of cases will make the law of the association of the two approach, but never quite reach, certainty.

Russell identified a further, related problem, one that was in some ways even worse news for empirical philosophy. The principle of induction could not itself be either proved or disproved. A scientist forms the belief that 'All swans are white' and then encounters a black swan. This new evidence of course means that the hypothesis about swans must be abandoned, but it does not in itself cause much of a problem for the principle of induction. The scientist knows perfectly well that expectations are sometimes defeated and does not give up on forming inductive expectations on the basis of this one disappointment. It is still reasonable to form other expectations about different things in the future. However, scientists can never have conclusive proof of the principle of induction because they can never get beyond a very high level of probability for any particular prediction. The sun rising again increases the probability of this individual prediction but cannot prove the principle of induction. Russell summed up this quandary for empirical investigations as follows: 'Thus all knowledge which, on a basis of experience, tells us something about what is not experienced, is based upon a belief which experience can neither confirm nor confute, yet which, at least in its more concrete applications, appears to be as firmly rooted in us as many of the facts of experience' (Russell 1912: 38).

In everyday life, where we work with the principle of induction all the time, the lack of certainty in both the principle and the individual predictions it generates is not a real problem; we live with it. It may be the case that we do not know for certain that it will rain today just because there is a black cloud, or even that the sun will rise tomorrow, but the degree of certainty we have is good enough for us. Indeed it would not be practical to live our lives in any other way. The question is whether science can also live with it. In the case of the Vienna Circle, the problem of induction was eventually sufficient to see the end of the principle of verification, which was replaced by a principle of confirmation. Knowledge was never certain, meaning that no statement could ever be conclusively verified. But statements could be confirmed, and gain increasing degrees of plausibility, by successive observations of the appropriate type. The old, unworkable principle of verification did not admit of degree; a statement was either verified or it was not. But statements could be confirmed to a greater or lesser extent; some statements could be considered to be more highly confirmed than others. The most highly confirmed statements might approach the status of being verified, but they could never actually reach it.

Carnap explicitly adopted confirmation. In an article published in 1936 he explained that 'If by verification is meant a definitive and final establishment of truth, then no (synthetic) sentence is ever verifiable ... We can only confirm a sentence more and more. Therefore we shall speak of the problem of *confirmation* rather than of the problem of verification' (Carnap 1936: 420, original emphasis). On Carnap's account the problems for verification had turned out to be even more severe than those inherent to any approach that relied on induction. Certainly, verification had succeeded in ruling out metaphysical statements on the grounds that they were meaningless, and therefore warranted no place in rigorous scientific discourse. But it had become apparent that the very same processes that ruled out metaphysical statements also ruled out observation statements and statements of natural laws. Scientists' statements about their own immediate experiences could always be subjected to more and more rigorous tests by devising more and more elaborate experiments. There was no identifiable end point to this process, so no observation could ever meet the criterion of verification. Statements about natural laws, the very currency of scientific discussion, were also incapable of verification for reasons already discussed. 'All swans are white' could never be conclusively verified because of the possibility that future observations of swans might not correspond to past observations. The necessary consequence of this would be that statements of science must be classified as meaningless, and therefore indistinguishable from the statements of metaphysics. This gave Carnap compelling reasons to adopt instead the principle of confirmation, which he was convinced avoided these problems. He insisted, however, that this was to be seen as a modification rather than a complete abandonment or replacement of the principle of verification.

Schlick had also taken on board the problems for induction. However, he responded to them without adapting his own philosophy as much as Carnap was doing, and he remained to the end perhaps the staunchest supporter of an essentially original version of logical positivism. It seems that he acknowledged that natural laws must be seen as rules concerning how statements were to be constructed; they were themselves a type of 'pseudo statement' (as explained in Popper 1935: 314). But in a paper that was not published until a few weeks after his death, he was still proposing an identifiably logical positivist line: 'The meaning of a proposition is its method of verification' (Schlick 1936: 341). Apparently under the influence of discussions with Wittgenstein, he now claimed that this tied in with the position that any answer to a question about the meaning of a sentence must make reference to the circumstances in which it would be used: 'we want a description of the conditions under which the sentence will form a *true* proposition, and of those which will make it *false*' (ibid., original emphasis). The big difference between Carnap and the more conservative Schlick was that Schlick still held to the requirement of verifiability, although he was now operating with a more nuanced and hedged definition of this term.

The members of the Vienna Circle had modified their positions and adapted their philosophies in an attempt to save logical positivism from the pitfalls attendant on the problems of induction. But worse was to come, in the form of a new philosophical conundrum, and this time it seemed to many that logical positivism was cornered. It was already acknowledged that the inductive method on which logical positivism depended was unable to deliver certain knowledge. But with the exposition of 'Hempel's paradox' it also lost its intuitive 'common sense' appeal. Hempel identified the seemingly unacceptable account of how we acquire knowledge to which logical positivism was committed. His paradox held even for the modified version of logical positivism that dealt in confirmation rather than verification.

Carl Hempel was sympathetic to the logical positivist enterprise. He was not himself a member of the Vienna Circle, but had attended a number of its meetings when visiting from the University of Berlin. He became aware of a particular problem with the relevant evidence underpinning empirical knowledge, but he was not necessarily advocating the abandonment of the approach, simply its more cautious application. He developed his position during various discussions and conference papers in the 1930s, and finally published it in 1945, by which time he had fled Europe and was establishing his career in the United States. Like Carnap in the late 1930s, Hempel championed the centrality of confirmation rather than verification. No finite amount of data could ever conclusively verify a hypothesis expressing a general law such as gravity, but it could constitute confirming evidence for it. Problems arose, however, when the scientist addressed the question of what sort of evidence was to count towards confirmation. Hempel considered the general law 'all ravens are black', and those observations that might be relevant to it. Sightings of black ravens would, of course, serve to confirm the law; the more black ravens that were seen the higher the degree of confirmation that the law would achieve, although it could never become a certainty. Conversely, the sighting of a raven that was any colour other than black would force the scientists to abandon this particular law.

Hempel drew attention to the fact that, logically speaking, the general law 'all ravens are black' is equivalent to 'All non-black things are non-ravens'. If this statement were true, and if something were observed that was non-black, that thing must also be a non-raven. Sightings of black ravens counted as cumulative confirmation for the statement 'all ravens are black'. Sightings of anything that was not black and was not a raven counted as confirmation for the statement 'all non-black things are non-ravens'. But if the two statements were logically equivalent those same sightings of non-black non-ravens must equally count as confirmation for the statement 'all ravens are black'. The types of evidence that could confirm a general law became vast, unwieldy and unintuitive. As Hempel himself explained it: 'Consequently, any red pencil, any green leaf, and yellow cow, etc., become confirming evidence for the hypothesis that all ravens are black' (Hempel 1945: 14). Hempel did not propose to abandon induction in the face of his own paradox. Indeed, he saw the paradox as more apparent than real; it could be surmounted by a more careful consideration of what was to count as a confirming instance for any general statement. He urged a cautious approach to the nature of confirmation. Certainly, all claims made in the sciences must remain tentative rather than definite. Confirmation should be discussed in terms of the appropriate types of observation statement used in scientific discussion, rather than in terms of any notion of raw observation. In effect, all apparently confirming evidence was not necessarily to be treated equally.

Verification, and the principle of induction on which it depended, were beset by a host of complications and difficulties by the time Karl Popper put forward his views on falsification. But on Popper's own account the apparent chronology is misleading. Popper's ideas were published in *Logik der Forschung* in 1935, later translated into English as *The Logic of Scientific Discovery*, and they are sometimes assumed to be a response to the problems that were by then well established for logical positivism, and an attempt to offer an alternative. Popper himself was always keen to stress that his views were developed considerably earlier than they were published, largely as a reaction against what he saw as a lack of scientific credibility in the theories of psychologists such as Freud. Popper found it hard to imagine what sort of evidence might be recognized as a challenge to these sweeping, fanciful theories, so for him they failed to offer any systematic predictions or explanations: 'There is no action which we could not explain in terms of those theories' (Popper and Eccles 1974: 75).

Despite these specific origins of his thinking, Popper was not shy in claiming credit for challenging, even for single-handedly overthrowing, logical positivism. In his intellectual autobiography he explained how during the 1930s he came to realize that 'to everyone of their main problems, I had better answers – more coherent answers – than they had', and that his publication of these answers eventually made logical positivism untenable (Popper 1976: 80 and 88). Although living and working in Vienna throughout the 1920s and up until 1937 when he fled to New Zealand, Popper attended no meetings of the Vienna Circle. He attributed this bluntly to the fact that membership of the Circle was entirely at Schlick's invitation and 'I was never invited' (Popper 1976: 84). According to his account, the members of the Vienna Circle failed to realize the full implications of his work and attempted to annex it as a helpful modification of logical positivism rather than the complete refutation that it seemed to him. Certainly, in contemporary reactions to the publication of *Logik der Forschung*, individual members of the Vienna Circle seem to have taken its ideas onboard calmly. Many saw Popper's work as very much in keeping with the direction in which logical positivism was in any case moving, rather than as the complete and devastating break with them that Popper himself seems to have envisaged (see, for instance, Carnap 1937a: 26). Carnap's later account of the relationship between the Vienna Circle and Popper suggested less distance than Popper himself liked to claim: 'His basic philosophical attitude was quite similar to that of the Circle. However, he had a tendency to overemphasise our differences. In his book he was critical of the "positivists", by which he seemed to mean chiefly the Vienna Circle ... He therefore antagonized some of the leading figures in our movement' (Carnap 1963: 31).

Members of the Vienna Circle were already discussing falsification in relation to scientific statements (see, for instance, Schlick 1936). But they tended to treat it as the simple opposite of verification in terms of the functions of empirical evidence. Many instances of black ravens would serve to verify, or perhaps increasingly to confirm, the statement 'all ravens are black', while any instance of a non-black raven would serve to falsify the same statement. Popper elevated the capacity for falsification to nothing short of the definitive criterion for any truly scientific statement. In subsequent commentaries on his work he emphasized repeatedly that he was not simply substituting a principle of falsification for a principle of verification. This was chiefly because, unlike the logical positivists, he was not interested in dividing statements into the categories of 'meaningful' and 'meaningless'. The true measure of a statement for Popper was not whether it was meaningful but whether it was scientific: that is, whether it said something substantive about the world that explained current data, made predictions about possible new data and could be challenged by identifiable future observations or experiments. Thirty years after the original publication of his ideas on falsification he complained that 'My position has repeatedly been described as a proposal to take falsifiability or refutability as the criterion of *meaning* (rather than of demarcation)' (Popper 1963: 188, original emphasis). For Popper, 'demarcation' was demarcation between scientific and nonscientific statements.

Popper began *The Logic of Scientific Discovery* with a litany of problems for induction. What he proposed was not another modification of induction in order to address these problems but a wholesale replacement of it. Falsification was to be accompanied by a deductive scientific method. With an inductive method, the data are primary. Observation of the data leads to the formulation of a generalization or universal law that can then be tested against further data. With the deductive method, the theory or universal law itself is primary. The scientist devises a theory which serves as a hypothesis that can then be tested by observation and experiment. Popper was rather elusive about how the hypothesis first came into being, apparently because this aspect of the process did not appear to him particularly worthy of attention. He was prepared to accept an almost mystical concept of inspiration, by means of which the scientist made an imaginative leap to form a hypothesis. 'The question of how it happens that a new idea occurs to a man – whether it is a musical theme, a dramatic conflict, or a scientific theory – may be of great interest to empirical psychology; but it is irrelevant to the logical analysis of scientific knowledge' (Popper 1935: 7).

What interested Popper was what happened to the theory next. Many different types of data might serve to confirm a theory. To the scientist working with the inductive method this was of central importance but to Popper it was of little interest. In relation to the deductive method it was crucial only that it should be possible to envisage what sort of data would serve to falsify a theory. The ability to make clear predictions about what sort of data would falsify it was the criterion of demarcation for a truly scientific statement. On the inductive method, 'all ravens are black' could be successively confirmed but could never achieve anything other than high probability. This was simply not a problem for the deductive method. 'All ravens are black' was a scientifically acceptable statement because it made meaningful predictions about future data. Many black ravens might strengthen the scientist's conviction, or in Popper's favoured terminology might 'corroborate' (Popper 1935: 10) the theory, but they did not do anything for the status of this as a scientific statement. Crucially, the statement was phrased in such a way that it was perfectly possible to envisage what would constitute falsifying counter evidence. The discovery of one non-black raven would be sufficient to falsify the theory. In response to such a discovery the scientist must either modify the theory to account for the new data or must abandon the theory altogether.

Popper was not slow to recognize the implications of what he was saying for the business of science itself. In some ways the picture was quite bleak. Induction might have proved incapable of producing certain knowledge or assured truth, but the case might at first seem hardly better for falsification. A deductive theory could never be proved true. It could never even, Popper explained, lay claims to probability. All that could be said for it was that it had not yet been falsified: that it had so far stood up to empirical testing. The business of forming a hypothesis, testing it, then modifying it or forming a new hypothesis, then testing the modified or new hypothesis, was in principle never ending. The goal of science was not to reach some established, proven truth, but to develop theories that presented a progressively more successful account of some aspect of the world, one theory supplanting another in a gradual movement towards greater understanding. Scientists' task was to try to prove themselves wrong. 'Once put forward, none of our "anticipations" are dogmatically upheld. Our method of research is not to defend them, in order to prove how right we were. On the contrary, we try to overthrow them' (Popper 1935: 178–9).

The acceptability of a deductive hypothesis, then, is always contingent, always subject to revision in the light of future data. For Popper, this was a price well worth paying for the sake of empirical credibility. Falsification and the deductive method constituted the only truly empirical scientific approach. Certainly, deduction took the scientist beyond immediate observation to the realms of extrapolation, imagination and speculation, but for Popper this offered the only possible chance of saying something interesting and significant. The problems for induction had already indicated that simple immediate personal experience was not enough to license the types of statements that scientists needed to be able to make. In fact, any scientific statement must go beyond the immediate evidence if it was to say anything about the world and offer anything more than a simple summary of personal experience. What made a theory truly empirical for Popper was the fact that it was vulnerable to experience, and subject to change or abandonment as the observable evidence dictated.

> I shall not require of a scientific system that it shall be capable of being singled out, once and for all, in a positive sense; but I shall require that its logical form shall be such that it can be singled out, by means of empirical tests, in a negative sense: *it must be possible for an empirical scientific system to be refuted by experience.*
> (Popper 1935: 18, original emphasis)

In Popper's version of empiricism, observations of the world were irrelevant to the formation of laws or theories and served little purpose in terms of confirming them, but were crucial in their potential to falsify them. The claims of science were still tentative. But whereas for the positivists the claims were tentative because they could never get past probability to achieve certainty, for Popper they were tentative because they were always contingent on the possibility of falsification. A scientific claim could never be proved; it could not even be described as more or less probable. It was a hypothesis that served a useful explanatory purpose for a particular period of time. It was almost to be expected that one day a piece of evidence would come to light that would cause the claim to be modified or abandoned.

A version of Popper's position has been widely accepted in the physical sciences, and by analogy in some areas of linguistics. But it would be wrong to suppose that the debate ended there, or that the subsequent decline of logical positivism is evidence that Popper's ideas were simply greeted with enthusiasm by a grateful scientific community and uniformly accepted. During the 1960s, journals such as *Philosophy of Science* were publishing numerous articles on the relative merits of induction and deduction (See for instance, the exchange between Canfield and Lehrer 1961 and Coffa 1968). By 1963, Hempel could comment that 'The neat and clean-cut conceptions of cognitive significance and of analyticity which were held in the early days of the Vienna Circle have thus been gradually refined and liberalized to such an extent that it appears quite doubtful whether the basic tenets of positivism and empiricism can be formulated in a clear and precise way' (Hempel 1963: 707). But Popper's account of the truly scientific statement was beset by problems of its own.

One type of challenge to Popper revolved around the nature of falsification itself, which some saw as so dogmatic and uncompromising as to be unworkable in practice. In an article published in 1945, Friedrich Waismann set out his understanding of Popper's position and then countered: 'That is unrealistic. What astronomer would abandon Kepler's laws on the strength of a single observation?' (Waismann 1945: 126). This objection was echoed in the philosophical generation after Popper and Waismann. During the 1950s Thomas Kuhn developed a sociological approach to studying the business of science. For Kuhn, Popper's ideas about falsification presented a stereotype of scientific procedure, in which sudden revelations and startling discoveries led to the overthrow of one theory in favour of the next. Kuhn argued that this sort of epiphany, although possible, was, in practice, very rare in science, which dealt much more frequently with the calm comparison of theories and with gradual progress as theories were adapted and modified.

Like Popper, Kuhn saw theories as produced imaginatively rather than as discovered by induction, but he took issue with the concept and the term 'falsification', as being too strong. He argued that a single piece of falsifying evidence, or even several such pieces, should not, and in practice did not, license the abandonment of a scientific theory, especially if there was nothing current to take its place: 'All theories can be modified by a variety of *ad hoc* adjustments without ceasing to be, in their main lines, the same theories' (Kuhn 1970: 13).

In a response to this particular presentation of Kuhn's arguments, the philosopher of science Imre Lakatos took a more charitable view of Popper's work. Kuhn was attacking naïve falsificationism, he argued. Popper may have begun as a naïve falsificationist, but he developed methodological falsificationism. Kuhn could not simply present arguments against naïve falsificationism, such as the argument that a single counterexample should not in practice be allowed to demolish a theory, and think that he had had the last word. Naïve, or dogmatic falsificationism certainly was untenable for Lakatos. It relied on a distinction between speculative propositions which formed the hypotheses of science, and observational ones, which might serve to falsify them. But in fact no clear-cut distinction of this type existed. Even apparently observational propositions relied on some theory. For instance, observations of the planets, which might be considered to offer the empirical data for theories of astronomy, were necessarily conducted using scientific equipment such as telescopes and therefore relied on optical theory. Lakatos saw these problems for falsificationism as more damning than the ones Kuhn had discussed, particularly because: 'The difficulties concerning the empirical basis which confronted "naïve" falsificationism cannot be avoided by "sophisticated" falsificationism either' (Lakatos 1970: 131). For Lakatos, science could claim to have made progress if a hypothesis were developed that explained everything its predecessor did and something new as well.

Kuhn's most celebrated original contribution to the history and philosophy of science was his 1962 book *The Structure of Scientific Revolutions*. In this he focussed on the series of rare but significant upheavals that scientific thinking repeatedly goes through, where an old paradigm, or way of thinking, is replaced by a new paradigm that itself becomes orthodoxy before eventually being overthrown by another revolution. He urged the importance of studying the psychological drives of scientific groups and generations when seeking to understand why particular models gain and maintain prominence. In some ways his approach echoes that of Otto Neurath 30 or more years before; for both philosophers it was important to consider what counted as received wisdom for any particular historical stage of the development of a science. Kuhn considered the stages of education that scientists went through and that inevitably shaped and might limit their ways of thinking. He repeated his criticism of Popper's particular claims, arguing that it was well established that no scientific theory would ever fully fit all the facts or explain all the puzzles: 'If any and every failure to fit were ground for theory rejection, all theories ought to be rejected at all times' (Kuhn 1962: 146). Rather, in so far as the concept of truth could be discussed in relation to the sciences, it lay in the consensus of the scientific establishment, which was of course subject to change over time.

Paul Feyerabend, Kuhn and Lakatos's near-exact contemporary, also emphasized the relativity of any scientific doctrine, a relativity which he linked to the different cultures, even the different languages in which science was conducted. The questions that science asked, he claimed, depended on the times and places in which they were asked, and were not guaranteed as stable. Feyerabend set out Popper's position that scientific investigation started with a problem that it then proceeded to solve, and commented: 'This characterization does not consider that problems may be wrongly formulated, that one may inquire about properties of things and processes which later views declare to be non-existent. Problems of this kind are not *solved*, they are *dissolved* and removed from the domain of legitimate inquiry' (Feyerabend 1975: 274, original emphasis).

During the 1960s and 70s, then, Popper's work on falsification and the deductive method was being questioned by some younger philosophers of science who wondered whether its claims were too dogmatic and whether the expectations it placed on working scientists were unrealistic. These philosophers also questioned whether scientific theories could really aspire to the empirical credibility that Popper claimed for them, or whether their status would always owe something to the culture and the hegemonic structure in which they were developed. At this same time, an approach to the study of language was being developed and was gaining ground that many saw as exerting its own hegemony, even tyranny, over contemporary linguistics. There has been much talk of revolutions and of messiahs, but Chomsky was doing something genuinely new and to many genuinely shocking when he unfolded the various stages of his linguistic programme during the second half of the twentieth century. It was not new to claim that linguistics should be pursued as a science. Early in the 1930s, Leonard Bloomfield had made this a founding assumption of his book *Language*. The difference was that for Bloomfield the science of language was clearly, explicitly, an inductive science (Bloomfield 1933, discussed in the final chapter of this book). For Chomsky, the study of language should go beyond the immediately available evidence of language data to posit unobservable entities and processes. Such hypotheses should be subject to testing against further data. Traces of this attitude were present as early as Chomsky's description of linguistics in *Syntactic Structures*:

> A grammar of the language L is essentially a theory of L. Any scientific theory is based on a finite number of observations, and it seeks to relate the observed phenomena and to predict new phenomena by constructing general laws in terms of hypothetical constructs such as (in physics, for example) 'mass' and 'electron'. Similarly, a grammar of English is based on a finite corpus of utterances (observations), and it will contain certain grammatical rules (laws) stated in terms of the particular phonemes, phrases, etc., of English (hypothetical constructs). These rules express structural relations among the sentences of the corpus and the indefinite number of sentences generated by the grammar beyond the corpus (predictions).
>
> (Chomsky 1957: 49)

Chomsky's defence of the deductive method was not as clear-cut here as it was to become later in his work. In fact, the talk of theories based on 'a finite number of observations' which are used in the process of 'constructing general laws' could almost have come from an inductive scientist. But Chomsky's readiness even at this stage to go beyond the observable was crucial. He was certainly not reluctant to posit unobservable processes and entities, for instance introducing during the 1960s the distinction between deep and surface structure and transformations mediating between the two (Chomsky 1965). He has also, of course, posited an innate language faculty, an unobservable mental structure that allows and constrains the process of language acquisition (throughout his work, but for an early version of this claim see Chomsky 1965: 37). Chomsky has always maintained that his study of language is empirical. It does not limit itself to the observable, but for Chomsky this is not the defining property of the empirical. Rather, the predictions and the hypotheses that are formed are subject to clearly identifiable processes of testing against the available evidence, and contain within themselves the possibility of being falsified by the appearance of some clearly specified type of counter evidence. He has continued to develop the idea of linguistics as a science and to urge its empirical credentials. (See, for instance, Chomsky 1976, 2000.)

Chomsky's empiricism is somewhat obscured by his readiness sometimes to use the terms 'empirical' and 'empiricism' as philosophical terms of abuse. When he does so it is usually to distance himself from a style of empiricism represented particularly among his contemporaries by W. V. O. Quine, whose work and whose long battle with Chomsky are considered in the next chapter. On such occasions, Chomsky links 'empiricism' to any doctrine opposing the notion of an innate language faculty. That is, he draws on a distinction between empiricism and rationalism. He argued in *Aspects of the Theory of Syntax* that 'It is a curious fact that empiricism is commonly regarded as somehow a "scientific" philosophy. Actually, the empiricist approach to acquisition of knowledge has a certain dogmatic and aprioristic character that is largely lacking in its rationalist counterpart' (Chomsky 1965: 207). He also distanced himself from the positivistic approach to knowledge inherent in this type of empiricism, reflecting on what he saw as the temporary and unsustainable attempts to 'limit the term "theory" to "summary of data"', which may have been fostered in part by 'strong verificationism' (Chomsky 1965: 194).

Chomskyan linguistics is generally seen as belonging firmly in the Popperian tradition where empirical science is deductive science and where the potential for falsification demarks genuinely scientific statements from the unscientific. Yet in his published writings Chomsky has said very little explicitly about deduction, he has rarely used the term 'falsification' and, despite his frequent references to the recent and distant philosophical past, he never cites Popper. Perhaps the nearest he came to Popper was in *Aspects of the Theory of Syntax*, where he argued that a successful linguistic theory should offer an account of data drawn from speaker intuition:

> on the basis of an empirical hypothesis concerning the innate predisposition of the child to develop a certain kind of theory to deal with the evidence presented to him. Any such hypothesis can be falsified (all too easily, in actual fact) by showing that it fails to provide a descriptively adequate grammar for primary linguistic data from some other language – evidently the child is not predisposed to learn one language rather than another. It is supported when it does provide an adequate explanation for some aspect of linguistic structure, an account of the way in which such knowledge might have been obtained.
>
> (Chomsky 1965: 26)

However, Chomsky has not returned to this notion of falsification frequently in his work and elsewhere he has written more generally of a theory being 'tested' against 'evidence' (for instance Chomsky 2000: 57). What remains central for Chomsky, and what is recognizably Popperian in spirit, is the insistence that the linguist is in constant search not of positive knowledge about a particular language but of interesting hypotheses. These hypotheses may be successively modified and may even supplant one another in the gradual process of gaining a clearer understanding of the subject matter: 'It is always reasonable to consider alternative approaches, if they can be devised, and this will remain true no matter what successes are achieved. The situation does not seem different in principle from what we find in other areas of empirical inquiry' (Chomsky 1986: 23–4).

The successive development and replacement of hypotheses in Chomsky's methodology has given rise to some striking and perhaps unfortunate terminology. From the 1960s onwards discussions of Chomskyan linguistics included references to 'Standard Theory', 'Revised Standard Theory', 'Revised Extended Standard Theory' and so on. These terms were used by Chomsky's commentators more than they were in his own works. A major textbook on transformational syntax from the early 1980s was subtitled 'a student's guide to Chomsky's extended standard theory' (Radford 1981). Chomsky himself apparently distanced himself from this terminology, referring for instance in 1975 to 'the so-called "extended standard theory"' (Chomsky 1975: 195). Just by using the term, however, and by the fact that he was endorsing the theory itself as he did so, he necessarily perpetuated the usage. In some ways this terminology was very appropriate to the Popperian tradition, in which expansions in the available data may force a theory through a series of revisions and even replacements, but some of Chomsky's critics have been troubled by it. To them it has suggested a certain intellectual arrogance, perhaps an implicit claim that the 'standard' did or should hold not just in the specific field of transformational-generative grammar, but in linguistic study in general.

In other words, Chomskyan linguistics was seen as exerting, or at least as claiming, undue influence on the mid-twentieth-century study of language. Enthusiastically received by some professional linguists and then taught exclusively at a number of prestigious academic institutions, it exerted its own hegemony in linguistics. It had become a linguistic paradigm, like the scientific paradigms discussed by Kuhn. The danger with such paradigms, of course, is that their significance and influence may be based more on social status and acceptance within a particular community than on intellectual merit or empirical credibility. Chomskyan linguistics, in its current minimalist version, is still dominant in some areas of linguistics, but other types of paradigms also have held or continue to hold sway in language study. Some of Kuhn's comments on scientific debates can perhaps be illuminating as to why linguistic theories with such different premises can exist simultaneously, and why real dialogue between them has frequently proved so elusive. He argued that 'The proponents of competing paradigms are always at least slightly at cross-purposes. Neither side will grant all the non-empirical assumptions that the other needs in order to make its case.' (Kuhn 1962: 148). This issue will be discussed in more detail in the final chapter.

If these issues are pertinent in the broad church of twenty-first-century linguistics, they are also pertinent to the apparently restricted area of empirical philosophies of language of the mid-twentieth century. The three philosophers whose work will be the subject of the next five chapters, W. V. O. Quine, J. L. Austin and Arne Naess, all claimed justification for what they were doing on the grounds that their approach to language was scientific. Yet the assumptions, methodologies and conclusions of all these different styles of language study were radically different from each other, and each was radically different from Chomskyan linguistics. At an initial glance the range of competing claims to empiricism is bewildering, and the extent of the differences between the paradigms making these claims seems inexplicable. Another observation of Kuhn's can perhaps serve as an interim epigram on this matter: 'The competition between paradigms is not the sort of battle that can be resolved by proofs' (Kuhn 1962: 148).

3
Holism

The mid-twentieth-century debate considered in the previous chapter was concerned primarily with the nature of scientific discovery and progress. In so far as it related to the work of the Vienna Circle, it confronted the problems raised by too dogmatic a commitment to induction, and questioned whether these were best solved by modifying or by overthrowing logical positivism. It engaged with the study of language to the extent that it was concerned with questions of how scientific hypotheses could legitimately be expressed and of the differences between describing a statement as 'meaningful' and describing it as 'scientific'. This debate has influenced the subsequent development of language study, largely because of the interest among some linguists in Popper's version of falsificationism, but most of its main protagonists were from scientific backgrounds, and they would certainly not have considered themselves to be theorists of language. Popper himself was openly dismissive of language as a focus of study in its own right, repeating in his writings different formulations of the stark dictum that 'I never quarrel about words' (Popper 1935: 131 [Addendum, 1972]).

Not all the philosophical contemporaries of the Vienna Circle were so dismissive of language. One of the leading voices in the response to logical positivism was that of W. V. O. Quine, and for Quine language was of central importance. He was well placed to comment on the Vienna Circle, having been invited to attend some of their meetings during 1933, and even on one occasion to speak on his own work. He also came from an impeccable background in logic, and had traveled from Vienna directly to Prague to study with Carnap. Quine maintained a resolutely empiricist stance on knowledge, and from this position he questioned what he saw as some of the dogmas that underpinned logical positivism. He therefore became one of the first, and has remained one of the most prominent, of those who objected to logical positivism on the grounds that it made some fundamentally unempirical assumptions about language.

Quine's proposed alternative, which he saw as more genuinely empirical, was what is sometimes described as a 'holistic' approach to knowledge and to language. Concentrating on individual propositions or individual sentences was artificial and simply wrong-headed; it was bound to produce misleading results. Instead, propositions must be considered as parts of a whole system or network of knowledge, and sentences as parts of a whole language for describing that knowledge. This position is reminiscent of Otto Neurath's later philosophy: what Moritz Schlick had seen as Neurath's abandonment of logical positivism. In particular, Neurath had claimed that the truth of any individual scientific statement could appropriately be assessed not in isolation but in relation to the whole currently accepted body or web of scientific knowledge, with which it could either conflict or conform. Both Neurath and Quine were reacting against the claim inherent at least in early versions of logical positivism that certain knowledge could be reached by examining and testing individual propositions. They both rejected the idea that propositions in isolation from each other had determinate meaning. For Neurath, so-called 'protocol sentences' were simply those whose truth was accepted by a particular speech community. For Quine too the beliefs and behaviours of a speech community were central to defining meaning and establishing truth. Quine maintained, however, that there was no direct influence of Neurath's thinking on his own.

Quine expressed his holism in 'Two dogmas of empiricism', a paper he presented in 1950 and published in 1951. From the first it has been widely cited and the subject of many responses, both favourable and critical. His central claim was that, despite its self-proclaimed empirical credentials, logical positivism rested on some thoroughly unempirical assumptions, particularly assumptions about language. For all their caution about admitting only statements that could be verified, the logical positivists had made a series of sweeping statements about meaning and truth that had no apparent base in the observable properties of human language. While insisting that the only use of language acceptable to the philosopher must be rigorously scientific, the Vienna Circle had failed to approach their discussion of language itself in a scientific manner.

The two particular dogmas of empiricism that Quine identified and challenged went right to the heart of logical positivism, a least as it had been practised in the heyday of the Vienna Circle. One was the claim that all meaningful statements were built up from atomic propositions, themselves subject to evidence from the individual's sense perceptions. Quine therefore denied that all knowledge could be reached by building on the evidence of the senses; he denied that all knowledge could be positive knowledge. The other dogma of empiricism to come under Quine's scrutiny was the viability of a distinction between analytic and synthetic statements. This was, of course, fundamental to the logical positivist enterprise. Establishing the existence of a separate class of analytic statements had allowed them to exclude certain necessary truths, including the statements of logic and hence of mathematics, from the criterion of verification. No apparent procedures for verification could be established for statements such as 'All bachelors are unmarried' or '2 + 2 = 4', but such statements were not for this reason to be dismissed as meaningless. Rather, meaningfulness was stipulated to be a property shared both by synthetic statements that could be subjected to an identifiable process of verification, and by analytic statements.

Quine claimed that this dogma too stood on unempirical foundations. In particular, it made sense only on the assumption that there was some independent, identifiable phenomenon called 'meaning' that was attached to words regardless of the specifics of use and context. Only on this assumption was it possible to comment in abstract terms of the truth of a statement such as 'all bachelors are unmarried'. The logical positivists were able to label this a necessary truth because of their unquestioned conviction that, in effect, 'bachelor' and 'unmarried man' each had a clearly identifiable meaning. For Quine the only empirically justifiable assumptions were that there were words and that there were objects in the world. To posit some intermediary, unobservable notion of 'meaning' was no better than a metaphysical statement, having no basis in observable reality. All that it was, in fact, possible to observe was the behaviour of individuals and of groups of individuals in communities: the contexts in which they habitually used particular words and the effects that the use of these words generally evoked.

The date 1950 might seem a long time after Quine's personal encounters with the Vienna Circle for him to produce a response to logical positivism. There is evidence, however, that Quine's thinking in this area developed much earlier than 1950 but that he deliberately delayed making his views fully public, perhaps out of deference to Carnap, who was by then established at the University of Chicago. Carnap, whom Quine respected enormously, still espoused the distinction between analytic and synthetic statements, although not in the context of the radical verificationist account of meaning associated with the early days of the Vienna Circle. In the preface to *From a Logical Point of View*, where 'Two dogmas of empiricism' was published, Quine acknowledged the contribution made to his ideas on analyticity by discussions with a number of fellow philosophers, including both Carnap and Tarski, from 1939 onward. In 1950 Morton White wrote of the distinction between analytic and synthetic that 'a revolt seems to have developed among some philosophers who accepted this distinction as one of their basic tenets a few short years ago' (White 1950: 317). He was coy about citing specific philosophers, offering as an excuse the fact that little explicit material had yet been published about this revolt, but he hinted that such sentiments had been shared by both Quine and Nelson Goodman for some time.

Certainly, there are some clues as to what was to come in a paper Quine published in 1943, although the attack on logical positivism was much more veiled and the comments on the distinction between analytic and synthetic much more guarded than they were later to be. In many ways 'Notes on existence and necessity' was a canonical paper on meaning and the logical problems associated with it, including the implications of Frege's distinction between 'sense' and 'reference'. Quine discussed analyticity, suggesting that this could only be defined using terms such as 'meaning', and expressing a worry that there was as yet no clearly identified way into the definition of such terms that was empirically sound. 'Just what the *meaning* of an expression is – what kind of object – is not yet clear; but it is clear that, given a notion of meaning, we can explain the notion of *synonymity* easily as the relation between expressions that have the same meaning' (Quine 1943: 120, original emphasis). He observed that synonymity was itself presupposed in any discussion of the distinction between the analytic and the synthetic.

Quine was happy to accept the Fregean notion of 'reference'. He conceded that, by observing the prominent features of the contexts in which people used particular words, it was possible to make empirical statements about the extensional links between words and objects. But he was increasingly uneasy about the notion of 'sense', the abstract, explanatory link between word and object. The notion of analyticity relied on sense. To say that 'All bachelors are unmarried' is necessarily true is to appeal to the fact that 'bachelor' has a sense, independent of any specific occasion of use, that includes the notion of 'unmarried'. Quine's unease found full expression in 'Two dogmas of empiricism', where he wrote of the distinction between analytic and synthetic: 'That there is such a distinction to be drawn at all is an unempirical dogma of empiricism, a metaphysical article of faith' (Quine 1951: 37). Richard Creath has reported that Carnap replied to Quine in a paper that was never published, arguing that Quine had underestimated just how vague ordinary language was, and that semantical rules are designed to address this vagueness (Creath 1991: 365).

Quine never accepted the distinction between analytic and synthetic back into his philosophy. There is some evidence that in later writings his attitude towards it softened a little, but only to the extent that it could be accommodated into a social account of language. For instance, in the mid-1970s he conceded that it might be possible to say that a sentence such as 'a dog is an animal' was analytic, to the extent that successfully learning to understand it entailed learning that it is true. 'Language is social, and analyticity, being truth that is grounded in language, should be social as well. Here then we may at last have a line on the concept of analyticity: a sentence is analytic if *everybody* learns that it is true by learning its words' (Quine 1973: 79). The notion of a clear-cut logical basis for the distinction, however, remained an anathema to him.

Quine's holism emerged in 'Two dogmas of empiricism' in part as a solution to the problem he had set himself by rejecting the distinction between synthetic and analytic. Without such a distinction, he was left without an explanation of why some of our beliefs seem firm and certain, not subject to change in the light of any possible future evidence. Analyticity offers a clear explanation for the firmness of our belief that 'All bachelors are unmarried'. The discovery of counter evidence that might challenge this belief seems unthinkable; the truth status of this sentence could not change unless the actual meanings of its words changed. Quine's holism supported his claim that, once the redundant notion of meaning was dispensed with, so too was the need to divide all sentences between two categories dependent on a supposed difference in the status of their truth values. Rather, he argued that all the statements that made up a system of belief formed a single network. It was true that some beliefs were more likely to be revised or abandoned than others, but this was a matter of degree rather than of absolute categories. The supposed distinction between analytic and synthetic statements reflected 'the relative likelihood, in practice, of choosing one statement rather than another for revision in the light of recalcitrant experience' (Quine 1953a: 43).

Revision when it occurred was never of the single statement in isolation but of the network of beliefs as a whole. In the course of such revisions, an individual was much more likely to select so-called synthetic statements for review than so-called analytic ones, but all were in principle open to scrutiny. So in a radical departure from the most central dogmas of the Vienna Circle, Quine argued that it was not appropriate to scrutinise each statement in a belief system for truth. Rather, 'our statements about the external world face the tribunal of sense experience not individually but only as a corporate body' (Quine 1951: 41). Experience of the world did impinge on belief systems, but it did so with respect not to the individual sentences that were accepted as true or rejected as false, but to the system as a whole. Quine was keen to point out that this view, at least, was quite in keeping with, and might almost be attributed to, Carnap; 'for in his later writings he abandoned all notion of the translatability of statements about the physical world into statements about immediate experience' (Quine 1951: 40). Quine offered a fuller and more developed statement of his views in a later work:

> The lore of our fathers is a fabric of sentences. In our hands it develops and changes, through more or less arbitrary and deliberate revisions and additions of our own, more or less directly occasioned by the continuing stimulation of our sense organs. It is a pale grey lore, black with fact and white with convention. But I have found no substantial reasons for concluding that there are any quite black threads in it, or any white ones.
>
> (Quine 1963: 406)

Quine's holism points to an ambitious project for explaining the nature and the mutability of scientific knowledge, and as such it has been seen as an important contribution to the philosophy of science, as well as a shaping force in the direction of analytic philosophy. As well as being reminiscent of Neurath's earlier ideas about the 'web of knowledge', it has features in common with Kuhn's work on scientific paradigms, published just over a decade later. For Kuhn, scientific orthodoxy was the collective received wisdom of a scientific establishment at a particular point in time, and it was that collective that was subject to change or even overthrow. In fact, Kuhn had met Quine while he was himself early in his career at the University of Harvard, and later admitted that Quine's ideas had been influential on his own thinking about the changes in scientific thought (Kuhn 1962: vi). What was distinctive in Quine's version, and also what gave it far-reaching consequences in the philosophy of language in particular, was the way in which he linked it to his refutation of the distinction between analytic and synthetic.

For Quine, the unempirical nature of the distinction meant that it could no longer serve to discriminate between the validity of different types of judgments or the truths of different types of sentences. For some contemporary commentators, this greatly enhanced the empiricist credibility of analytic philosophy. Morton White, considering the general possibility of abandoning the distinction, noted that 'Analytic philosophy will no longer be sharply separated from science, and an unbridgeable chasm will no longer divide those who see meanings or essences and those who collect facts' (White 1950: 330). The irony of the accusations that beset logical positivism becomes apparent again. In the early, enthusiastic days of the Vienna Circle, its members saw a firmer clarification of the distinction between analytic and synthetic distinction as the key to a truly scientific method. But according to White's summary, it was this very distinction, supported as it was by an unscientific discussion of 'meaning', that had divided versions of analytic philosophy such as theirs from true science.

Within the philosophy of language itself, the distinction between analytic and synthetic sentences became established as a topic of huge significance during the middle part of the twentieth century. On a first glance, however, the literature in this area may not appear very promising. Philosophers are seen in earnest discussion of a small group of uninspiring, rather odd-sounding example sentences, often concerning the unmarried status of bachelors or the capacity of material bodies to take up space. But how philosophers have analysed such examples has had profound implications for major questions about meaning and about the certainty of knowledge. The renewed interest in the distinction which had been in philosophical currency at least since the time of Kant was due in a large part to the Vienna Circle's dependence on it, followed by Quine's attack. Apparent squabbling about the status of a few obscure examples masked the significance of the philosophical battles that were being fought. If Quine was initially reluctant to push the implications of his ideas for fear of injuring or offending Carnap, he may well have had a point. For old-school logical positivists there was a lot at stake.

However, not all of Quine's philosophical commentators saw him as an outright opponent of logical positivism, or even as having done it any real damage. Carl Hempel regarded Quine's criticisms of the Vienna Circle, particularly in 'Two dogmas of empiricism', as some of the most important and powerful in terms of the future of logical positivism. For Hempel, Quine was not so much overthrowing logical positivism as determining the new direction it was to go in, moving from a dogmatic insistence that all knowledge must be ultimately based on experiential data to a more fluid notion of truth. In Hempel's words, Quine offered, 'a coherentist, or holistic, conception of scientific claims as forming a system of mutually interdependent assertions, some of them accepted on the basis of immediate observation, others inferentially linked to them and to one another, all offering mutual support to each other, but every one of them always open to reconsideration and change' (Hempel 1993: 8).

Michael Dummett, too, saw 'Two dogmas of empiricism' as essentially reforming rather than refuting the work of the Vienna Circle. Quine had broken the link between the generally accepted belief that scientific knowledge should be based on observation and the claim, which was not in fact a necessary corollary of this, that every sentence must be subject to individually tailored support from empirical evidence. 'The great contribution of that essay was that it offered an essentially verificationist account of language without committing the logical positivist error of supposing that the verification of every sentence could be represented as the mere occurrence of a sequence of sense-experiences' (Dummett 1976: 71). Gerald Holton has added his voice to this assessment of Quine as essentially benign towards logical positivism: 'Quine's work can be seen as a critique and a restructuring of the logical positivism of the Vienna Circle, so to speak from the inside, and particularly, as Quine has acknowledged, as a result of his contact with Rudolf Carnap' (Holton 1993: 60).

Other critics have concentrated on Quine's treatment of the problematic term 'meaning'. Alexander Miller has argued that what he describes as Quine's 'meaning scepticism' has not been conclusively supported, but has continued to highlight the problems with 'meaning facts'. Quine and others have failed to come up with compelling arguments in favour of meaning scepticism, but, 'it is fair to say that there is little consensus in contemporary philosophy of language as to what meaning-facts are, or even as to the constraints that an account of the meaning-facts ought to satisfy. It is perhaps in their highlighting of this that the true value of meaning-sceptical arguments resides' (Miller 2006: 111).

Reflecting on the debate about analyticity of the last few decades, Jerry Fodor and Ernie Lepore have lamented the tendency to conflate this with the issue of synonymy. 'On our view, synonymity is necessary but not sufficient for analyticity' (Fodor and Lepore 2006: 117). Establishing that two words or phrases in a language can be said to share a meaning is for Fodor and Lepore a necessary starting point for establishing the existence of analytic sentences, but is not the same process. They blame Quine for encouraging the conflation by his own usage, particularly in 'Two dogmas of empiricism'. It is true that Quine seems always to have argued, or even to have assumed, that synonymity and analyticity were two aspects of the same problem, or two corollaries of the same unempirical assumptions about meaning. For Quine, two expressions could be said to be synonymous only on the erroneous assumption that expressions in some way 'had' a meaning, independent of particular occasions of use. If this version of meaning is permitted, then 'bachelor' and 'unmarried man' could each be said to 'have' a meaning, and these meanings could be compared and be found to be identical. This in turn explained why 'All bachelors are unmarried' was said to be analytic. In an essay produced slightly later than 'Two dogmas of empiricism', Quine offered a suggestion as to the proper analysis of synonymy. This saw expressions as arranged on a scale rather than sharply divided into categories of the synonymous and the nonsynonymous. 'Quite possibly the ultimately fruitful notion of synonymy will be one of degree: not the dyadic relation of *a* as synonymous with *b*, but the tetradic relation of *a* as more synonymous with *b* than *c* with *d*' (Quine 1953a: 63). In other words, Quine proposed an analysis of synonymy that had much in common with his analysis of analyticity. In later writings Quine was even more explicit on the connection, referring for instance to 'the semantical notion of analyticity which is interdefinable with synonymy' (Quine 1970a: 393).

Quine's ideas on the plausibility of analyticity and the feasibility of synonymy assured his position as an important commentator on logical positivism, and a powerful advocate of holism in the study of language. They also fed into the views collected in *Word and Object*, in which he outlined a set of ideas about 'the indeterminacy of translation'. Put simply, this set is based around the claim that it is never possible to establish a single, accurate translation between two different words or sentences. As it stands this may not strike linguists as a particularly challenging or even a particularly original claim. It is widely accepted that exact translation between languages is not possible because of the different nuances and connotations, and perhaps even the different culturally determined perceptions of the world, inherent in different languages. But Quine's case was much stronger than this. He argued that it was impossible to claim equivalence of meaning, not just between two expressions in different languages, but also between two uses of apparently identical expressions by speakers of the same language, perhaps even by the same speaker on two different occasions of use.

Quine's indeterminacy of translation was closely linked to his holism, and also to his resolutely empirical stance on the study of language. His refusal to allow any notion of independently existing meaning, intermediate between a word and an object, ensured that meaning could be described only in terms of individual circumstances of use. It followed from this that no description that accurately recorded usage could be said to be any better than any other. There were no measures of which was the best system because there was no linguistic reality to judge competing theories, or translations, against. Even within a single language, there was no guarantee that a word or expression had exactly the same meaning for one speaker as for another. Their linguistic behaviours might appear to coincide with respect to this word or phrase, and if so that was all that the observing linguist could say about sameness of meaning. But it would be wrong to assume that there was a unique linguistic system underlying those two sets of behaviour, because each speaker's understanding of the word or expression had been built up from a different individual set of experiences and social encounters. Early in his exposition, Quine illustrated this point with an analogy that at first appears bizarre but is in fact illuminating: 'Different persons growing up in the same language are like different bushes trimmed and trained to take the shape of identical elephants. The anatomical details of twigs and branches will fulfill the elephantine form differently from bush to bush, but the overall outward results are alike' (Quine 1960: 8). Even comparisons within the speech of one individual were complicated by the fact that people's experiences continued throughout their lives to shape their understanding of the world and the mechanisms by which they applied words to objects and properties.

In unfolding his ideas about the indeterminacy of translation, Quine described language in more overtly behaviouristic terms than he had done before. It was possible to talk about the meanings of terms to the extent that it was possible to talk about 'affirmative stimulus meaning' (Quine 1960: 32): in effect the set of circumstances or occurrences in which the speaker of a language would be prepared to assent to the term. This set of circumstances was available for inspection by the linguist, who could build up a generalization about when assent was given. But this would not produce a definitive account of the meaning of the word. An individual's willingness to affirm a term might vary for reasons not yet discovered by the set of observations the linguist had made. And certainly once observations were made involving other speakers it was entirely possible that they might assent to or withhold assent from the term in different sets of circumstances from the initial speaker. Stimulus meanings, then, were not fixed for an entire language but might vary between speakers.

Quine also employed his behaviouristic vocabulary in the discussion of the problem of synonymy. He had early argued that it was not possible to claim that two expressions were synonymous in the sense of 'having' the same meaning, because such an explanation relied on exactly the notion of meaning that he deemed unempirical to the point of being metaphysical. He now argued that synonymy could be discussed as long as it was considered exclusively in terms of '*stimulus synonymy*, or sameness of stimulus meaning' (Quine 1960: 46, original emphasis). That is, if an individual appeared to assent to one expression in the same set of circumstances as that individual assented to another expression, the linguist had good reason for concluding that the two expressions shared the same stimulus meaning. It might also be possible for the linguist to extend this analysis and claim that two expressions had stimulus synonymy for an entire community if this pattern of assent held for all members of that community. The linguist could observe the circumstances in which members of the community would assent to 'bachelor' and the circumstances in which they would assent to 'unmarried man'. For as long as these coincided the linguist worked with the hypothesis that the two had stimulus synonymity. This assumption was reached by induction over observation so it remained possible that the stimulus meanings of the two expressions might diverge in some future set of circumstances. Quine did not here link these claims explicitly to his rejection of the distinction between analytic and synthetic, but it is clear how such a link could be made. Since an accumulation of observations of the stimulus meanings of 'bachelor' and 'unmarried man' was all the linguist had to go on, there could be no special intrinsic status for the truth of 'All bachelors are unmarried'. It was simply that this sentence had to date stood up to more empirical evidence than most.

As part of his exposition of the indeterminacy of translation, Quine set out the mental exercise of 'radical translation' (Quine 1960: 28). He urged his readers to consider the task before a field linguist intent on analysing, understanding and translating a newly discovered language. There were to be no clues from similarities between words and structures as there might be in translating between cognate languages. No help could be assumed even from gesture in this alien culture. The process of translation was to be entirely radical, empirical and experimental. Quine suggested that the best starting point would be attempting to find translations for words or phrases that seemed likely to be linked to immediately observable stimuli, and in support of this he enlisted his now famous 'gavagai' example.

The story that Quine told about the field linguist's battles with the expression 'gavagai' was long and complicated, and the conclusions he drew from it far-ranging. In brief, the field linguist hears a speaker of the language utter 'gavagai' when in the presence of a rabbit that is apparently observable by them both. The linguist forms the hypothesis that the stimulus meaning for 'gavagai' is the same as the stimulus meaning for 'rabbit', or perhaps 'Lo, a rabbit' in English. This hypothesis is all right as far as it goes, but must of course be subject to further observations and possibly tentative experiments on the part of the linguist. The linguist might, for instance, utter 'gavagai' in different circumstances, sometimes when there is a rabbit present and sometimes when there is not, and try to establish in which cases the natives appear to assent to it. The linguist slowly builds up a picture of the stimulus meanings of this and of the other expressions of the language, but must be aware of two things. Firstly, all hypotheses about stimulus meaning must remain tentative. The linguist can never know for certain that 'gavagai' can be translated as 'rabbit', merely that the natives' tendencies to assent to 'gavagai' have so far coincided with the linguist's own tendencies to assent to 'rabbit'. Secondly, each tentative hypothesis about stimulus meanings in the language under study is dependent on and to some extent affects all other such hypotheses. For instance, the linguist notices that in response to 'gavagai?' in the presence of a rabbit the natives tend to reply 'evet', while in the absence of a rabbit they tend to reply 'yok'. It seems reasonable to assume that 'evet' corresponds to 'yes' and 'yok' as 'no'. But these assumptions depend on the prior assumption that 'gavagai' has the same stimulus meaning as 'rabbit', which can itself be only a working hypothesis.

Quine drew a sharp distinction between statements about stimulus meanings in the language under study, and guesses about translations between this language and English. The former were genuine hypotheses, but the latter were what he called 'analytical hypotheses'. The difference was that in the first case there was an objective truth that the linguist was attempting to find however fallible and incomplete the methods. In the second case there simply was no objectively correct translation for the linguist to be right or wrong about, because there was no meaning existing in the absence of individual stimuli and that could be shared by the two expressions in different languages. As Quine expressed it: '"Gavagai" and "There's a rabbit" have stimulus meanings for the two speakers, and these are roughly the same or significantly different, whether we guess right or not'. But in the case of an analytical hypothesis: 'there is not even, as there was in the case of "Gavagai", an objective matter to be right or wrong about' (Quine 1960: 73).

Quine concluded that a workable hypothesis about how it might be possible to translate between the two languages was all that the linguist could ever hope to achieve. This should not be seen as cause for despondency, however, because that was all there was to achieve. Two hypotheses about how to translate between the two languages might be empirically equivalent, that is they might each be equally effective in describing the collective linguistic behaviour of the natives, yet they might contain different analytical hypotheses about how particular words and phrases were to be translated from one to the other. Quine saw this as unavoidable and unproblematic. The 'indeterminacy of translation' was a natural corollary of freeing the study of language from metaphysical commitments. Quine related his theory of indeterminacy of translation back to his ideas about holism, when he explained that worrying about the correctness or otherwise of individual analytic hypotheses was wrong-headed because it assumed some objective reality as to the meanings of individual parts of the language. Rather, the values of different features of the language simple were the contributions they made to the language system as a whole. Translations of a language only worked and could only be assessed in entirety: 'When two systems of analytical hypotheses fit the totality of verbal dispositions to perfection and yet conflict in their translations of certain sentences, the conflict is precisely a conflict of parts seen without the wholes' (Quine 1960: 78).

The indeterminacy of translation related back to Quine's holistic view of language, but it also had implications for the nature and process of language acquisition, implications that Quine tackled in *Word and Object*. For Quine, the child faced with learning a first language was in the same position as the field linguist engaged in the process of radical translation. The task was one of building up evidence of the situations that provoked the use of a particular expression until the child was able to assent to the expression in the same contexts as did other speakers of the language. Quine was at his most explicitly behaviourist when discussing language acquisition: 'the child's early learning of a verbal response depends on society's reinforcement of the response in association with the stimulations that merit the response, from society's point of view, and society's discouragement of it otherwise' (Quine 1960: 82). The child's pattern of behaviour was gradually shaped by a process of reinforcement until it was indistinguishable from that of the rest of the speech community. Conformity of behaviour, rather than the attainment of some particular mental state or some determinate linguistic knowledge, was the goal and the measure of successful language acquisition.

Quine's thesis about the indeterminacy of translation has generated a lot of debate, perhaps because it appears to have so much to say not just about the nature of language itself, but about the practical business of studying and comparing languages. The 'gavagai' example has come under particularly close scrutiny. The is perhaps not surprising; the example is quirky and has a 'story tale' appeal in itself, as well as introducing some striking claims about what we can legitimately say about other people's use of language. However, Quine claimed that his critic's fascination with 'gavagai' skewed the discussion and drew attention away from the most important aspects of his ideas (Quine 1970b: 178). These were to do with the nature of scientific knowledge in general, but also with the particular problems and difficulties that beset the study of language. It was true that any scientifically interesting statement must do more than simply recount immediately available evidence, and hence that such statements would always be underdetermined by the data. This was a problem that had been encountered by the Vienna Circle. But for Quine 'The point is not just that linguistics, being a part of behavioral science and hence ultimately of physics, shares the empirically underdetermined character of physics' (Quine 1970b: 180). Rather, there were peculiar properties of the study of language that led to the indeterminacy of translation. Terms should be seen as 'inscrutable': that is, there simply was no reality about their true meaning, or their true mental representation, to form the subject of linguistic hypotheses.

It is in this matter of the relationship between linguistics and the physical sciences that the distance between Quine's work on language and Chomsky's is perhaps most apparent. Chomsky was 20 years younger that Quine, but the two stood as representative figures at the head of different schools of thought in the study of language from about 1960. Indeed, they conducted an intense and public written debate over the course of more than three decades, a debate that Chomsky in particular fashioned into an argument about linguistic method. The two sides of the argument can be, and have been, characterized variously as inductionism and deductionsim, behaviourism and mentalism, or empiricism and rationalism. Each pair of terms necessarily suggests some important features of the two positions, while glossing over others. As discussed in the previous chapter, Chomsky's position can be characterized as opposed to empiricism to the extent that he has seen himself as working in a rationalist tradition, but in other respects he has stoutly defended the empirical credentials of his approach.

Similar problems present themselves for a simplistic equation of Quine with the inductive method and Chomsky with the deductive. Certainly, Chomsky's enthusiasm for forming hypotheses about language that go beyond the available data but can be subjected to identifiable processes of testing and possibly of falsification, aligns him with the deductive method. For Chomsky, it is the possibility of going beyond the immediately available evidence that makes a statement about something as complex as natural language interesting. He has written on a number of occasions about the necessity of including in a theory abstractions, idealizations and reductions (Chomsky 1980: 217–9, 2000: 49). He has also criticized Quine for his refusal to include these in his accounts of language.

It is, however, far from clear that Quine accepted a straightforwardly inductive approach to scientific method. His place in the tradition of logical positivism, although complex and ambivalent, would seem to suggest this. Certainly, he commented explicitly that the picture of a language built up during the process of radical translation was formed on inductive evidence, in other words by generalizing over a collection of individual instances and building up an account of linguistic behaviour that was at least confirmed by all currently available evidence (Quine 1960: 30). His inductionism was closer to that of the later Vienna Circle than that of classical logical positivism, however, because of his awareness that inductive generalizations would always necessarily be underdetermined by the data, if they were to be more than simple listings of personal experiences. In a 1974 article on Popper's methodology he was even surprisingly supportive of Popper's views on falsification. He did not say anything explicit in this article about deduction, but he did digress in order to offer a solution to Hempel's paradox. This was Hempel's claim that, because of the logical equivalence of 'All ravens are black' and 'All non-black things are non-ravens', anything that is not a raven and is not black must offer confirmation of the proposition 'All ravens are black', posing a profoundly counterintuitive problem for induction. Quine argued that black ravens do partially confirm 'All ravens are black', but unblack non-ravens do not partially confirm 'All unblack things are non-ravens'. This is because 'raven' and 'black' are what he called 'projectible predicates' while 'unblack' and 'non-raven' are not. He continued: 'I would equate projectibility of predicates to the naturalness of kinds, and I would account for our native primitive intuition of natural kinds by Darwinian natural selection. The intuitively natural groupings that favor successful inductions are the groupings that have survival value in the evolution of the species' (Quine 1974: 219).

In the course of an article in praise of Popper, Quine seems here to be proposing a surprisingly strong defence of induction. At its most extreme, it could be read as a suggestion that human beings are evolutionarily adapted to the inductive method. Even if Quine was not going this far, his words certainly imply that cognitively tendencies that have emerged during the process of evolution are beneficially employed during inductive reasoning. It has been beneficial from a survival point of view for human beings to recognize 'ravens' as a natural grouping more readily than to recognize 'all things that are not ravens'. Therefore a brown cow, for instance, simply does not hold as much weight as a black raven as confirmatory evidence that 'all ravens are black', because our attitude to cows does not most naturally and beneficially classify them as 'non-ravens'.

Chomsky certainly concentrated on what he perceived as Quine's inductionism. Just as Quine had done with the Vienna Circle, Chomsky accused Quine of being unempirical in relation to language. In this case, the accusation took the form of a charge that Quine was ignoring what was usual in scientific method. Chomsky took exception to the special case that Quine made for language. That is, Quine argued that statements about meaning equivalences could only ever be analytical hypotheses rather than genuine scientific hypotheses; observable linguistic behaviour existed and could be studied, but underlying mental states or cognitive meanings did not and could not. For Chomsky, Quine was being unempirical in singling out language as a topic that could not be studied like the subject matter of any other natural science, by a process of hypothesis formation and testing. Quine's insistence on merely collecting and observing the data limited what could be done with it in a way that was artificial and also arbitrary because this was not a restriction imposed on any other natural science: 'It is quite certain that serious hypotheses concerning a native speaker's knowledge of English, or concerning the essential properties of human language – the innate schematism that determines what counts as linguistic data and what intellectual structures are developed on the basis of these data – will "go beyond the evidence". If they did not, they would be without interest' (Chomsky 1969: 66). For Chomsky 'going beyond the evidence' was not simply a matter of making generalizations that were necessarily underdetermined by the data. It meant forming hypotheses that were not licensed by the data, although they could subsequently be tested against it.

Chomsky has become gradually more explicit in his claims that linguistics is a natural science and as such should be investigated in the same ways as any other natural science. In his early work he often drew analogies with physics. Because of his view of language as a genetically programmed cognitive endowment, he has increasingly characterized linguistics as a branch of biology (see, for instance, Chomsky 1976: 123, Chomsky 1986: 27). He has viewed Quine's approach, on the other hand, as being in contravention of all that is expected of scientific study: 'Quine and those influenced by his paradigm are enjoining the "field linguist" to depart radically from the procedures of the sciences, limiting themselves to a small part of the relevant evidence, selected in accordance with behaviourist dogma; and also to reject the standard procedures used in theory construction in the sciences' (Chomsky 2000: 54).

Chomsky also disagreed with Quine about a particular implication of the indeterminacy of translation. For Quine, it made no sense to argue that one translation of a language into another, or one set of analytical hypotheses about meaning in a particular language, was better or more successful than another. As long as the two accounts were both empirically adequate, there was no further level of adequacy to strive for. This was because there was no objectively real meaning for the linguist to model. The question of which of the two different translations best modelled what was really going on in the mind of a speaker of another language 'is a question whose very significance I would put in doubt' (Quine 1970b: 181). For Chomsky, on the other hand, with his commitment to the reality of linguistic mental structures, it was crucial to seek an explanation that not only fitted the available linguistic facts but also did so in the most adequate manner. From his earliest work he elaborated the notion of what made a grammar adequate, arguing that there were different types and degrees of adequacy by which rival grammars could be compared. A grammar could achieve descriptive adequacy if it described the facts of the language. To reach explanatory adequacy, however, it must describe them in such a way that it explained how those facts were consistent with certain universal properties shared by all human languages, and hence how it was possible for speakers to learn that language. That is, it must describe the language in a way consistent with Chomsky's notion of Universal Grammar (for instance, Chomsky 1965: 30–7).

Quine also persisted in his approach, maintaining throughout their protracted debate that his was the truly empirical method for studying language, while Chomsky's was simply unscientific. In an article from the mid-1970s he urged his readers to 'recognize that the semantical study of language is worth pursuing with all the scruples of the natural scientist. We must study language as a system of dispositions to verbal behaviour, and not just surface listlessly to the Sargasso Sea of mentalism' (Quine 1975: 91). For Quine, mentalism entailed a morass of entities entering into the account of language that were unexplained and unsupported by the available evidence.

Quine and Chomsky each attacked the other on the basis that the methodology implied by his linguistics was fundamentally flawed, and that its errors were revealed when it was compared with the mainstream natural sciences. Unlike Quine, Chomsky established an entire school of linguistics in the form of transformational generative grammar in all its varieties. Chomsky and his followers put his ideas into practice; they attempted to develop actual grammars that met his various conditions of adequacy, including the requirement of conformity to Universal Grammar. 'Chomskyan linguistics' was dominant in some linguistics circles for several decades and polarized opinions among linguists. Some of the common criticisms of Chomsky will be considered in the final chapter. One such criticism hinged on his methodology and in particular his enthusiasm for reductions and idealizations. It is argued that in abstracting away from actual utterances, Chomsky could say little that was constructive about how language was actually used for communicative purposes in social situations (see, for instance, Leech 1983: 54, Fairclough 1989: 7, Honey 1997: 45, Gibbon 1999: 19–20).

Quine's influence in present-day linguistics is perhaps less obvious. His name does not have the same currency, or the same tendency to provoke extreme reactions, as Chomsky's does. In fact he is rarely cited by linguists and, despite his long and fervent opposition to Chomsky, is not often evoked by those opposed to Chomsky on methodological grounds. Nevertheless, his work can arguably be seen as a philosophical guarantor for any approach to linguistic study that sees empiricism as tied up with practical fieldwork. Quine himself never engaged in actual linguistic fieldwork, but he frequently urged it as the only sure means of progress in language study, even if he had a tendency to describe it in vaguely exotic terms with the use of expressions such as 'jungle'. Nevertheless, he remains a potential, if dated, champion for those branches of linguistics that eschew mentalism in favour of close regard to contexts and patterns of use.

Some of the other philosophers among Quine's near contemporaries who objected to the assumptions about language made by logical positivism attempted actual studies of language use, generally motivated by specific philosophical purposes. These studies concentrated on a variety of different aspects of language, and might be judged to have met with a variety of degrees of success. But what is perhaps most striking is the difference between the stances the philosophers took as to what would count as an appropriately empirical method for studying language. The next four chapters will be concerned with the works first of the Oxford philosophers of ordinary language and then of the Oslo school of philosophy, concentrating particularly on their acknowledged leaders J. L. Austin and Arne Naess. A study of these two schools of thought suggests that the issue of what counts as empirical in language study is far from clear-cut or self-evident. It is interesting because of the parallels it suggests with present day linguistics. Here, too, widespread acceptance that empiricism is a laudable measure of linguistic study is accompanied by unease and outright disagreement as to what such empiricism is to consist of. As in the case of the mid-twentieth-century philosophical disagreement, this debate concerns both the question of what counts as the proper method and also the closely related matter of what counts as the appropriate data.

4
Ordinary Language Philosophy

The logical positivism of the Vienna Circle exerted a firm, but relatively brief, hold on British philosophical imagination. This hold was loosened soon after the Second World War as a result of a growing conviction among many British philosophers that, despite its obvious appeals, logical positivism was ultimately untenable as a philosophical approach. A number of philosophers commented on what was wrong with logical positivism in general, and with what it said about language in particular. In this way they presented for themselves the task of establishing an alternative stance on the place of language in philosophy, and indeed on the type of subject matter than language constituted. One set of responses to this task formed the basis of what soon became known as 'ordinary language philosophy'.

The name perhaps most readily associated with ordinary language philosophy is that of J. L. Austin. It would be wrong to see him as the sole progenitor of the movement. Many other philosophers have been rightly credited with playing a role in its development; for instance G. E. Moore, Gilbert Ryle and the later Wittgenstein all wrote influentially about the place of ordinary language in philosophy. Nevertheless, the focus of this chapter will remain chiefly with Austin himself. It was in his work that the influence of logical positivism on empirical approaches to the philosophy of language made itself most strongly felt (for a discussion of the wider philosophical background to ordinary language philosophy, see Chapman 2005: chapter 3). Austin gained the respect of his colleagues for work that set out deliberately and self-consciously to refute some of the more extreme claims of logical positivism. As a result of this respect and of Austin's own austere charisma, a style of philosophy emerged at Oxford that was for sometime acknowledged an orthodoxy. Moreover, in response to the demands made by ordinary language Austin developed a new and, in his opinion a least, genuinely empirical philosophical methodology. It was shaped by his particular enthusiasms and proclivities and seen by many as idiosyncratic, even eccentric. Nevertheless, the application of this methodology at Oxford triggered a debate in the wider philosophical community about what was the best way to go about the empirical study of ordinary language, and even whether ordinary language was amenable to empirical study at all. Finally, Austin's ideas about speech acts, together with subsequent developments of these ideas, have been an important catalyst in the development of pragmatics, and more generally of the discussion of the relationship between meaning and use, in linguistics.

The British enthusiasm for logical positivism in the years immediately before the Second World War arose almost exclusively from the publication of A. J. Ayer's *Language Truth and Logic*. Following this, many British philosophers developed views similar to those expressed in early articles in *Erkenntnis;* this new approach was capable of revolutionizing philosophical thought by revealing the misconceptions and confusions underlying many traditional philosophical problems. To some *Language, Truth and Logic* offered a coherent expression of worries about traditional philosophy that they were already experiencing but had not yet fully voiced. These worries generally centred around a dissatisfaction with metaphysical speculation that was often highly subjective and sometimes moralizing. Ayer's presentation of logical positivism offered a principled way of rejecting this type of philosophy; philosophical discussion was from now on to be conducted only on the basis of a rigorous, objective analysis of the terms in which it was expressed. Some British philosophers retained this faith in analysis even after their initial enthusiasm for logical positivism had abated. Ayer himself summed up this story succinctly in his own retrospective reflections on *Language, Truth and Logic*, explaining: 'that it crystallised certain tendencies which had been struggling before the war for wider acceptance and that it served also as a springboard for the development after the war of the various trends that were rather inaccurately fused under the heading of linguistic philosophy, even though they came to be at variance with it at many cardinal points' (Ayer 1987: 24).

Austin was in many ways representative of what Ayer described. He was initially impressed by logical positivism. Its intolerance for metaphysical speculation chimed with his own discomfort with the unreflecting use of language in much of traditional philosophy. But he was also uneasy about some of its more dogmatic claims, and this unease resolved itself into a reaction against logical positivism as he gradually developed his own philosophical approach. This journey from guarded enthusiasm about the logical positivism expounded in Ayer's book to open hostility to its strictures seems to have been common among many of those who later became leading lights of ordinary language philosophy. In his intellectual autobiography Paul Grice described Ayer's impact on Oxford philosophy: 'Many people, myself included, were greatly interested in the methods, theses, and problems which were on display, and some were, at least momentarily, inspired by what they saw and heard. For my part, my reservations were never laid to rest' (Grice 1986: 48). Describing the influences on him in the early years of his academic career, P. F. Strawson commented: 'Nor should I fail to mention A. J. Ayer whose *Language, Truth and Logic* I had read, enthralled, in the gardens of St John's as an undergraduate – even though, by now, I no longer found satisfying his undiluted classical empiricism' (Strawson 1998: 8).

Austin's early anxieties about logical positivism centred on what he saw as its disregard for how topics discussed by philosophers were dealt with in nonphilosophical language. His own method of bringing non-philosophical language to bear on philosophical problems developed gradually, and only fully after the Second World War. But even in the 1930s he was uneasy with logical positivism's insistence on the use of technical terms without regard for the resources already available in language. In effect Austin was arguing that this made for a very unempirical approach to philosophy. Technical terms were coined and defined by diktat. Philosophical discussion then proceeded on the basis of these definitions, without recourse to how the relevant terms were used outside philosophical discussion, or even regard to whether they were used at all.

An early focus of dispute between Austin and Ayer was over just such a technical term: the use of the expression 'sense data' and its role in discussions of the philosophy of perception. Ayer later published his account of perception in the follow-up to *Language, Truth and Logic*, another short and polemical book entitled *Foundations of Empirical Knowledge*. In this he set out his own version of a philosophical view of long standing: that we never directly perceive material objects, only sense data. Statements about material objects can legitimately enter into philosophical discussion only if they can first be 'translated' into statements about sense data, the philosopher's term for the impressions we receive through our senses when we have the sensation of interacting with material objects, and which form our only truly empirical encounter with the physical world (Ayer 1940).

Austin was highly suspicious of these ideas. His formal response to them was interrupted by his war service, but on his return to Oxford he wrote a series of lectures explicitly aimed at refuting Ayer's claims. These were first delivered in 1947, continued throughout the 1950s, and were eventually published posthumously under the title *Sense and Sensibilia*. Austin stressed in these that he was not interested in putting forward an alternative philosophy of perception, but merely in getting rid of some of the false assertions that tended to dog this area because of the unquestioning acceptance of technical terms. His attack was two-pronged. First of all he argued that many of the expressions on which Ayer's position depended were little better than nonce coinages that existed only within the closed world of philosophical discussion. People described their encounters with the everyday world without any perplexity and without these terms. The expression 'sense data' simply did not turn up in everyday discussion. People very rarely talked about 'material objects', and even the verb 'perceive' occurred infrequently compared with such much more common and much less problematic alternatives as 'see'. Austin's first claim, then, was that the insistence on translating perfectly workable and effective ways of talking into philosophical terminology was not in itself justified. It simply introduced unexplained and problematic notions, such as sense data, that did not bother the vast majority of people in their interactions with the world.

Austin's second approach was to engage in the careful scrutiny of how some of the more everyday words that occurred in philosophical discussions of perception were actually used outside philosophy. He concentrated on some of the terms that, he argued, Ayer used carelessly. He produced examples of these words in a variety of everyday-sounding expressions, encouraging the audience of his lectures to consider exactly when they would use verbs such as 'looks', 'seems', 'appears', or what ranges of experience they would describe as 'apparent', 'imaginary' or 'real'. He argued that just as philosophers such as Ayer promoted unnecessary distinctions and complications by means of philosophical coinages, they were also guilty of missing the subtleties of expression available in everyday language. For instance, discussing the word 'real', Austin claimed that philosophers had missed some important insights by failing to notice that 'it does not have one single, specifiable always-the-same *meaning*', nor was it even systematically ambiguous between a number of different meanings (Austin 1962a: 64, original emphasis). Rather 'real' was what he called an 'adjuster word'; its function was to exclude possible ways of being not real, and there were many different ways in which something could be said to be 'not real'. To say that the colour of someone's hair was 'not real' because the hair was dyed was to say something very different from saying that the colour of something seen by artificial light in a shop was 'not real' because it would look different in natural daylight.

Early in his career Austin also developed doubts concerning some the claims about semantics made by the Vienna Circle. He expressed these in a lecture in 1940. Perhaps surprisingly, given his readiness to disagree explicitly with Ayer and his general enthusiasm for demolishing opposing philosophical views, Austin did not attack logical positivism by name. But his target would have been obvious to his Oxford audience because he focussed on a central tenet of the Vienna Circle: the viability of the distinction between analytic and synthetic sentences. Austin argued that the distinction was just another example of the pointless complications that philosophers would embroil themselves in if they failed to attend to how language actually worked. Philosophers should be cured of trying to divide sentences into the analytic and the synthetic because the distinction was itself meaningless. It was meaningless because it depended on the phrase 'the meaning of a word', which was in turn a staple of traditional philosophical discussion that failed to relate to how language actually worked. The distinction between analytic and synthetic was one of the dogmas of logical positivism that would later form a target for Quine's attacks on the unempirical assumptions of the Vienna Circle about meaning. Quine's argument would be that the distinction was based on the unempirical assumption that words had an inherent meaning, independent of specific occasions of use. In 1940, Austin told his audience that 'there is *no* simple and handy appendage of a word called "the meaning of (the word) 'x'"' (Austin 1940: 30, original emphasis). Philosophers of language should stop worrying about this obscure phrase and concentrate instead on the question of why people called different things by the same name. He urged his audience to consider the word 'head' as one example of this problem. What he rather surprisingly called 'the different meanings of the word "head"' would show a complex network of relationships to each other, but would actually encompass a wide variety of objects and concepts (Austin 1940: 42–3). In other words, there was no single, identifiable entity to which we could give the name 'the meaning of the word "head"'.

Austin's contention was that this realization left the distinction between analytic and synthetic untenable. If words could not be said to have 'a meaning', then it was not possible to say that one word 'means the same as' another, or had a particular constituent as 'part of its meaning'.

In effect, although Austin did not spell this out, it was no longer viable to describe a sentence as analytic because it made no sense to claim that its subject meant the same as its predicate, or that the meaning of its predicate was contained in the meaning of its subject. In fact, he argued, the distinction was not just meaningless; it was unworkable and unhelpful. There were many sentences that ordinarily did not fit into a simple dichotomy between analytic and synthetic, and the artificial and unmotivated assumption that all sentences must do so was unnecessarily holding philosophers back when they could be investigating the ways in which language actually worked.

Austin's mistrust of the attempt to class all sentences as either analytic and true, or synthetic and contingent was one aspect of his general unease with the traditional philosophical notion of 'truth'. Classical logic, and the various branches of philosophy that drew on it, depended on a bivalent definition of truth. There were two truth values: true and false. If a statement was not true it was false. If it was not false then it was true. This was the definition that underpinned Frege's development of mathematical logic and Russell and Whitehead's assimilation of mathematics to logic. It was also central to the work of the Vienna Circle. Non-analytical statements were to be admitted into philosophical discourse only if it proved possible to establish that they held one of these two truth values. Tarski's semantic definition of truth, endorsed by Carnap, had added a precise definition of what it was to say that a sentence was 'true'. Austin found the philosophical notion of 'truth' to be one of the most problematic, perhaps because it was one of the least empirical. A simple division between 'true' and 'false' did not do justice to the range of responses that people actually had to statements. In a paper on the subject in 1950, he argued that there are many other adjectives, besides 'true' and 'false' that are used to express judgements on statements: 'We say, for example, that a certain statement is exaggerated or vague or bald, a description somewhat rough or misleading or not very good, an account rather too general or too concise. In cases like these it is pointless to insist on deciding in simple terms whether the statement is "true or false"' (Austin 1950: 97–8).

Austin's unease over the philosophical insistence on a rigid distinction between 'true' and 'false' was one factor in his rejection of what in the same article he described as 'the descriptive fallacy'. This was the philosophical claim, or rather the unsupported assumption, that the significant business of language was to describe the world: to make statements of fact. These statements were then subject to the judgement of being either 'true' or 'false'. Austin rejected the descriptive fallacy on the grounds not just that statements may not necessarily be either true or false, but also that making statements was by no means the only, and might not even be the most important, function that language performed. This argument was to underpin his most important philosophical ideas. In the article on truth he drew attention to commands and questions, as well as value judgements and works of fiction; none of these valid uses of language were concerned with describing the world, and none could appropriately be judged to be either true or false. Philosophers, he argued, should dispense with the unsupported and stultifying fallacy that language described the world. Instead, they should consider the wide variety of different ways in which language was actually used. Further, the only valid way to study the term 'true' itself was to consider the many ways in which 'is true' was used in English.

Austin's early lectures and papers, then, hint strongly at an interest in investigating language as it was actually used rather than as it had traditionally been discussed by philosophers. On occasions he made this interest explicit. In his 1940 lecture on the meaninglessness of 'the meaning of a word', Austin proposed that a full investigation into the question of why we call different things by the same name would involve careful and meticulous study of language. Taking a sideswipe at what he called 'the Polish semanticists' he urged that 'it demands the study of *actual* languages, *not* ideal ones' (Austin 1940: 38, original emphasis). In a later paper entitled 'Unfair to facts' he engaged in the philosophical debate about the nature and status of facts by 'observing certain rather easily overlooked boundaries between what may and may not be done with the word "fact"' (Austin 1954: 104), and even by consulting the Oxford English Dictionary to find out about the etymology of the word.

The examination of ordinary language was in fact rapidly becoming established as Austin's distinctive philosophical approach. It became an accepted norm of Oxford philosophy, so much so that in 1955 a report in *The Times* could comment on 'the new linguistic way of doing philosophy which has become the Oxford Movement of our time' (*The Times*, 26 September 1955: 10). The case that Austin made for this approach was two-fold. Firstly, and in direct opposition to the claims of formal philosophers such as Russell and Carnap, he argued that ordinary language was a legitimate and a worthwhile focus of serious investigation in its own right. This is the defence of language that would perhaps accord most with the outlook of present-day linguistics. The use of language constitutes a significant aspect of human behaviour and can tell us a lot about how human society and interaction operates, so it should be beyond question that it is an important topic of study. But this was not Austin's primary motivation in urging the serious study of language. He saw it as a valuable philosophical tool: as a means potentially of clarifying areas that had been made unnecessarily complicated by the use of philosophical, as opposed to ordinary, language. This was why he opposed what he saw as the unquestioning use of philosophical terms that did not occur in ordinary language, terms such as 'sense data' and 'analytic/synthetic'. He set out this position stridently in 'A plea for excuses', a paper from the mid-1950s about the language in which excuses, fault and blame are discussed. His case for ordinary language is often quoted, but bears repetition:

> Our common stock of words embodies all the distinctions men have found worth drawing, and the connections they have found worth marking, in the lifetimes of many generations: these surely are likely to be more numerous, more sound, since they have stood up to the long test of the survival of the fittest, and more subtle, at least in all ordinary and reasonable practical matters, than any that you or I are likely to think up in our arm-chairs of an afternoon – the most favoured alternative method.
>
> (Austin 1956a: 130)

For some philosophers working in Oxford in the 1950s this type of observation engendered an enthusiasm and an optimism similar to that felt in Vienna in the 1920s. The logical positivists had believed that they were going to do away, forever, with many of the traditional puzzles and perplexities of philosophy by showing that they were expressed in terms that were unempirical, and therefore that they presented puzzles only because they were meaningless. The ordinary language philosophers now believed that a careful enough attention to the patterns of language would reveal that those same problems had been perpetuated only because no one had taken time to consider the language in which they were expressed, and to see how far it strained or distorted ordinary usage.

This is not to say that Austin espoused, or that ordinary language philosophers universally endorsed, an unquestioning adherence to ordinary language as the only mode of philosophical discussion. Many people, including Bertrand Russell, were quick to assume that they did. Writing in *Mind* in 1957 Russell complained that many contemporary philosophers 'Are persuaded that common speech is good enough not only for daily life, but also for philosophy. I, on the contrary, am persuaded that common speech is full of vagueness and inaccuracy, and that any attempt to be precise and accurate requires modification of common speech both as regards vocabulary and as regards syntax' (Russell 1957: 387). However, in writing in support of serious attention to ordinary language, Austin repeatedly urged it as a potential starting point in philosophical discussion, not as a limitation on how that discussion should be conducted or what findings it should be permitted to reach. His aversion was to philosophical jargon that had been coined hastily and without prior consideration of the complexities of the language already available. He was willing to introduce new terms into a debate, but only after the resources of ordinary language had been thoroughly investigated and found to be wanting for some particular technical purpose. Even in his 1940 attack on the distinction between analytic and synthetic, making clear that philosophers should consult actual language, not a preconceived notion of language, he conceded that it would not do 'having discovered the facts about "ordinary usage" *to rest content* with that, as though there were nothing more to be discussed and discovered. There may be plenty that might happen and does happen which would need new and better language to describe it in' (Austin 1940: 37, original emphasis). In a slightly later article he argued that 'essential though it is as a preliminary to track down the detail of our ordinary uses of words, it seems that we shall in the end always be compelled to straighten them out to some extent' (Austin 1952: 181) and he continued to stress this point throughout his work.

Given Austin's repeated insistences that philosophical inquiry should begin with the rigorous analysis of language, and given his apparent contempt for 'armchair' speculation, he might have been expected to write about methodology. The present-day linguist might hope to find a discussion of how language should be studied, and by what criteria the rigour of this study should be judged. In fact, there is very little in Austin's published work about how his distinctive style of philosophy should be approached, beyond a few hints in papers such as 'A plea for excuses'. Austin did have a method, although it seems he shied away from any claims to have established a 'philosophical methodology', or to have identified the single correct way of approaching philosophical problems. The results of Austin's method are apparent in a number of his published writings, including the papers on word meaning, on truth and on facts. What is not always in evidence, however, is how he got to those results, or what for him counted as acceptable data about how language was ordinarily used.

Austin's method of doing philosophy was familiar to many of his colleagues because he was keen to involve those around him as much as possible in his research. His 'Saturday mornings' were famous in Oxford: term-time meetings to which he invited selected colleagues to termtime meetings for more informal philosophical discussion than were permitted by the requirements of weekday teaching commitments. These meetings were not devoted exclusively to putting Austin's methodology in practice. On a number of occasions they served as reading groups focussed on a particular work of contemporary philosophy, or as forums for more general discussion. But at least some of them were spent on the process that Austin liked to describe as 'linguistic botanising', and they therefore illustrate Austin's preference for collaboration in research, although not necessarily in writing.

As Austin's chosen title suggests, the task that he set himself and his colleagues was one of collecting and categorizing. He was almost certainly interested in the scientific overtones of the term; he was known to have been an admirer of the physical sciences, and to have regretted his own lack of expertise in them. But his was to be a science of the meticulous gathering and analysing of data, not of the construction of hypotheses or of generalizing theories. Austin's data were words, and also evidence about what speakers know of the ordinary use of words. By 'ordinary' he meant uses that were not philosophical. He was not interested in privileging colloquial over formal language, nor conversational over technical. The basic opposition he was concerned with was that between all these types of usage on the one hand and philosophical usage on the other. His thesis was that philosophy should depart from the ways in which words were used by nonphilosophers only with great caution, and only after a careful analysis of ordinary language.

When confronting a philosophical topic in need of elucidation, the first step in Austin's approach was to draw up a list of relevant vocabulary. Near synonyms of a key term, and also its apparent contradictions or opposites, were often a good starting point. It is possible to reconstruct fragmentary examples of such lists from published work such as 'A plea for excuses'. Austin tackled questions of fault and responsibility by considering, amongst other types of words, adverbs that might describe actions. His list included 'voluntarily', 'involuntarily' 'deliberately', 'unwittingly' 'spontaneously', 'freely' and 'impulsively'. According to Austin's method, lists of this type were collected mainly from the investigating philosopher's own knowledge of the language, but certain aids in this process were available. Chief amongst these was the dictionary. Austin offered his audience the following advice on how to proceed:

> First we may use the dictionary – quite a concise one will do, but the use must be *thorough*. Two methods suggest themselves, both a little tedious, but repaying. One is to read the book through, listing all the words that seem relevant; this does not take as long as many suppose. The other is start with a widish selection of obviously relevant terms, and to consult the dictionary under each: it will be found that, in the explanations of the various meanings of each, a surprising number of other terms occur, which are germane though of course not often synonymous. We then look up each of *these*, bringing in more for our bag from the 'definitions' given in each case; and when we have continued for a little, it will generally be found that the family circle begins to close, until ultimately it is complete and we come only upon repetitions.
>
> (Austin 1956a: 134–5)

Austin also suggested that, in the case of pleas and excuses, sources such as law and psychology books could be consulted for further expressions used to classify actions. Data received from the sources, however, were to be enhanced by use of the researcher's 'imagination'; the sources clearly had no higher status than as a prompt or guide to the researcher's knowledge of the language.

These hints in 'A plea for excuses' were just about all that Austin disclosed officially of his working method. His close colleague J. O. Urmson later reconstructed the next stages in the methodology, building on his own experiences of working with Austin and on some fragmentary notes discovered after Austin's death. Austin had given these the title 'Something about one way of possibly doing one part of philosophy' (Urmson et al. 1965: 77). The next step was to seek for connections, similarities and differences among the data. The imagination had a vital role to play here, too. The researcher or group of researchers were to think up contexts in which the different expressions would naturally occur. Such context would include sample utterances and simple scenarios: is it possible to say that a particular action was performed 'voluntarily'? Could the same action be described as having been done 'spontaneously' or 'freely', and if so would there be any differences in meaning? The imagined contexts might extend to constructed dialogues in which the expressions under consideration appeared either natural or unlikely. Such considerations allowed the expressions to be grouped and classified together, and significant differences in shades of meaning to emerge. As Urmson put it, when it came to giving accounts of particular expressions under consideration, 'it is an empirical question whether the accounts given are correct and adequate, for they can be checked against the data collected' (Urmson et al. 1965: 80). This in turn allowed the researcher to suggest a general account of this particular area of human experience: of the distinctions recorded in the language that were presumably a reflection of the distinctions people over the generations had found in the world and in human behaviour. Only at this point in the process, Urmson explained, was it permissible for researchers to consult what had traditionally been said in philosophy about the particular topic, and what vocabulary had been employed. Armed with carefully sorted and catalogued evidence about the distinctions and connections drawn outside philosophy, they were at last able to determine whether philosophical usage was justified, how the traditional problems were to be addressed, and maybe even how they could be dissolved.

Austin was apparently adamant that, if conducted thoroughly and rigorously, this method would yield genuinely empirical evidence about language. The data were not anecdotal or *ad hoc* if they were collected in suitable quantities. Even some of his more sceptical colleagues seemed impressed. Stuart Hampshire vouched for the fact that in the case of language it might ultimately be possible, given sustained effort by a group of philosophers, to 'collect a sufficient range of graded examples to permit, for the first time, some really well-founded generalisations' (Hampshire 1960: 40). The most important aspect of the data for Austin, though, was not the amount collected but that fact that they were obtained collaboratively. The fact that a group of philosophers were working together on the task of collection and arrangement obviated possible concerns that the data might be subjective or skewed by one idiolect. Austin claimed that the degree of consensus and agreement among a group was usually remarkably high. If the data were collected, debated and agreed on collaboratively they could be claimed as objective and empirical. Some years after Austin's death, his colleague Geoffrey Warnock mounted a spirited defence of his method along these same lines. Warnock drew attention to what he clearly saw as the empirical credentials of Austin's 'fieldwork': 'Does it not make sense to, as it were, try things out as you go along on other critical people – the closest, perhaps one can get to an "experimental" test?' (Warnock 1989: 9). Warnock went on to urge that an agreement reached among colleagues after careful discussion should be treated as acceptable evidence of how things actually were.

Austin's approach tended to polarize opinion. Among some of his colleagues and many of his students he was celebrated, revered even, as a pioneer of a fresh and empirically rigorous new style of philosophy. But he also attracted an unusually high level of criticism, which was often quite rancorous; many articles and a number of books were written with the express aim of opposing his approach. Amongst his critics it was very often Austin's working method that attracted the harshest comment. Some complained that analysis of ordinary language was simply the wrong way to go about philosophy; philosophical terminology had been introduced for a purpose and generally served that purpose well. Many, however, focussed specifically on Austin's unique method of collaborative data collection. They argued that whatever the strength of the case for proceeding from ordinary language, Austin was simply not doing what he claimed. He was not working with a genuinely objective and empirical sample of ordinary language; there was something faulty, even phoney, about his method.

One line of argument was concerned with the introspective nature of Austin's data. For some critics, the fact that a group of philosophers met together to discuss their findings was simply no compensation for the fact that the findings in question were drawn from their own opinions of how they would themselves use language in a variety of hypothetical situations. This general argument was summed up succinctly in an article published a few years after Austin's death but while ordinary language philosophy was still seen by many as dominant. Jerry Fodor cautioned that 'We do not always say what we say that we would say' (Fodor 1964: 199). Fodor argued that speakers' intuitions were acceptable as evidence, but only when they were at least in principle capable of objective checking; only in this way could they become truly empirical. Fodor was suspicious of arguments that relied on what philosophers decided they would say in hypothetical but unrealistic situations, since such intuitions were simply not amenable to testing.

Fodor was responding to ordinary language philosophy from a position within linguistics. In a slightly earlier article, co-written with Jerrold Katz, he characterized Austin's approach as being distinct from linguistics largely because of its focus on meaning. Fodor and Katz did not take issue with the methodologies of ordinary language philosophy; they described the possible alternative of a researcher going about transcribing speech and noting what was said and how frequently as a 'caricature' of empirical language study and as being alien to the methods of both linguistics and ordinary language philosophy. 'Rather, to say that the Oxford philosopher engages in empirical investigation is to say that his claims about English should be subject to the same modes of confirmation and disconfirmation that linguists accept' (Fodor and Katz 1963: 71). A few years later C. G. New was less conciliatory, comparing Austin's methodology unfavourably with that of contemporary linguistics. He commented tersely that 'What we think we do with words is not necessarily what we actually do with them' (New 1966: 155).

Philosophers, too, were worried about the use of data drawn from introspection. Benson Mates argued that all individuals, however learned or skilled, must be treated as unreliable reporters on their own linguistic usage. People were generally not good judges of how they themselves used language, so their reports must always be treated as subjective and unempirical. Mates cast further doubt on the reliability of Austin's favoured style of data by claiming that 'the intuitive findings of different people, even of different experts, are often inconsistent' (Mates 1958a: 165). Stanley Cavell responded to Mates's arguments with an article, in general, more sympathetic to the aims of ordinary language philosophy. However, his contribution to the debate did include a hint towards another contemporary criticism of Austin's method. Cavell made the following comparison between philosopher's ordinary language and what he called 'ordinary ordinary language': 'The philosopher, understandably, often takes the isolated man bent silently over a book as his model of what using language is. But the primary fact of natural language is that it is something spoken, spoken together' (Cavell 1958: 198).

Cavell did not develop this criticism in much detail. As it stands in his published article it appears to be concerned mainly with the difference between written and spoken language, and to advance the argument that an inquiry into what is genuinely ordinary in language use should be concerned with the latter. But it also touches on a concern about Austin's chosen sample of subjects and it therefore relates to a criticism that was voiced by a number of Austin's contemporaries: that Austin's group was simply not representative of speakers of the language as a whole, with the result that any findings from it must necessarily be skewed. Ordinary language philosophy's claims to empiricism relied on the use of a sample of speakers of the language, but that sample was uniform and self-selecting. The results of this type of investigation could not hope to offer a genuine picture of the state of the language because the sample in question was both small and also socially and intellectually elite. Along these lines, C. W. K. Mundle complained that Austin's accounts of language 'describe how English is spoken by the few people who are as fastidious as himself and as sensitive to the nuances and etymology of its words' (Mundle 1979: 82). Austin and his circle were criticized for being inward-looking and parochial.

Other critics were worried by what they saw as Austin's excessive reverence for ordinary language as it was spoken at the particular time at which he was working and by the implication that they drew from this that it could not and would not change. Austin had argued in 'A plea for excuses' that the distinctions and connections embodied in ordinary language had 'stood up to the long test of the survival of the fittest' (Austin 1956a: 130). Warnock later voiced this praise of ordinary language in his own words: 'language does not develop in a random or inexplicable fashion. It is to be *used* for a vast number of highly important purposes; and it is at the very least unlikely that it should contain either much more, or much less, than those purposes require' (Warnock 1958: 150, original emphasis). The critics of ordinary language philosophy remained unconvinced. Quine complained that some of his contemporary philosophers were 'treating ordinary language as sacrosanct. They exalt ordinary language to the exclusion of one of its traits: its disposition to keep evolving' (Quine 1960: 3). Critics objected to what Ernest Gellner described as the 'idolatry of ordinary language' (Gellner 1959: 61), and the implication that it had reached a state of stability and perfection. This particular charge is perhaps unfair. Austin did not claim that ordinary language could not be improved upon, rather that philosophers should be cautious rather than rash in any attempts to do so themselves. Furthermore, the Darwinian overtones of Austin and Warnock's account did not commit ordinary language philosophers to the view that language would not change in the future. As Quine acknowledged in his own choice of expression, evolution is a continuous process.

There is, however, a particular tendency in Austin's work that seems rather at odds with his enthusiasm for language as it is ordinarily used, and that is perhaps related to his alleged elitism. Given Austin's professed confidence in the profundity and subtlety of what people ordinarily say, it is perhaps surprising to find occasional comments in his lectures and papers that suggest a distinctly prescriptive attitude to linguistic usage, or an assumption that some speakers are simply better at the business of using language than others. Nevertheless such comments are to be found. Austin suggested on one occasion that if colloquial speech can sometimes be 'a bit loose' this is something that speakers are aware of – unless, of course they are 'anyway rather insensitive about such matters' (Austin 1962a: 35n). On another occasion he claimed that using 'could' incorrectly when 'might' should be used 'might, I think, be held to be a vulgarism' (Austin 1956b: 155).

Dissatisfaction with Austin's reliance on intuition led some philosophers to suggest other types of data that might lend more weight to his claims. In an address to the Aristotelian Society in 1960, Nathan Isaacs professed himself generally sympathetic to the aims and approach of ordinary language philosophy. Nevertheless, he drew attention to the marked lack of agreed knowledge or clarified thought to have emerged from it, given its ambitions and its comparative longevity. He suggested that for such an approach to succeed there was a need for some preparatory groundwork, and that this was not being done. Some hard factual evidence was needed about the contexts in which specific key terms were used and the functions they performed. Such work was overlooked because of 'the assumption that philosophers somehow have their own sufficient access to whatever *psychological* data or notions they wish to examine or use (an assumption long since abandoned as regards, for example, physical or astronomical or biological data!)', and specifically the assumption that data about ordinary language were 'given' (Isaacs 1960: 220, original emphasis).

Bertrand Russell, too, gave voice to this criticism. Russell's opposition is not surprising; Austin's enthusiasm for ordinary language as a guide to the structure of reality was the opposite of his own distrust of language as illogical and potentially misleading. Russell remained openly and implacably hostile towards ordinary language philosophy throughout the 1950s, attacking it as narrow-minded and unproductive and arguing that it trivialized philosophical inquiry. Repeating the accusation of elitism and insularity, he suggested during one such attack that 'common usage' could only really be investigated by means of large-scale data collection and analysis: 'What in fact they believe in is not common usage, as determined by mass observation, statistics, medians, standard deviations, and the rest of the apparatus. What they believe in is the usage of persons who have their amount of education, neither more nor less' (Russell 1956: 138).

The many perceived problems with Austin's method are summarized in the series of rhetorical questions fired off by Keith Graham in his book-length critique of ordinary language philosophy:

> But if we, i.e. a small group of socially and culturally homogeneous philosophers meeting in an Oxford college, do pronounce from this position on what we, i.e. all or most competent native English speakers should say in different situations, how can we be sure that our pronouncements are correct? Does the method not cry out for some form of empirical verification? If we hold that most people would say

so-and-so, should we not test this claim by observing their linguistic behaviour or at least by asking them whether they agree?

(Graham 1977: 40)

Graham pinpointed the root of the problems for ordinary language philosophy as its assumption that report rather than observation was an appropriate source of data in language study. In fact, there are some tantalizing hints that Austin was interested in the possibility of using tape recorders to gather data about usage (see, for example, Tennessen 1965: 234 and 248 n. 3). However, there is no reference in Austin's own writings to this possibility, and no evidence that he ever actually engaged in this procedure.

Throughout the 1950s the major British philosophy journals published a raft of articles and notes on the nature and place of ordinary language and on the question of whether it could legitimately be investigated by intuition (see, for instance, Cobitz 1950, Haggstrom 1952 and the exchange comprising Hare 1957, Henle 1957 and Korner 1957). The debate reached something of a crescendo in 1959 when it spilled over into the letters and editorial pages of *The Times*. The trigger was the publication of Ernest Gellner's *Words and Things*. Gellner was a former student of Austin's, now thoroughly disillusioned with ordinary language philosophy in general and working in the comparatively new discipline of sociology at the London School of Economics. His book was explicitly intended to expose what he saw as the errors, pretensions and outright deceptions inherent in Austin's approach. He rehearsed many of the arguments already put forward in the debate during the 1950s, and added a particular sociological criticism, linking the style of philosophy to the social class and background of the individual philosophers who practised it. He argued that 'Anyone accustomed to a certain conversational tradition, one which avoids both ideas and technicality, but indulges in a kind of conspicuous, lighthearted triviality, can take part in a linguo-philosophical discussion without much training: he will easily recognise its rules' (Gellner 1959: 266–7).

Words and Things was published with an enthusiastic Introduction by Bertrand Russell. Gilbert Ryle, then editor of *Mind* and regarded by many as something close to an elder statesman of ordinary language philosophy, wrote to the book's publishers explaining that he would not permit it to be reviewed in his journal on the grounds that it was abusive and therefore not an appropriate contribution to an academic debate. Russell took issue with this, so much so that he wrote to *The Times* to draw attention to Ryle's actions. He accused Ryle of suppressing discussion of the book simply because it disagreed with his own philosophical views, adding that 'if all books that do not endorse Professor Ryle's opinions are to be boycotted in the pages of *Mind*, that hitherto respected periodical will sink to the level of the mutual-admiration organ of a coterie' (*The Times*, 5 November 1959: 13). Ryle replied alleging that Gellner defamed several easily identifiable Oxford philosophers. A number of letters followed this exchange, from readers of *The Times* both within and outside of the philosophical establishment. These debated the relative merits of the autonomy of a journal editor, the importance of open academic debate, and perhaps most significantly the perceived insular and self-sustaining world of contemporary Oxford philosophy.

Three weeks after Russell's initial letter, victory seemed to be declared in his favour, when an editorial in *The Times* brought the discussion to a close. This commented on the degree of antagonism that ordinary language philosophy had clearly generated. It suggested various reasons for this, including its almost cult-like status among its practitioners, and citing allegations of elitism and isolationism. Philosophers of ordinary language, the editorial suggested, regarded philosophical problems as 'a sort of cerebral neurosis' which they must cure: 'The fact that they practised the therapy chiefly on themselves did not reconcile those of different views to the bland and seemingly patronizing attitude inherent in this doctor-patient relationship' (*The Times*, 24 November 1959: 13). In the end, in this very public debate, the view of ordinary language philosophy as insular, self-validating and remote seems to have held sway.

Despite Austin's hints that their approach would offer new and decisive insights into old and muddled discussions, ordinary language philosophers did not engage much in wider philosophical debates. One exception to this rule was H. L. A. Hart, whose area was jurisprudence. Hart acknowledged Austin's contribution in 'A plea for excuses' to the understanding of the complexity of human action. He employed a small-scale piece of linguistic botanizing when writing about legal responsibility and excuses: 'If an individual breaks the law when none of the excusing conditions are present he is ordinarily said to have acted of "his own free will", "of his own accord", "voluntarily", or it might be said, "He could have helped doing what he did"' (Hart 1958: 28).

Another exception, and one more closely related to the traditional terms of the philosophy of language, was an article by Paul Grice and P. F. Strawson which took on Quine's attack on the distinction between analytic and synthetic statements. Strawson himself had published widely and influentially. In most of these publications he had revealed himself as not so much an Austin-style philosopher of ordinary language as a formal philosopher in the analytic tradition with an unusual sensitivity to natural, as opposed to artificial logical languages. Collaboratively with Grice, however, Strawson defended the distinction between analytic and synthetic against Quine's charge that it was unempirical by drawing attention to the ways in which people ordinarily talked about meaning. It was true that the words 'analytic' and 'synthetic' themselves did not appear very often in everyday talk. Nevertheless, to insist that the distinction had no meaning would entail insisting that other related words and phrases, ones that were current in ordinary language, must also be meaningless. If there were no such thing as an analytic statement then there could be no such thing as synonymity, since 'all bachelors are unmarried men' could be said to be analytic if 'bachelors' and 'unmarried men' could be said to be synonymous. If there were no such thing as synonymity, then it could make no sense to talk about two words or expressions 'meaning the same' as each other, or even to talk about expressions having meaning at all. These implications would presumably not have troubled Quine; they were very much in line with what he was explicitly arguing about meaning. But Grice and Strawson argued that such implication should be troubling because people did routinely use expressions such as 'means the same as' and 'means'. 'Is all such talk meaningless?', they asked, 'Is all talk of correct or incorrect *translation* of sentences of one language into sentences of another meaningless? It is hard to believe that it is' (Grice and Strawson 1956: 201, original emphasis).

Despite these forays into legal language and into the debate about analyticity, the ideas which have formed ordinary language philosophy's chief legacy are Austin's own development of the theory of speech acts, and Paul Grice's theory of conversational implicature. Each has generated a huge responsive literature in philosophy and more recently in linguistics. There is a clear link between Austin's views on the practice of philosophy and the theory of speech acts. He made it clear in his most famous presentation of these ideas that he quite literally went through the dictionary looking for performative verbs. Grice was a lot more ambivalent towards linguistic botanizing, but the habit of attending to ordinary use, and to the things that speakers actually do with their language, are not hard to trace in his best-know works. In both cases, however, assumptions were made and distinctions drawn that were not obviously empirical in nature.

Most of the responses to ordinary language philosophy considered in this chapter dwelt on the nature and the legitimacy of Austin's chosen type of data. The next chapter considers further criticisms levelled at Austin, and also at Grice, for basing their work on some unempirical assumptions about language itself: very similar assumptions, in fact, to those for which Austin and his followers vociferously criticized the Vienna Circle. To the extent that it draws on Austin's and Grice's works and relies on these same assumptions, present-day pragmatics might be open to the same charges. Since Austin and Grice faced their contemporary critics, however, the debate between Quine and Chomsky has problematized the notion of empiricism in relation to the study of language and shown that it is capable of at least two very different interpretations. Chomsky's interpretation, inspired by falsification rather than by verification, might offer a response to such criticisms for present-day pragmatics and in retrospect for ordinary language philosophy.

5
Speech Acts and Implicatures

Austin insisted that any serious philosophical discussion must take account of the distinctions, connections and classifications apparent in the ways in which language was ordinarily used. This conviction developed, at least in part, from his dissatisfaction with the logical positivism of the Vienna Circle. He found there too much eagerness to adopt technical philosophical terminology, too much readiness to dismiss ordinary language as vague, messy or simply meaningless, and too dogmatic an assumption that the chief business of language was to make statements that might be evaluated for truth: a philosopher's conception of truth at that. In response to these perceived defects in logical positivism, Austin not only urged the philosophical utility of ordinary language, he elevated its analysis to the status of a philosophical methodology. A meticulous examination of what native speakers know about a relevant range of vocabulary, ideally conducted collaboratively, was an essential starting point to any philosophical inquiry.

Austin may have written more about the potential benefits of this approach than about any specific results he had obtained from it, but he does seem to have had ambitious aspirations for its future. The testimonies of his close colleagues vouch for this. Speaking shortly after Austin's death, Geoffrey Warnock told the writer Ved Mehta that Austin saw the tendency in philosophy to produce just a few examples to illustrate any theory as stultifying and unscientific. It meant in effect that philosophers always had to begin afresh, rather than being able to build on the work of their predecessors. Mehta quoted Warnock as saying that Austin 'envisaged the future task of philosophers as the compilation of a super-grammar – a catalogue of all possible functions of words – and this was perhaps why he enjoyed reading grammar books so much' (Mehta 1963: 54). Another colleague, J. O. Urmson, summed up Austin's attitude as follows: 'Austin regarded this method as empirical and scientific, one that could lead to definitely established results …. He seriously hoped that a new science might emerge from the kind of investigations he undertook, a new kind of linguistics incorporating workers from both the existing linguistic and philosophical fields' (Urmson 1967: 25). No such specific 'new kind of linguistics' has emerged in the decades since Austin's death and the decline of ordinary language philosophy. Large-scale analyses of patterns of linguistic usage are conducted in present-day linguistics, but by means of the computational interrogation of corpora of electronically stored text that would have been impossible in Austin's day. The relationship between Austin's method and corpus linguistics will be considered in more detail in the final chapter. Austin's continuing reputation in linguistics, and his only significant contribution to the discipline, depends not on his views on methodology or on his enthusiasm for the possibilities of a new scientific approach to language, but on the particular set of ideas that came to be known as the theory of speech acts.

Austin's ideas about speech acts developed out of his more general approach to language, and traces of his distinctive methodology can be found in his published work on the subject. But the theory of speech acts represents arguably some of his least straightforwardly 'ordinary language' thinking. It relies on the coinage of a number of specific technical terms, including 'performative', 'illocutionary' and (a special sense of) 'felicity'. It posits the existence of a distinction between different types or levels of meaning that are not obviously available to intuitive inspection. And perhaps most strikingly of all it seems to depend on the existence of a concept of meaning independent of context, just the concept of which Austin was most wary in his response to logical positivism. Many of the contemporary or near-contemporary commentators on the theory of speech acts dwelt on what they saw as these empirically unjustified aspects of Austin's work.

Despite these initial reservations on the part of philosophers and linguists, Austin's account has been an important factor in the establishment of pragmatics as a linguistic discipline. In this context, his work is often coupled with that of Paul Grice, another Oxford philosopher of the mid-twentieth century to produce some surprising, controversial, but ultimately influential, ideas. Grice differed from Austin on many points of method and of conclusion. But his theory of conversational implicature developed against a recognizably 'ordinary language' interest in the regularities of use. Strikingly, it too posited a distinction between types or levels of meaning. Pragmatics, often heralded as the branch of linguistics most centrally concerned with 'meaning in use', has from its outset been concerned with the nature, demarcation and viability of such a distinction. Pragmatics is a broad discipline with many different branches and subfields, but in the case of 'formal' pragmatics, at least, the data most readily relied on are intuitive, although usually without Austin's claims to systematicity and scientific objectivity.

Formal pragmatics is therefore vulnerable to the accusations levelled by many of Austin's contemporary critics: of being unempirical in two different ways. Firstly, the data are drawn from intuition rather than observation. Secondly, there is a notion of unobserved and essentially unobservable 'core' or 'literal' meaning at the heart of many pragmatic theories. Austin's trenchant position that intuitive data could be empirical was discussed in the previous chapter, and other defences of intuitive data will be considered later in this chapter and in the final chapter. The question of the validity of literal meaning remains controversial. Austin and, to a lesser extent, Grice seemed reluctant and almost embarrassed about its presence in their work. More recent pragmaticists are in general less coy, explicitly acknowledging the presence of literal meaning in pragmatic theories although rarely confronting directly the potential charge of being unempirical. The more complex and multifaceted notion of empiricism now available to discussions of language might, however, suggest ways of countering this charge.

Austin himself used the term 'speech acts' very little, but through subsequent developments of his work it has come to be used as a convenient and easily recognized title for a particular set of ideas. Austin had been developing these ideas since his early career before the Second World War, when he was still casting around for a distinctive voice and approach. They were afforded a passing mention in a paper on 'Other minds' in 1946. Austin was concerned in this with the problem of whether we can ever claim knowledge of what is going on in another person's mind, a problem he linked to the more general question of how it is that people ever claim to know anything at all. In the course of his discussion of this issue he drew attention to a similarity between beginning an utterance with 'I know' and beginning one with 'I promise'. In each case the speaker is making not so much a factual commitment, as a claim to be in a suitable position to make such a statement. In these and other cases, including 'I order', and 'I do' when said during a marriage ceremony, there are certain attendant expectations about the situation: 'But now, if the situation transpires to have been in some way not orthodox ... then we tend to be rather hesitant about how to put it' (Austin 1946: 70).

In each case it does not seem straightforwardly appropriate to say that the speaker lied. These ideas, even some of these examples, resurfaced and were developed in Austin's teaching at Oxford during the early 1950s. The form in which they are now best known is the book *How to Do Things with Words*, the posthumously published text of the William James lectures that Austin delivered at the University of Harvard in 1955.

Austin's exposition of his ideas in the William James lectures was unusual. In effect he began by describing a possible account of meaning, which he labelled the 'performative hypothesis', and then spent the rest of the lectures identifying problems for it and dismantling it. The performative hypothesis clearly seemed to Austin to be an important starting point in explaining his ideas, just at it had been a necessary first step in developing them. It remains a good point of entrance to the William James lectures, because it is here that the link between speech acts and Austin's more general philosophical system and method is most apparent. The performative hypothesis can be seen as a response to Austin's unease with the 'descriptive fallacy'. Despite the pronouncements of some recent philosophers, describing the world in ways that could be labelled 'true' or 'false' was only one, and perhaps not even a very significant one, of the things that people ordinarily did when they used language. Austin labelled those uses of language that did describe the world 'constatives'. This was not a coinage but a rejuvenation of an archaic and erudite term. He contrasted constatives with performative utterances, a category to include his old examples 'I do' and 'I promise ...' as well as many others. 'Performative' was a deliberate neologism on Austin's part, but he was careful to justify it; 'no term in current use that I know of is nearly wide enough to cover' all different types of performative (Austin 1962b: 7). Performatives, Austin explained, were not descriptive of the world and they could not correctly be judged to be true or false. Rather, in relation to the circumstances in which they were uttered on any particular occasion, they could be judged to be appropriate or inappropriate. They could be successful or otherwise in performing certain acts, or bringing about certain states of affairs. There were specific conditions for success or for 'felicity' attached to any performative. In some cases these were part of a social ritual; 'I do' works as a performative in a marriage ceremony only if the person speaking it is presently unmarried, for instance. In other cases they were concerned with less clearly demarcated conventions and relationships; 'I promise' performs a genuine promise only if the speaker is sincere.

Austin's distinctive philosophy was apparent in the founding assumptions of speech act theory, in particular in relation to his response to the descriptive fallacy. It was apparent also in the manner in which he approached the study of speech acts. He proposed as a valuable research programme the identification of all verbs that could be used performatively in English, and here his enthusiasm for linguistic botanizing was of central importance. The canonical form of a performative was that it included a verb in the first person singular present indicative active. 'I do' and 'I promise' fit this description, as well as a host of others including 'I order', 'I warn' and 'I bet'. Austin proposed that a list of all verbs that could occur in this form with a performative meaning could be produced by looking through a dictionary. He conceded that such a list would not identify every possible performative use of language, because the canonical form accounted for only explicit performatives. Other types of utterance had performative function without the presence of a first person singular present indicative active verb. But these were implicit performatives and, crucially, could be re-expressed as explicit ones; 'come here at once' could be re-expressed as 'I order you to come here at once', 'That bull is about to charge' as 'I warn you that that bull is about to charge', and so on.

Austin found it harder than he had originally envisaged, however, to establish a clear-cut distinction between truth and falsity on the one hand, and acceptability and unacceptability on the other. The distinction between constatives and performatives began to break down under the weight of this difficulty, a process which is chronicled in the William James lectures. The acceptability of a performative such as 'I apologise' is not free from all entanglements with truth values; in fact it relies on the truth of a number of statements, including 'I am apologising'. Austin recognized that the categories of utterances that had provided his starting point for the description of speech acts were dissolving into each other. He concluded the fourth of the 12 William James lectures with the admission that 'Perhaps indeed there is no great distinction between statements and performative utterances' (Austin 1962b: 52). Quine later pronounced himself as unsurprised by the failure of the performative hypothesis, since even a Tarskian definition of truth could accommodate performatives: 'There are good reasons for contrasting and comparing performatives and statements of fact, but an animus against the true/false fetish is not one of them' (Urmson et al. 1965: 90).

In the later William James lectures Austin, more or less, gave up on the performative hypothesis. However, he retained much from his original justification of performatives, and incorporated this into a different classification of speech acts. Using language was still primarily a means of doing something rather than merely describing something. The majority of utterances were still to be labelled as either acceptable or unacceptable in context, with conditions for felicity drawing the distinction. But Austin no longer tried to divide utterances into different categories. Instead he set about identifying and describing three different acts that took place whenever any utterance was produced. In effect, he was elaborating a much more complex account of meaning than had been assumed by philosophers under the influence of the descriptive fallacy. He argued that philosophers had spent too much time considering the performance of an act *of* saying something and not enough time on the much more interesting topic of the performance of an act *in* saying something. Austin labelled the first of these the 'locutionary act'; identifying a locutionary act on any occasion involved establishing what was said, taking account of the literal meaning of the words uttered in their context. The act performed *in* saying something constituted the 'illocutionary' act. This was determined by literal meaning, but also by a host of other phenomena, including the conventions prevalent in the society and the specific intentions of the individual producing the utterance. Finally, utterances also had a perlocutionary dimension. The perlocutionary act was the outcome or result of the production of the utterance. This might coincide with the speaker's intention but would not necessarily do so. So for a single utterance it might be possible to define the locution as 'He said to me, "You can't do that"', the illocution as 'He protested against my doing it' and the perlocution as 'He pulled me up, checked me' (Austin 1962b: 102).

Throughout the William James lectures Austin produced examples to support or to illustrate his case. They are all typical outputs of linguistic botanizing: intuitive responses to self-imposed questions about what would or could be said in various hypothetical situations. For instance, Austin confidently informed his audience that 'We do not say "I am promising"', and that it is possible to test for a performative by asking for instance 'Does he *really* [welcome him]?' (Austin 1962b: 64 and 79, original emphasis). Such examples themselves may seem uncontroversial enough, but they can of course be treated as genuine examples of usage only if intuitive understanding is admitted as empirical evidence. Towards the end of the lectures Austin suggested that in would be important to establish an exhaustive list of illocutionary forces, and that such a task would be 'a matter of prolonged fieldwork' (Austin 1962b: 148). As was the case with so many of Austin's aspirations towards thorough and systematic study of data, this plan was left unfulfilled at the time of his death, and there is no evidence that he had either begun or seriously contemplated the task.

Austin's data, then, raised some obvious and potentially damaging questions about the credibility of his ideas. However, contemporary reaction to the publication of *How to Do Things with Words* did not in general dwell on this aspect of the theory of speech acts. After all, Austin's enthusiasm for listing words and expressions, and for contemplating when and how they would be used, was an aspect of his work that his commentators had already decided to be a virtue or anathema, regardless of the particular issues to which it was applied. But his contemporaries did have a lot to say about the empirical justification for another aspect of the William James lectures, namely the decision to posit different types or levels of meaning within one speech situation. If Austin was right, it was no longer possible to ask simply what a particular expression meant, or even what the utterance of an expression in a particular situation meant. An account of any utterance must now make reference to three different components; a full description of meaning must take account of the locution, the illocution and the perlocution. Some commentators had assumed philosophers of ordinary language clung to a simplistic belief in their supposed motto 'meaning is use' (for instance Gellner 1959). This assumption is still repeated in more recent literature (see, for instance, Dascal 1994: 324). But the content of the William James lectures suggests that if Austin could ever have been accused of such an allegiance, the charge no longer held. There was no single notion of 'meaning' to be identified and fully delineated by considering usual conditions of use. Meaning now consisted of three distinct layers of significance, and analysis must involve teasing apart these three layers in the apparently uniform act of producing an utterance. This in turn raised the question of whether Austin's more elaborate theory of language was justified by the complexity of his data. If not, he might lie open to the charge of indulging in the type of unempirical assumptions about language that he deplored in logical positivism.

The main focus of discussion was the distinction between locutionary and illocutionary acts. The viability of this distinction depended on the assumption that every expression had a unique, identifiable linguistic meaning, determined by the conventions of the language. This linguistic meaning, together with some local details such as deictic references, provided the force of the locutionary act. This combined with the apparent intentions of the speaker and certain further conventions to give a distinct illocutionary act. The relevant conventions were those concerning the ways in which the language was used in a particular society. For instance in British English, requests and even orders are often issued by means of interrogatives. Speakers are more likely to say 'Can you pass the salt?' than 'Pass the salt' or even 'I request that you pass the salt'. The illocutionary force, however, would still be paraphrased along the lines of 'she requested that he pass the salt'.

To many of Austin's commentators, what he described as illocutionary force seemed to be the intuitively correct notion of meaning, and the only one with a legitimate role to play in an account of language. 'Can you pass the salt?' just meant, in most normal contexts, that the speaker was requesting the hearer to pass the salt. Such commentators saw Austin's separation out of the more literal meaning determined by the conventions of the language, or the locutionary meaning, as an unnecessary and unjustified complication that was without empirical foundation. Max Black summed up this attitude succinctly when he argued in 1963 that 'The only proper unit for investigation seems to be what Austin has called an illocutionary act and the supposed locutionary act is at best a dubious abstraction' (Black 1963: 410). Austin's colleague P. F. Strawson also touched on this issue in his discussion of speech acts, although he did not elaborate on it: 'It may be felt that Austin has not made clear just what abstractions from the total speech act he intends to make by means of his notions of meaning and of locutionary act' (Strawson 1964: 380).

There is some evidence in *How to Do Things with Words* that Austin was aware of this problem, and attempted to downplay it. He reassured his audience that: 'The total speech act in the total speech situation is the *only actual* phenomenon which, in the last resort, we are engaged in elucidating' (Austin 1962b: 147, original emphasis). It would appear from his choice of emphasis that it was only the total act in context for which he would want to argue a real existence. The locutionary and illocutionary acts were indeed abstractions from this, but abstractions that were necessary to the task of explaining and fully describing the actual speech act.

Despite this reassurance, Austin was not very explicit in his reasons why the different levels of meaning were a necessary expository device, and critics remained wary of them. To some, it was the illocutionary act itself that seemed to be an unnecessary and unhelpful complication. Jonathan Cohen expressed severe misgivings about the justification for hypothesizing illocutionary force as something distinct from meaning. He proposed instead to collapse much of what Austin would see as the illocutionary act into the locutionary act itself. He criticized 'Any attempt to prise off this aspect of meaning, and regard it not as meaning but as something else' (Cohen 1964: 429). Mats Furberg defended Austin against Cohen's attack, arguing that the meanings of words were indeed governed by conventions not affected by individual intentions. In other words, the distinction between locution and illocution remained significant because it was sometimes necessary to acknowledge meaning other than the face value interpretation a hearer would normally place on an utterance. Even when used indirectly, 'words retain their old meaning' (Furberg 1969: 460). 'Can you pass the salt?' retained its interrogative nature, and literally enquired about the abilities of the hearer, despite the intention to make a request with which it was most often uttered. Furberg's intention was to offer support to the motivation for speech act theory. But in doing so he outlined a clearer independent existence for the locutionary and the illocutionary than Austin was ready to concede; Austin himself might have been reluctant to endorse Furberg's argument.

The separate existence of locutionary and illocutionary meaning was brought out even more forcefully by John Searle in his development of speech act theory. Searle went some way towards the extensive project that Austin had hinted at, in that he concerned himself with listing different possible types of illocutionary force. But Searle's version of this 'fieldwork' task was still the result of data collection that was unashamedly intuitive: perhaps more unashamedly than in Austin's case, since Searle made no claims to collaborative interrogation of the language. Searle insisted that intuitive data told researchers all they needed to know about the rules that underlie how language was used. He drew attention to 'the existence of certain data, data of the form, "It would be odd or impermissible to say such and such"' (Searle 1969: 144). Searle also introduced the notion of 'indirect speech acts', ensuring that the existence of different levels of meaning became even more deeply ingrained in the theory of speech acts. The primary illocutionary act of the salt-passing example is the one that will be prominent in most contexts: the act of making a request. But this is derived from the secondary illocutionary act of asking a question, also present whenever the expression is produced, and also important to the elucidation of meaning. On specific occasions of use, in fact on most such occasions, the secondary, literal illocutionary meaning will be ruled out because the necessary felicity conditions for a question successfully to be asked are not in place. Searle had formalized Austin's conviction that speech acts maintained both a force close to their literal meaning and a force dependent on personal intention and social convention.

Formalized theories were certainly not Austin's strong point. He offered an explanation of meaning that included some levels of abstraction, but he was hesitant and guarded in his introduction of these levels, and he did not attempt anything recognizable as a scientific model to explain his subject matter. In fact, Austin's style of philosophy became for some a byword in the avoidance of formal systems. Jerrold Katz later summed up this attitude when he described 'the traditional suspicion on the part of ordinary language-style philosophers toward the use of formal systems in connection with natural language' (Katz 1977: xi). This suspicion was not shared by all those who were at the time labelled 'philosophers of ordinary language'. It was certainly not shared by Paul Grice. In fact Austin's reluctance to go beyond observation and description to give a more formal account of language was for Grice a source of growing disillusionment with the whole ordinary language enterprise. For him, Austin's piecemeal observations compared unfavourably with the more ambitious programmes of Chomsky and of Quine (see Grice 1986: 59–60. For a more detailed discussion of Grice's reaction to Austin's philosophy see Chapman 2005).

Grice's own programme was very ambitious, attempting to retain traditional formal logic as a basis for explaining meaning in natural language, and to ascribe the obvious divergences from logic in everyday usage to a set of principled regularities in human interactions. Grice's theory of conversation, as it has become known, did not develop as a reaction to speech act theory. He was working on it long before the delivery of Austin's William James lectures, and he was focussing on different aspects of the problem of meaning. Austin was attempting to rebut the descriptive fallacy that led philosophers to concentrate on statements at the expense of other uses of language. Grice, in effect, left the descriptive fallacy unchallenged; he made the working assumption that language was primarily used to convey information, and that a theory of language use must be able to explain the process by which this was achieved. His concern was rather with how a formal account of linguistic meaning could be squared with the overwhelming evidence that what is conveyed in context is often very different from, even at odds with, what is apparently specified by the language. In developing his theory Grice drew on a number of established philosophical problems. He was not attempting to dissolve such problems by showing them to be ill-conceived; he was attempting to solve them. Nevertheless, his theory of meaning in use shared with Austin's the controversial feature of introducing different levels of meaning. Both depended on the viability of looking beneath the surface of native speakers' intuitive understanding of utterances in context to establish structured differences in types of meaning.

The best known account of the theory of conversation, the nearest we have to a finished version, comes from another set of William James lectures, this time the ones that Grice delivered in 1967. These were published piecemeal and incompletely during the 1970s, and were finally collected together as part of *Studies in the Way of Words* in 1989. In the most frequently cited of these, 'Logic and conversation', Grice proposed to retain traditional logic as a starting point for explaining linguistic meaning, while acknowledging that on its own it could not account for what is conveyed in the many different contexts and situations in which language is used. To separate these two aspects of meaning he adopted the intuitively appealing, but now notoriously troublesome, terms 'what is said' and 'what is implicated'. The trouble started as soon as Grice defined his terms: 'In the sense in which I am using the word *say*, I intend what someone has said to be closely related to the conventional meaning of the words (the sentence) he has uttered' (Grice 1975: 25). The fundamental vagueness of this definition was never fully resolved in Grice's writings. He allowed in general terms for information about the reference of deictic expressions and about basic lexical and grammatical disambiguation to be added in to 'what is said', but never clarified its relationship to the problematic notion of literal meaning.

Like Austin, Grice coined terminology, convinced that the existing resources of the vocabulary were not adequate to his purposes. Neither 'implication' nor 'suggestion' nor 'indication' could quite sum up the particular aspect of meaning he was focussing on, so he introduced the technical term 'implicature'. His definition of 'what is implicated' was, if anything, even harder to pin down than that of 'what is said'. He gave a fairly concise account of conventional implicatures, where the actual words used in 'what is said' themselves also determine 'what is implicated'. But in the case of conversational implicature, where some general properties of discourse are in play, Grice relied mainly on a series of examples to get his point across. Conversation was characteristically a cooperative process and the expectation of cooperation explained the mechanisms by which participants derived 'what is implicated' from 'what is said'. Cooperation was manifest in the maxims that enjoined participants to provide the right 'quantity' of information, to ensure that the information was of good 'quality', to produce utterance that had a certain 'relation' to what else was going on in the conversation and to express themselves in a certain 'manner' of clarity and concision.

It was largely left to Grice's later commentators to untangle the implications of his theory of conversational implicature for the relationship between logic and language. They have explained, for instance that 'and' can retain the basic meaning of logical conjunction, with extra information concerning sequence or causality arising as a result of expectations of cooperation. The literal meaning of 'and' in 'The lone ranger jumped onto his horse and rode off into the sunset' and in 'The capital of France is Paris and the capital of England is London' is exactly the same. The strong suggestion of temporal sequencing in the first case is the result of the operation of the maxim of manner; hearers expect that speakers will describe events in the order in which they occurred (Levinson 1983: 98. For more on the implications of Gricean implicature for logic and language, see Horn 1989, chapter 4 and McCawley 1981, chapter 8). Despite introducing his theory with reference to logic, Grice himself concentrated in his examples on 'particularised conversational implicatures', where specific aspects of context determined what was conveyed. Examples of this type are in many ways the most appealing, and have had the greatest impact on how linguists have subsequently discussed contextual meaning. 'War is war' may be an uninformative statement of identity at the level of 'what is said', but the expectations of quantity demand that this is not the final interpretation but rather a series of implicatures about the nature and outcome of war are understood. 'You are the cream in my coffee' can only be interpreted as literally false, but the expectation of quality demands that an alternative interpretation is found, and that a metaphorical meaning is established at the level of 'what is implicated' (Grice 1975: 33–4).

Philosophers of ordinary language had come a long way by 1967. The initial rallying cry to philosophers was to pool their intuitive resources in order to establish how different expressions in the language were used and ultimately to dissolve philosophical problems. Now Grice was insisting that looking at how an expression was used could be misleading as to its actual literal meaning, itself determined by the formal rules of the language and even of logic. Grice's enthusiasm for logic as the foundation of meaning was something of which, superficially at least, Carnap might have been expected to approve. It is perhaps not surprising then that some commentators have seen Grice's William James lectures as evidence that he was breaking away from the ordinary language tradition, and even as a significant event in the failure of ordinary language philosophy as a movement (see for instance Grice's obituary in *The Times*, 30 August 1988). But Grice's theory of conversation owed a lot to his philosophical background. It was based on a careful consideration of what speakers said and hearers understood in a range of different situations and circumstances. It also insisted that everyday uses of language were worthy of philosophical attention. If logic could not explain everything that was understood from an utterance that was no reason to abandon logic, but nor was it a reason to give up on trying to explain the utterance. This is where the apparent kinship with Carnap falters. Grice insisted that a principled account of contextual meaning in natural language was worth pursuing and was attainable.

The cost to Grice, as far as his ordinary language credentials were concerned, was the increased formality of his account of meaning compared with anything that Austin had suggested. Almost a decade before Grice delivered his William James lectures, Bernard Mates had claimed that philosophers of ordinary language were 'inclined to overlook the semantic-pragmatic distinction' (Mates 1958a: 169). With the William James lectures, Grice had exonerated himself from this charge. Moreover, he did not advance any support for his distinction between 'what is said' and 'what is implicated' that would have met Austin's professed standards of empiricism. His examples are compelling but they were presented in a seemingly *ad hoc* manner to illustrate his case, rather than systematically to prove or to support it.

There are problems and vaguenesses with Grice's account of 'what is said' and 'what is implicated', but he had attempted a principled demarcation between the two, and had suggested formal mechanisms for deriving the latter from the former. He would therefore seem to be immune from Katz's generalization that philosophers of ordinary language shied away from formal systems and theories. His separation of literal meaning from the complex mass of interpretation in context explains Marcelo Dascal's argument that, together with Searle, Grice questioned the assumptions of the method of ordinary language philosophy: 'The method consists in inferring that a certain condition characterizes the *meaning* of a word or phrase from the fact that this condition is required for the appropriate *use* of certain sentences containing that word or phrase' (Dascal 1994: 324, original emphasis). Closely related to this is Michael Dummett's observation concerning theories of meaning that retain logic despite evidence of use that seems to run contrary to logic. Dummett did not mention Grice, but pointed out that such accounts did not simply accept that use determined meaning: rather, such an account 'challenges that principle by giving reasons for thinking that we must have a prior understanding of the *sentence* before we can be in a position to ask what the point of a particular utterance of it may be' (Dummett 1979: 107). Despite the importance in Grice's work of the distinction between what Dummett described as 'the sentence' and 'a particular utterance', there is a case to be made for Austin himself as the instigator of the move away from a straightforward equation of meaning with use, if any such equation was ever, in fact, made in ordinary language philosophy. His theory of speech acts depended on a degree of separation between the two that was more marked and more formalized in Grice's theory of conversation. Kent Bach has pointed out that, unlike the later Wittgenstein's belief in use as the guide to meaning, 'Austin developed a systematic, though largely taxonomic, theory of language use. And Paul Grice developed a conception of meaning which, though tied to use, enforced a distinction between what linguistic expressions mean and what speakers mean in using them' (Bach 2006: 147).

Linguists working in the field of pragmatics have generally relied on the validity of this distinction. Perhaps not surprisingly, they have been beset by many of the same problems that beleaguered Austin and Grice as, with different degrees of reluctance, they distanced themselves from equating meaning and use. Many of the criticisms and objections raised by Austin's and Grice's commentators would apply equally well to these more recent writers. Firstly, and perhaps most obviously, there is the reliance on intuitive data. There is a tradition of 'field' pragmatics that draws on the recording of naturally occurring data, and a recent rise in 'experimental' pragmatics, which claims allegiances to clinical psychology. Nevertheless the overwhelming emphasis in pragmatics has been on data that is collected by intuitive judgement on the part of the researcher and possibly of some native speaker informants. Ira Noveck and Dan Sperber comment on pragmaticists that 'The only source of evidence most of them have ever used has been their own intuitions about how an invented utterance would be interpreted in a hypothetical situation' (Noveck 2004: 7–8).

An explicit defence of this method was offered by Searle in his extended discussion of speech acts. He argued that the individual native speaker's intuitions were not a poor substitute for the statistical analysis of extensive empirical data because what the linguist was studying was not a sample of the actual uses made of language, but the rule-governed activity of language itself. Individuals' judgements about what they would say are simply the best way of accessing these rules. Solitary reflection is the best way to learn about linguistic characterizations: 'And those characterizations can have a generality which goes beyond this or that instance of the use of the elements in question, even though the characterizations are not based on a large or even statistically interesting sample of the occurrences of the elements, because the rules guarantee generality' (Searle 1969: 13). Searle backed this up with an argument that all studies of language, even those that claimed to be the most empirical, must ultimately rely on the intuitions of speakers.

Some, like Esa Itkonen have not been impressed. Writing in 1983 he reflected on the tendency of ordinary language philosophy to rely on thought experiments based on the question, 'what would you say if ...?'. Itkonen reflected that 'Today, of course, practitioners of linguistic pragmatics conduct their own research by giving answers to the same question. Now, as Wittgenstein points out, a thought experiment is not an experiment, and therefore a discipline which manages to depend solely on thought experiments could not possibly qualify as empirical' (Itkonen 1983: 301).

The second charge of being unempirical levelled at Austin and Grice, to which pragmatics is also vulnerable, arises from the separation of literal from contextual meaning. Much of the history of pragmatics has depended on the assumption that such a separation is possible, or theoretically desirable. Yet the only thing that linguists or indeed native speakers in general have access to is evidence about how particular utterances are interpreted in their specific contexts. Analysis of this interpretation into different components of meaning has to be done formally rather than intuitively. Intuitive decisions about what counts as literal or as contextual meaning are bound to failure because literal meaning is a formal, hypothesized concept. It would be impossible to ensure that apparent intuitions about this were not contaminated by intuitions about utterance interpretation as a whole. As Simon Handley and Aidan Feeney have put it, 'Gricean errors' would be bound to intrude (Handley and Feeney 2004: 229).

Pragmatics has at its heart a phenomenon that is incorrigibly unobservable. On one account this makes much of pragmatics inherently unempirical. Since Austin and Grice faced these charges, however, Chomsky has drawn attention in his debate with Quine to a quite different notion of empiricism, whereby it is legitimate to hypothesize about things that cannot directly be observed if such hypotheses are consistent with the available evidence, offer a coherent explanation of that evidence and make further, substantial predictions. On this account, introducing an unobservable notion of literal meaning does not in itself render theoretical pragmatics unempirical. It is an explanatory device, such as early Chomskyan deep structure or the physicist's electron. An unobservable 'what is said', for instance, buys the pragmaticist an explanation of why a word such as 'and' can apparently take on such a range of different meanings in context without being simply a set of homophones, such as 'bank' or 'pen'. It may well be that the account offered by a particular pragmatic theory is flawed or is later assailed by new types of data. But this is a different issue from the charge that positing the unobservable is simply unempirical. As is the case with any type of theory, if a pragmatic theory makes predictions it is vulnerable to data.

This possible defence of Austin and Grice, and by extension of more recent pragmatic theories, draws on Popper's notion of falsification. Neither Austin nor Grice made any reference to Popper in their work, and it is far from clear that either would have defended his own account of language in these terms. But Chomsky's version of linguistic theory has subsequently laid open to linguists the possibility of supporting an account of what cannot be observed with reference to what can be observed. The major problem is the question of whether pragmatic theories do in fact make testable predictions. Recent work in experimental pragmatics has grappled with this issue. Ira Noveck has commented ruefully that 'The idea of submitting Grice's hypothesis to experimental investigation is extremely attractive', indicating the difficulties of isolating testable predictions from Grice's work (Noveck 2004: 301). Raymond Gibbs has gone further, endorsing 'the belief that the best ideas in linguistic-pragmatics are those that can be experimentally examined and potentially falsified (where failing to falsify allows one to claim scientific evidence in support of a hypothesis)' (Gibbs 2004: 69). He argues that pragmatic theories can be evaluated and ranked according to their amenability to this type of testing.

Some linguists have detected testable predictions in the work of the ordinary language philosophers. Sam Glucksberg has taken the case of metaphors and argued that Grice's work predicts that non-literal interpretations 'are generated only when an utterance is "defective"', that is, when a literal interpretation renders some sort of oddity (Glucksberg 2004: 73). According to Glucksberg's reports of his own and other's experiments, Grice's theory does not fare very well when this particular prediction is subjected to experimental testing. Testable predictions have also been advanced, and as a result problems have been indicated, for aspects of the theory of speech acts, for instance, in relation to indirect requests (Glucksberg 2004) and to promises (Bernicot and Laval 2004).

Other pragmaticists urge caution in relation to extrapolating claims about processing from theoretical accounts of the distinction between meaning and use, and testing these against data from experimental psychology. One particular problem is that such theoretical accounts, at least those developed in philosophy, generally aim at concision and consistency rather than psychological credibility. It is appropriate to ask whether they account for a range of interpretations but not whether they accord with the psychological experiences of interpreting subjects. Anne Bezuidenhout and J. Cooper Cutting have argued persuasively that experimental results are not an appropriate measure of the success of Grice's theory of conversation because, 'Grice was interested in giving a conceptual analysis of the concepts of saying, meaning and so on, and not in giving a psychological theory of the stages of utterance processing' (Bezuidenhout and Cooper Cutting 2002: 443).

Whatever its claims to empirical credibility, the nature of literal meaning is itself contested. The recent history of pragmatics makes clear that a working hypothesis that includes literal meaning does not entail a belief in context-free meaning that is complete in itself but waiting to be enriched by pragmatic principles. It is not clear that either Austin or Grice would have gone so far as to endorse such a belief, since each allowed some contextual assistance in producing locutionary force and 'what is said', respectively. In recent decades a central topic of debate in pragmatics has been the extent to which features of the context, and even guidance from pragmatic principles themselves, must intrude into semantics in order to provide something equivalent to a Gricean 'what is said'. The literature here is vast and has for some time been dominated by the opposing schools of thought of 'relevance theory' and the 'neo-Griceans' (See, for instance, Sperber and Wilson 1995 and Carston 2002; Levinson 1983, 2000, Horn 1989 and Bach 2001).

Aside from this opposition, there have been a number of recent contributions to the debate over the viability and status of literal meaning. On the side of keeping literal meaning minimal and autonomous, Emma Borg argues against what she calls 'dual-pragmatics', or the possibility of contextual intrusion into semantics, arguing that this can be achieved if semantics is freed from having to explain communicative skills (Borg 2004). Herman Cappelen and Ernest Lepore argue for 'semantic minimalism and speech act pluralism'. Other than determining the value of deictic expressions, 'the context of utterance has no effect on the proposition semantically expressed', while 'what is said (asserted, claimed etc) depends on a wide range of factors other than the proposition semantically expressed', and what is asserted can, in fact, be a proposition that is incompatible with the semantically expressed proposition (Cappelen and Lepore 2005: 2 and 4).

Searle, on the other hand, has propounded 'contextualism', which defends the notion of literal meaning but argues that this can never actually be free of certain background assumptions; it is always relative to context. To arrive at even the most basic literal meaning we necessarily draw on a host of background experiences and cultural assumptions. Nevertheless the concept of literal meaning remains viable: 'Literal meaning, though relative, is still literal meaning' (Searle 1978: 132). François Recanati also defends contextualization in semantics. He points out that, 'In general, the literal truth-conditions posited as part of a minimalist analysis turn out to be very different from the intuitive truth-conditions' of utterance interpretation (Recanati 2004: 10). In an earlier article he argued that variation in propositional content did not necessarily equate to variation in linguistic meaning, so that the fact that expressions could be interpreted in different ways in different contexts did not have to be explained either in terms of implicature or in terms of semantic ambiguity. 'Modified Occam's Razor shows that an account in terms of implicature is preferable to an account in terms of *semantic ambiguity*', but saying that propositional content varies with context is not the same thing as conceding semantic ambiguity. (Recanati 1994: 163, original emphasis). (For a much fuller account of different approaches within pragmatics to the notion of conventional meaning, see Thompson 2007).

The existence of an unobservable, context-free literal linguistic meaning has remained, then, an essential, if controversial, feature of many versions of present-day pragmatics. This feature can explain the unlikely alliance that has been struck between pragmatics and formal, Chomskyan linguistics. At first glance, the two might be expected to be mutually suspicious, even mutually incompatible. Convenient summaries of pragmatics include statements that it is concerned with 'meaning in context' or 'language as communication'. Chomsky has notoriously declared himself uninterested in considerations of context, which fall outside the study of language proper. He has also claimed with varying degrees of emphasis that the relationship between language and communication is tangential and accidental. Nevertheless, pragmatics and Chomskyan linguistics have found each other's existence extremely convenient. When ideas from ordinary language philosophy were taken up by linguists, they were received with particular enthusiasm by those working in the formalist tradition. Here the reliance on intuitive data was already well established, and indeed explicitly advocated as the best means of investigating the particular set of knowledge that constituted a language. Such linguists saw the suggestions of separate, identifiable principles of interpretation in context as support for the distinction between competence and performance, and perhaps also as justification for dismissing the latter from consideration within core linguistics. Chomsky supported the version of generative grammar, then current, by arguing that if certain aspects of meaning 'can be explained in terms of general "maxims of discourse" (in the Gricean sense), they need not be made explicit in the grammar of a particular language' (Chomsky 1972: 113).

Grice's particular development of ordinary language philosophy was perhaps the most likely to appeal to Chomsky because of its open endorsement, if rather hazy definition, of a literal 'what is said' as well as a contextual 'what is implicated'. Austin's claims to be concentrating on the total speech situation, together with his rather embarrassed defence of the locutionary act, put a clearer distance between him and Chomsky. Chomsky did not attempt to reconcile speech act theory with transformational grammar, and drew attention to the essential differences between Austin and himself. Commenting on Austin's appeal to linguists always to take account of the situation of use, he cautioned that, 'We cannot go on to conclude, as he does, that this description tells all we might want to know about the meaning of the word' (Chomsky 1976: 301). For Chomsky, Austin was avoiding any discussion of the system underlying the usage.

In his development of speech act theory, Searle urged much more explicitly the claim that Chomsky detected in Austin that use and context were important to meaning. He claimed that the theory of speech acts was not to be seen as an 'adjunct' to a theory of language, consigned to pragmatics to take up the explanation of meaning once semantics has left off. Rather, the speech act was the central unit of linguistic analysis, so consideration of this necessarily involved a full account of language. It might well have implications for syntactic analysis as well: 'It is not at all surprising that the theory of speech acts should have syntactical consequences, since, after all, that is what a sentence is for. A sentence is to talk with' (Searle 1975: 179). Jerold Katz tried to bring together elements of ordinary language philosophy with those of Chomskyan linguistics, by incorporating information about illocutionary force into syntactic structure. Katz argued that the theory of speech acts and the theory of generative grammar had followed largely separate and mutually suspicious paths, but that this state of affairs was not necessary (Katz 1977: xi). The suspicion of speech act theory among generative grammar must have arisen, at least in part, in response to Austin's discomfort with literal, context-free meaning and Searle's rhetoric against it.

Despite the suspicion described by Katz, the accounts of how speakers convey their meanings that are the most high-profile products of ordinary language philosophy share common ground with generative grammar. Austin's theory of speech acts and, more explicitly Grice's theory of conversational implicature depend on the distinction between literal meaning and meaning that is affected by contextual factors. This dependency has been a target for some critics of ordinary language philosophy, who have used it to question the empirical credentials of a movement that was supposed to be reclaiming for philosophy the language that could be observed in everyday usage and recognized by the collaborative efforts of speakers. It also set ordinary language philosophy apart from another, contemporary philosophical movement that also advanced some striking ideas about how language should be studied and what philosophers should be saying about it. This was the school of Oslo philosophy, the subject of the next two chapters. Like ordinary language philosophy, Oslo philosophy was, in part, the product of a response to logical positivism. But in this case the response was not to the version mediated by A. J. Ayer, but to first-hand experience of the Vienna Circle at work on the part of Arne Naess.

6
Oslo Philosophy

Arne Naess was appointed to the chair in philosophy at the University of Oslo in 1939 and proceeded to use this position as a basis from which to develop what he described as 'empirical semantics'. He established this as the dominant form of philosophy in Oslo by means of a determination and a charisma to rival J. L. Austin's. Austin and Naess make for an interesting comparison, both personally and intellectually. They had much in common. They were near contemporaries, Austin born in 1911 and Naess in 1912. Both showed promise as philosophers from their student days and went on to hold chairs at their respective universities, Oxford and Oslo. Both were initially attracted by the logical positivism of the Vienna Circle, but became disillusioned with what they saw as the unempirical assumptions and methodologies underlying this supposedly most empirical of philosophical movements. In response, both Austin and Naess attempted to define a new and more truly empirical style of philosophy, each becoming recognized as the leader of a specific, geographically localized philosophical movement. Both Oxford ordinary language philosophy and the Oslo school of philosophy flourished in the years immediately following the Second World War, attracting attention, notoriety and some harsh criticism. Austin and Naess even both finished their professional philosophical careers suddenly and at the height of their success, although they did so in very different ways. Austin succumbed rapidly to cancer and died early in 1960. Naess resigned his chair in 1970 in order to devote himself to the environmental movement that he had founded, which has become known as 'deep ecology'.

Nevertheless, the differences between the two men are in many ways more significant than their similarities. Their points of departure from the Vienna Circle may have been similar, but their directions of travel, in terms of the ways in which they planned to develop a new way of doing philosophy, were very different. One of the most striking aspects of their story is the extent to which two movements with such similar pedigrees, each attempting to make the study of language appropriately and properly empirical, could propound and vigorously defend such different methodologies. Austin accumulated data drawn largely from introspection and subjected it to analysis by means of intuition, imagination and, ideally, group discussion. Naess collected data by questionnaire-based interviews of members of the public and by scouring pre-existing texts; his analysis of this data was formal and statistical. Ordinary language philosophy and Oslo philosophy both attracted comment for the insistence on consulting everyday as opposed to philosophical usage, but Austin and Naess remained implacably opposed to each other's way of doing things. This difference is symptomatic of the nature of language study; time and again researchers have disagreed not just over how linguistic data should best be analysed but even over what actually constitutes the true data of linguistic study. A version of the debate between Austin and Naess is still being played out in present-day linguistics, often with a similar degree of entrenchment and, unfortunately, sometimes with a similar level of contumely.

Austin has an established place in the history of linguistics, especially in relation to the development of pragmatics. He is also remembered, although not always fondly, in the philosophy of language. Very few linguists have heard of Naess, although what he was trying to do in Oslo in the 1940s and 50s in some ways prefigures developments in more recent linguistics such as sociolinguistics and corpus linguistics. He is known in philosophy, but mainly for his work in deep ecology, which now overshadows his earlier philosophy of language both in its fame and influence and in the amount of time he has devoted to it. Yet his credentials in the philosophy of language are impeccable. He was one of the relatively few outsiders to be invited to attend meetings of the Vienna Circle. His work was taken seriously and was cited, although not always with approval, by many of the major players in mid-twentieth-century analytic philosophy, including Carnap, Tarski, Ayer, Popper, Quine and Austin.

In some circles, Naess's philosophy of language is overshadowed not just by his ecological work but by a different and less intellectual activity: his mountaineering. He climbed many of the most difficult peaks across the world, and became notorious for his fondness for remote and inaccessible places in which to make his home. Even while he was in full-time employment, Naess liked to get away from the university, to explore and to tread fresh, sometimes literally untrodden, paths. Austin, on the other hand, belonged firmly in the Oxford common room. Admittedly he was remarkable among his colleagues for eschewing the usual rituals of college life and of high table, but he did so in order to return to his family home in the Oxfordshire countryside where he relaxed by playing the violin and reading dictionaries. A similar difference can be seen in the two philosophers' approaches to the study of language. Austin exhorted philosophers to leave their armchairs, but his search for linguistic data took him no further than a seminar room full of like-minded colleagues. Naess left his armchair much further behind. He looked for his data in undergraduate lecture halls, in laboratories and on the streets of Oslo.

From an early age, Naess discovered twin interests in philosophy and in the experimental sciences, but his philosophical career really took off when he travelled to Vienna in 1934, soon after graduating from the University of Oslo. He was apparently attracted, in part, by what he had heard of recent philosophical developments but just as much by the prospects of good mountaineering in Austria. Be that as it may, he was almost immediately invited to participate in the meetings of the Vienna Circle. He stayed in Vienna, and continued attending meetings of the Circle, until the autumn of 1935. He was impressed by some aspects of what he heard there, particularly by the clarity and the cooperation that characterized the discussions. He disagreed, however, with much of the philosophy of the Vienna Circle, particularly the claim that philosophical problems were largely pseudo-problems. For Naess, there would always be some philosophical problems that could not be dissolved by any amount of linguistic analysis. Complete clarity of expression, where all possible interpretations could be enumerated and delineated, was rarely attainable. Ordinary language was necessarily and incorrigibly complicated. Naess's disagreement over the nature of pseudo-problems meant that he was also uneasy about the Vienna Circle's sweeping application of the label 'meaningless' to anything that did not meet the rigours of verification. To dismiss a problem from discussion because it had been labelled meaningless was not a legitimate philosophical manoeuvre for Naess; if a problem could be expressed in language then it deserved proper scrutiny. So even as he attended meetings of the Circle, he was already reacting against philosophical discussion that appeared to ignore the ways in which language was ordinarily used and understood. Naess formed the opinion that only careful study of many instances of use could tell the philosopher anything about the meaning of a word; isolated philosophical analysis never could. This led him to the conclusion that the logical positivists were not so empirical in their approach as they appeared to believe. In particular, their philosophy relied on some intuitive and wholly unempirical assumptions about ordinary language.

In an interview conducted in the early 1990s, Naess recalled of the Vienna Circle that 'They imagined they had perfect knowledge of ordinary language about their mother tongue. So, to me, they were antiempirical, as they thought that their analysis of the use of "or", for example, was much deeper than what you could get from statistics' (Rothenberg 1993: 28). It seems that Naess did not have much success at the time in getting across to the members of the Vienna Circle the nature of his disagreements. They assumed that he was basically supporting, perhaps extending, but certainly not significantly altering their existing doctrines. This reaction is very similar to the response about which Popper complained so vehemently. Indeed, Naess thought of Popper when he was reflecting many years later on the Vienna Circle's attitude to his own criticisms of logical positivism. He commented that, just like Popper, he had been labelled by the Circle as a thinker whose ideas did not significantly differ from their own. During the 1930s, Naess explained, he worked on a criticism of the apparent empiricism of Neurath and Carnap that he produced in written form between 1937 and 1939. This 'was *intended* to be directed against *fundamental* theses and trends in the Circle, but was understood by Neurath as a proposal for modifications which were already accepted in principle and were to be made official in future publications' (Naess 1968a: 13–14, original emphasis). Having been reassured about these future publications, Naess gave up on his plans to publish this work.

In his account of this incident Naess omitted to mention that his treatise on Neurath and Carnap was subsequently published in Oslo in 1956. In a contemporary review of this book Eivind Storheim acknowledged the gap of some 20 years between writing and publication, and pointed out how regrettably late this first-hand commentary on logical empiricism had been made available. Storheim indicated that Naess accused Carnap of accepting implicitly and without empirical justification hypothesis about the equivalence between expressions of natural language and of logic, for instance between 'if ... then' and →. It is also evident from Storheim's review that in the mid-1930s Naess was dissatisfied with what he saw as the limitations placed on methodology by the Vienna Circle's particular attitude to the correct form of expression for positive knowledge. Naess urged that any method of gathering information that was relevant should be considered permitted, in contrast to

Carnap's insistence on data that could be expressed in language suitable for physics. Storheim summed up this position as: 'Naess thus gives priority to research areas not to any specific "scientific" method' (Storheim 1959: 190).

Like Quine, Naess detected unempirical assumptions underlying the apparently empirical dogmas of the Vienna Circle, and detected these particularly in relation to language. In his response to this, Quine developed a distrust of any notion of 'meaning' that went beyond an account of the linguistic behaviour of a speech community. Such an account could be attained by suitably rigorous study on the part of the 'field linguist', an activity towards which Quine himself showed no inclination. There is a hint of Naess's response in his reference during the 1990s interview to 'statistics'. He too saw meaning as encapsulated in linguistic behaviour, and for him this put the onus on philosophers themselves to study that behaviour. This entailed systematic observation and statistical analysis. It is not clear exactly at what stage Naess began to develop his own philosophical methodology along these lines, and whether, as this comment would seem to suggest, he was already thinking about statistics in the early 1930s. Certainly, in the later 1930s he travelled to Berkeley, California, and spent some time in psychological research. At that time and in that department psychology was more or less synonymous with behaviourism. Naess was already familiar with this movement, and indeed had produced a doctoral dissertation that displayed decidedly behaviouristic leanings. He shared these leanings with Quine, whose own work on language would be increasingly influenced by behaviourism. Again, however, Naess's involvement was more immediate and more practical than Quine's. At Berkeley he devised and conducted numerous experiments involving rats in mazes in order to study decision strategies, and analysed his results statistically.

During his time in the laboratories of Berkeley, Naess also experimented with the practice of observing the psychologists observing the rats. He developed a conviction that to be truly empirical, researchers must dispense with any psychological premises and just observe the behaviour before them. So he collected records of the behaviour of the psychologists, for instance the movements of their heads and the times at which they took notes, together with as much detail as possible about background events. In effect, he was drawing up a sociology of the laboratory, or a sociological study of the behaviour of scientists. The work proved unfeasibly onerous and was soon abandoned, but it had caused Naess to think about the types of research being conducted in the comparatively new disciple of sociology, and these included the questionnaire method of collecting data. Naess soon decided that this was the most appropriate method for the study of language. At the time the use of questionnaires was very new and rather *avant-garde* in sociological research. It was only just emerging as a powerful tool in the more practical areas of market research and political polling. George Gallup pioneered his methods as a market researcher during the early 1930s, and founded the American Institute of Public Opinion in 1935. From here the methodology of the Gallup Poll developed; the first prediction of the outcome of a political election using this method was produced, against received wisdom but correctly, in 1936. George Gallup's commitment to scientific sampling is reminiscent of Naess's approach to philosophy. So too is his mission statement, despite the fact that Gallup was concerned with political opinion rather than linguistic usage: 'If democracy is supposed to be based on the will of the people, then someone should go out and find out what that will is'. In philosophy at that time the use of questionnaires was unheard of.

In the later part of the 1930s Naess began conducting what he saw as truly empirical philosophical research. His main theme was the conception of truth, a philosophical problem of very long-standing, and much strongly expressed, disagreement. Most recently, of course, the logical positivists had enthusiastically adopted Tarski's logical re-expression of the correspondence account of truth, because it offered them the prospect of incorporating truth into their account of meaningfulness. According to Popper's recollections, Naess's work on truth was based on a desire to find a way to justify his disagreement with Tarski. At a discussion at the Copenhagen Congress in 1936, Neurath argued against Tarski's theories about the concept of truth, 'and he inspired (if my memory does not deceive me) Arne Ness [sic.], who was also present, to undertake an empirical study of the usages of the word "truth", in the hope of thus refuting Tarski' (Popper 1963: 201). Certainly, Naess was wary of the apparently unquestioning acceptance that Tarski must be right about what 'truth' really meant, especially when considered in the context of other theories of truth accepted equally readily by earlier schools of philosophy. He proposed to investigate what people really understood by the term 'truth': people who were unencumbered by philosophical allegiances and who had perhaps never before given any serious thought to traditional philosophical problems. His chosen method was the use of questionnaires. As he pointed out, it was difficult to come across instances of non-philosophers talking spontaneously about truth, let alone enough instances to provide statistically interesting findings.

In 1938 Naess presented his results, or as he saw it his results so far, in a short monograph published in Oslo. *'Truth' as Conceived by Those Who Are Not Professional Philosophers* is a difficult book to summarize, and an even harder one to evaluate. This is perhaps because it is esoteric in the extreme, really quite unlike anything that was being published in philosophy at the time and certainly quite unlike anything that would fit the expectations of philosophical research today. It was produced by a philosophically ambitious young man who had a firm grounding, indeed many personal acquaintances, in the leading philosophical trends of his day, but who had also become attracted to trends in other disciplines not traditionally considered congruent with philosophy: particularly trends in psychology and sociology. As such, the book is packed with an assemblage of ideas and approaches, proposals for further research, unexpected connections and intriguing insights. It draws together a number of intellectual trends of the early twentieth century that have not often collided, offers some genuinely novel and interesting findings, and is in many ways ahead of its time, in terms both of its research methodology and of the claims it makes about apparent philosophical certainties. At the same time, from a present-day perspective at least, it is woefully under-referenced, its methodologies are poorly supported and rarely fully explained, and while criticizing the whole host of previous philosophers of truth for failing to offer adequate evidence for many of their central claims, it falls into exactly the same pattern itself.

Naess's central aim in *'Truth' as Conceived by Those Who Are Not Professional Philosophers* was clear and, to the present-day linguist, uncontroversially worthwhile. Philosophers had for centuries made assumptions about what could be summarized as 'the common sense view of "truth"'. These philosophers felt confident in making pronouncements about what those outside of philosophy – 'the uneducated', 'the man in the street' – believed about the term 'truth'. A whole array of competing philosophical theories of truth had been presented by means of the rhetorical device of comparing them favourably with this common sense view. Other theories, such as Tarski's had been heralded as according closely with the everyday understanding of 'truth'. Yet there was no evidence, and Naess expressed repeated and perhaps overemphasized incredulity at this fact, that any of these philosophers had undertaken research into what non-philosophers did actually think about truth. Naess proposed to make a start on this missing research in order to perform a long overdue assessment of what philosophers said about non-philosophers, and also of the actual difference to be found between conceptions of truth traditionally classed as 'philosophical' and those traditionally classed as 'non-philosophical'.

Naess's survey of the field is perhaps the least successful part of his study. Here he complained about what philosophers had said in the past, but frustratingly omitted to cite his sources. He assured his readers that he had conducted a statistical study of philosophical accounts of truth and that 'the papers of ca. 200 philosophers have been inspected', (Naess 1938: 13) but he failed to mention which papers were involved, how they were interrogated, or how the results were analysed statistically. Naess was more forthcoming when he reported on his own empirical research. He and his assistants had interviewed a group of 250 subjects on the theme of truth, basing their questions on a set questionnaires but varying them as the situation demanded. The subjects were selected for their lack of philosophical training. They were predominantly young, some still at school, but included both male and female respondents from a variety of educational backgrounds. They were also apparently extremely accommodating, voluntarily being subjected to rigorous interrogation about their conception of truth, in some cases over periods of several hours.

Naess presented a number of different research methods that he and his assistants had experimented with in a search for the most effective way of eliciting relevant data. These methods were not all afforded equal space in his monograph; he variously described, outlined or hinted at the different techniques that had been tried. For instance, the researchers had investigated the differences between obtaining spoken answers and written ones and had tried out different types of question and different wordings for individual questions. Throughout, Naess was anxious to emphasize that the necessarily tentative and provisional nature of his findings did not make his study unscientific. In fact, all empirical research was necessarily characterized by conclusions that were suggested rather than definite, because such research involved samplings and reductions.

The main set of findings reported in *'Truth' as Conceived by Those Who Are Not Professional Philosophers* related to the question, presented and responded to orally, that Naess settled on as most successful. The interviews were all conducted in Norwegian, although not all the subjects were native speakers. Naess translated the relevant question as 'What is the common characteristic of that which is true?' (Naess 1938: 23). A huge variety of responses were obtained. These responses were in some cases gathered during protracted conversations with the subjects and only short selections from a few of these were published in the book.

Naess distilled the responses into brief summaries, some of which he listed. He then arranged these responses into 37 different groups, insisting that the nature and the labels of the groups were driven entirely by what he found in his data, not by any philosophical preconceptions. Here is a sample of the responses and of the groups. The descriptions of the groups have in some cases been abbreviated:

> response: agreement with reality
> group: what is true is identified with a *relation of agreement* or accordance between something and a *r[eality]-factor*
>
> response: agreement with the facts of the case
> group: what is true is identified with a *relation of agreement* between something and fact(s)
>
> response: something that really is
> group: what is true is identified with an *e[xistence]-factor* or a *r[eality]-factor*
>
> response: that it actually is so
> group: what is true is identified with what is the case
>
> response: that they can be proved
> group: what is true is identified with that which can be proved
>
> response: agreement between statement and observation
> group: what is true is identified with the relation of agreement or correspondence between something and *observation*
>
> response: things I have not yet found any reason to doubt
> group: what is true is identified with what cannot be *doubted*
>
> response: what I perceive directly by my senses
> group: what is true is identified with what is arrived at by using one's *senses*
>
> response: what all people have found immediately obvious
> group: what is true is identified with what someone has found *obvious* or *evident*
>
> response: scientists' statements
> group: what is true is identified with what some *authority* or other says
>
> response: what the majority says
> group: what is true is identified with what is determined by counting noses in a certain way

response: it serves life
group: what is true is identified with what in some way or other serves life or corresponds to it, what is good to mankind, what is expedient to man

response: a thing that must and ought to be accepted by all
group: what is true is identified with something that *must be* thus or thus

(Naess 1938: 42–4 and 66–8, all emphasis original)

Naess drew two main conclusions from these findings. Firstly, philosophical commentaries on 'the non-philosopher's view of truth' had been not merely ill-informed, but fundamentally misguided. There was simply no such thing as a unique definition of truth readily recognized and widely accepted by the class of all people who happen to be non-philosophers. The variation in definitions provided by Naess's subjects was at least as wide as that in the definitions of professional philosophers themselves. But Naess went further than this. His second conclusion is perhaps the more startling. He claimed not just that non-philosophers had as many definitions of truth as philosophers, but that the definitions in question were remarkably similar. Making allowances for variations in vocabulary and in sophistication of expression, non-philosophers identified just the same range of concepts of truth as philosophers. Naess was able to draw attention to response types that looked a lot like pragmatism, logical positivism, correspondence, relativism and so on.

The comparison between philosophical and non-philosophical concepts of truth was not Naess's only concern in *'Truth' as Conceived by Those Who Are Not Professional Philosophers*, although it was his main theme. In fact, the slim volume is crammed with details, descriptions and patterns of a host of different experiments. Naess seems to have been so enthusiastic about the possibilities of his form of empirical research that he was eager to do as much and as varied work as possible while he had his subjects in place. The results of these supplementary experiments are generally tentative. He experimented with comparisons between subjects according to different parameters, suggesting for instance that there were no marked correlations between the distribution of reply types and either age or education. He did, however, find evidence in his data that 'feminine persons have a greater tendency to believe in absolutes that masculine' (Naess 1938: 124). In one of his most engaging, but perhaps also most provocative, subsidiary experiments, he engineered philosophical debate by inviting subjects to evaluate each other's responses. He found that evaluations were predominantly hostile: 'It appears that critical statements are more than five times as frequent as those assenting' (Naess 1938: 144). Naess drew immediate parallels with apparently more high-minded discussions of the subject.

'Truth' as Conceived by Those Who Are Not Professional Philosophers is wide-ranging and ambitious in the number of experiments it reports and the issues it explores, but it does not go beyond an analysis of the single concept of 'truth'. Towards the end of the book Naess was at pains to point out that he nevertheless saw his methodology as a potentially important one for all areas of philosophical study. This was the case, at least, if the methodology of questionnaires could be combined with the use of what he called 'free association', where subjects were encouraged to speak more freely about their understanding of a particular term. Naess was no less ambitious for the prospects of his methodology that Austin was for his; both philosophers saw their respective approaches as having the potential to form the basis of a whole new style of philosophy. Naess stated categorically, but without elaboration, that 'There are scarcely any of the traditional philosophic problems which are not suitable for this procedure' (Naess 1938: 162).

Naess finished his monograph with a meditation on why philosophers had said the things they had about the common conception of truth, apparently in the absence of any evidence. Related to this, he pondered the question of why certain definitions of truth had achieved the status of being seen as 'philosophical', with all the kudos that this description implied. Philosophers had a vested interest in the existence of a non-philosophical view of 'truth'. It was sometimes used as a weapon in the philosophical armoury; philosophers were in the habit of accusing their opponents of producing definitions of truth that went against common sense and understanding. Pragmatism, in particular, had often been confronted with this argument, although Naess's findings now seemed to have demonstrated that pragmatism had its place in the popular understanding of 'truth'. Naess's discussion of why certain philosophical theories gained credence and were perpetuated took the form of a speculation into the sociology of philosophy, and of philosophical dogmas. As such, it foreshadowed things that Kuhn would say about scientific paradigms some three decades later. It is also reminiscent of Neurath's web of scientific knowledge, accumulated and sustained by what counts as received wisdom at any given time. Naess suggested that potential new philosophers succeeded and were accepted by existing philosophers if they took part in the established debate about truth theories. Adopting a particular stance allowed the new philosopher to join in philosophical discussion, but also meant that the philosopher 'will never find any reason to investigate the many problems of history and logic of science, the psychology and sociology of research for *their own sake*' (Naess 1938: 175, original emphasis). The approach that Naess was advocating, on the other hand, opened up the possibilities of genuinely empirical, therefore scientific, research into topics that had characteristically existed only in isolated philosophical discussion.

The reception of Naess's eccentric monograph among professional philosophers was not enthusiastic. This is hardly surprising given some of the things that Naess had said about them. But his critics were not outraged, or at least did not in general openly express outrage, at his accusations of unempirical generalizations, or at the potentially seditious suggestion that philosophy might be conducted just as successfully by schoolchildren. Rather, they were exercised by his idiosyncratic mixing of science, philosophy and sociology, as well as by the nature of his scientific method itself. Contemporary reviews ranged from the mildly patronizing to the more openly critical. Writing in *The Journal of Philosophy*, Ernest Nagel opened his review with the evaluation: 'This is an interesting book, not without amusing features', but went on to predict that Naess: 'will no doubt remain an outcast from the philosophical community' (Nagel 1939: 78 and 79). Jared Moore, however, criticized both Naess's presentation of his data and his conclusions as unclear and unsystematic. 'The author tries desperately hard to be "scientific"', he comments, 'but seems to have little to show for it when all is done and recorded' (Moore 1939: 490).

At home in Norway, criticisms were more personal. When Naess was proposed for the chair in philosophy at the University of Oslo, members of faculty, including his own former advisor, objected strongly to the appointment entirely on the grounds that he had recently published *'Truth' as Conceived by Those Who Are Not Professional Philosophers*. One wrote that: 'The investigation is through and through characterized by a rather ironical attitude towards professional philosophy' (E. Kaila in an evaluation of the applicants to the professorship in philosophy at the University of Oslo, September 3, 1938, quoted in Grimm 1955: 118). Reflecting on this episode much later in life, Naess himself explained the opposition in terms of both his unfashionable methodology and his controversial choice of subjects:

> I used questionnaires. At that time, 1937–8, they were looked upon as the absolute bottom of doing research. They couldn't be taken seriously at all. And then it implied that I had an undignified, really atrocious

view of one of the great problems of humanity – namely, the problem of truth. Taking seriously what those schoolboys and housewives were saying was a kind of caricature of philosophy.

(Rothenberg 1993: 49).

Nevertheless, in 1939 Naess was appointed to the chair. At 27 he became Norway's youngest-ever full professor of philosophy despite, rather than because of, *'Truth' as Conceived by Those Who Are Not Professional Philosophers*. The appointment panel may not have liked his only major monograph, but Naess had other factors in his favour, not least the esteem in which he was held by some of the most eminent philosophers of his day. The Vienna Circle had disbanded by this time, but Naess was still in touch with some of its former members. The extant logical positivists were on the whole surprisingly enthusiastic about the publication of his study of truth. Yet again they treated work that might have been seen as problematic for logical positivism as if it simply supported their position. According to their responses, if Naess's study was not actually produced using the methodology favoured by the Vienna Circle, it nevertheless supported rather than challenged their ideas.

Naess's closet philosophical relationship was with Carnap, whom he greatly admired. Carnap expressed support for Naess's enterprise in empirically studying everyday conceptions of truth, although he did so in a manner that held Naess's work at a distance. Naess recalled that Carnap described the empirical work as 'pragmatic': 'and he seriously wished me success, placing me in that coffer' (Naess 1993: 17). There is perhaps a hint here that Carnap was employing what would later become known as the 'pragmatic waste bin'. If some feature of language or some method of studying it could be identified as 'pragmatic', it could safely be ignored by more serious-minded researchers. This avuncular, but rather dismissive, attitude of Carnap to Naess's undertakings does not seem to have been anything new. As early as the Paris Congress Carnap had intervened when Naess proposed to offer empirical evidence to refute Tarski's claims about truth. Naess later reported that at this time he already had some preliminary empirical findings to offer the congress, a report that argues against Popper's claim that it was only at the Congress that Naess was inspired to find ways of refuting Tarski. It may well be that Popper was simply unaware of the existing empirical evidence, because it never came before the Congress. Before the session on truth got underway: 'Carnap contended that the empirical material and the inferences drawn form it would cause confusion, not clarification. The objections by Neurath should suffice, and as they were well discussed beforehand, the plenum discussion would be fruitful and orderly. I agreed, having the feeling that nobody would think it even meaningful to do empirical *research* on ordinary language' (Naess 1981: 145, original emphasis).

If Naess's work on truth was motivated by a desire to challenge Tarski, then some form of response, refutation or self-defence might have been expected from Tarski in return. Tarski did respond to Naess, albeit by means of a few passing references in his 1944 paper 'The semantic conception of truth', in which he reported and then commented on his work from the early 1930s. His attitude to Naess appears rather ambivalent, certainly far from straightforwardly hostile. He appealed to *'Truth' as Conceived by Those Who Are Not Professional Philosophers* in support of his own mistrust of any insistence on identifying 'the right conception of truth'. He went on to acknowledge that the everyday, as opposed to the philosophical or scientific, meaning of 'true' was fluid and vague. But he offered this rather hedged defence of his own theory:

> In spite of all this, I happen to believe that the semantic conception does conform to a very considerable extent with the common-sense usage – although I readily admit I may be mistaken. What is more to the point, however, I believe that the issue raised can be settled scientifically, though of course not by a deductive procedure, but with the help of the statistical questionnaire method. As a matter of fact, such research has been carried on, and some of the results have been reported at congresses and in part published.
>
> (Tarski 1944: 360)

Here Tarski footnoted Naess's book. So far he appeared to approve of Naess's approach and the controversial introduction of questionnaires into philosophy, although interpreting Naess's work in a way that was rather favourable to his own. Naess did find evidence of a Tarski-style definition of truth in common usage, but he found equally strong evidence for many other types of definition too. But Tarski went on to sound a note of caution, suggesting that answers obtained by Naess's method might be skewed by the fact that schoolchildren, and even philosophically untrained adults, could simply misunderstand questions put to them. According to Naess, Tarski did later concede on a postcard that Naess might be right; Tarskian truth might amount to only one particular and specific type of use of the word 'true'. But Tarski added: 'that his theory did not pretend to cover more than one way, a fundamental way of using the term from the point of view of logic' (Naess 1993: 18).

After being appointed to the Oslo chair, Naess continued his philosophical work in much the same vein. He now had more influence, as well as more funding at his disposal, and he set about establishing what became known as the school of 'Oslo philosophy'. The group of philosophers who made up this school were devoted to the study of 'empirical semantics'. The chief aim of empirical semantics was the investigation of how language is ordinarily used and understood in order to facilitate a scientifically justifiable discussion of certain philosophically significant terms. Naess had for some time been interested in defining a version of philosophy that was identifiably Norwegian, for instance referring at the Cambridge Congress in 1937 to 'our Norwegian group of empiricists'. He did so in the process of extending an invitation to the Congress to meet in Oslo in 1940. According to Naess's memoirs of the Vienna Circle, the 1940 Congress was indeed planned for Oslo. However, it never took place because by then international events had intervened. Nevertheless, Naess's portrayal of the contemporary philosophical scene in Oslo is significant. He admitted that Norwegian empiricism was little heard, but claimed that this was simply because of the secure background of science then in place: 'We have no strong stimulus to defend ourselves against real or imaginary metaphysicians' (Naess 1937/8: 384).

Naess conducted empirical work on language throughout the 1940s and 1950s, although he also began to develop interests in other areas. He maintained that what he was proposing was nothing less than a new direction for philosophy that would make it more empirical and scientific, and therefore more useful, than abstract and subjective speculations. He continued to use questionnaires, which became more elaborate, with specific linguistic examples offered for consideration as well as more general questions about usage. In 1953 he published a short monograph in which he reported on research of this type to investigate synonymity. The opening sentences of this book were an ambitious mission statement for empirical semantics:

> In contemporary philosophical literature questions are raised and answered which admittedly are empirical. Why not try to test the answers by procedures used in contemporary science? That is one way philosophy can be a mother science. But one cannot expect professional psychologists, physicists or others to do the job – they have

their own favourite questions. The philosophically inclined must carry it out himself.

(Naess 1953: 5)

As discussed in the previous chapter, Austin was notoriously more ready to extol the potentials of his methodology than to use it to develop his own philosophical theories. Naess did do something rather more concrete with his empirical semantics, in the form of his theories of interpretation and preciseness. These will be the focus of the next chapter. In the case of his work on the concept of truth, however, he seems to have been reluctant to exploit the potential that his methodology apparently offered. Admittedly, his stated purpose in conducting his empirical investigation of 'truth' was to find out what non-philosophers actually understood by the term. Ingemund Gullvåg has complained that some contemporary criticism of this work: 'was based on the misunderstanding that Naess wanted to *participate* in and contribute to the philosopher's debate on truth, and set out to "find out what truth is" by asking non-philosophers. It was not understood that his aim was much more destructive in regard to traditional philosophy in general' (Gullvåg 1982: 38, original emphasis). Nevertheless, Naess's insistence that empirical semantics offered potentials for a new and scientific way of conducting philosophical study would seem to suggest that the findings of such an investigation should have fed into the philosophical investigation of truth itself. Naess did not go far towards developing his own theory of truth. The only contribution he made in this area was a short paper published in 1961 in which he offered an account of truth and of knowledge that was apparently sceptical, although he quibbled about this description. The paper was titled 'Can knowledge be reached?' and Naess's answer to this was an unequivocal 'no'; certain knowledge could never be obtained and nor was it possible to describe someone as 'reaching' or 'approaching' knowledge. Similarly, no statement could ever be said definitively to be true: 'If to reach truth, or to grasp truth, is to reach or grasp with a guarantee that it is not falsity, we can say: *Truth or falsity cannot be reached by increasing evidence*' (Naess 1961b: 224, original emphasis).

However, Naess maintained his interest in the conception of 'truth', developing it in the direction of particular related concepts. One such concept was synonymity, the subject of his brief 1953 monograph. The link between synonymity and the conception of truth was by means of the question of what effect, if any, the word 'true' had when it was added to a proposition. In the 1953 study, Naess asked subjects to comment on whether sentences of the form 'p' and 'it is true that p' could ever be used to express the same assertion. His work on synonymy was to develop into a significant component of his philosophy of language and to lead to some striking theoretical claims. These will be discussed in the next chapter. Naess was motivated in this work, in part, by the increased interest he had perceived among philosophers in the concept of synonymity. In particular, he was inspired by Quine's (1943) observation that philosophy lacked an adequate account of synonymy, and Mates's later call for research into what expressions were in fact synonymous in an ordinary language before such an account could be attempted. It is true that in the paper Naess referred to, Mates had argued that 'We need empirical research regarding the ordinary language in order to determine which expressions are in fact synonymous' before anything like a workable definition of synonymity could be achieved (Mates 1950: 209). But Mates had also argued that the research in question would be compromised by the fact that it would have to presuppose some notion of synonymity in the first place, and had gone on explicitly to reject some of the definitions that Naess had already put forward as the result of his empirical research. Nevertheless, Naess used a selective reading of the articles by Quine and Mates as the basis for a plea for trend-bucking empirical study on the part of philosophers: 'It is invigorating and might make subsequent occupation of the armchair both more pleasant and profitable' (Naess 1956: 4).

By the time Naess was writing this, Quine himself had decided that synonymity had never been adequately defined because it was a chimera, based on an untenable notion that words had meanings that could be objectively compared. Naess did not acknowledge this, but he did urge against too hasty an assumption that there must be a unique definition of synonymity to be discovered. Empirical research in this area, as in any other, favoured the gradual building up of a concept from many observations, rather than starting with the construction of a general criterion or definition. He bemoaned the fact that 'the training of graduate students of philosophy seldom includes empirical research techniques and this further increases their already strong tendency to find systematic observation and step-by-step generalization from obtained data, irrelevant or unenlightening' (Naess 1956: 8). The general moral that Naess drew from his empirical work on synonymy, like that from his work on truth, was rather negative. He cautioned against demanding or expecting too strict a notion of identity in cases where the word 'synonymous' was used. An inquiry into such uses revealed that: 'expressions may be said to be synonymous without implying an assertion covering all occurrences' (Naess 1957: 88).

Naess may have claimed to be offering a direct and practical response to Quine's exposition of the need for a definition of synonymy, but Quine himself was not impressed. Given the differences in the reactions of the two philosophers to what they both saw as a lack of empiricism in the philosophy of language, it is perhaps not surprising that Quine took a dim view of Naess's hands-on approach. He characterized Naess's 'unimaginative' answer to the question about the nature of synonymity and the applicability of the term as being 'ask the natives'. And, 'he suited the action to the word, disseminating questionnaires and claiming significantly uniform results' (Quine 1970a: 392–3). Interestingly, Quine claimed to detect suggestions of a similar answer in the work of Chomsky. In this he was presumably attempting to equate Chomskyan reverence for native-speaker intuition with Naess's reliance on questionnaire answers. For Quine, both were suspect when it came to complicated technical matters such as the possibility of synonymity, and he proceeded to call into question the legitimacy of Naess's conclusions.

By the 1960s many of the members of the Oslo school had moved into other areas. Naess himself was becoming increasingly interested in ethics, in scepticism and in the moral issues that would lead him into the ecology movement. In 1958 he had founded *Inquiry*, a new journal which had the explicit aim of bringing together philosophy and social science. But this seems to have been more an attempt to revive the flagging state of empirical semantics than an indication of its current prowess. In an opening editorial statement, Naess stressed the interdisciplinary nature of the new journal, designed as it was to meet a gap in the periodicals market. Nothing currently served philosophers who were interested in the science of society or social scientists concerned with theory, analysis or ethics. He aired again his hopes for the new combination of disciplines, this time seeing them as extending beyond the borders of philosophy and into more practical fields: 'The combination of philosophical perspective, analytical clarity and patient empirical research might contribute to the positive solution of (important contemporary) political, ethical, cultural and social questions' (Naess 1958: 3). In later commentaries on this period, Naess made it clear that he saw this move as prompted by the Second World War, and in two very different ways. Firstly, the upheavals of invasion and occupation left many philosophers with a sense that they needed to engage more closely with socially relevant issues. Secondly, grants from America encouraged collaborative links with academic refugees from Germany and Austria who had taken sanctuary in the USA, many of whom were social scientists (Naess 1980: 159).

The Oslo School may have declined, and Naess himself may have moved increasingly to other interests, but he did not abandon his belief in the validity of empirical semantics, or in the imperative that philosophers were under to base their discussions on the rigorous analysis of the use and interpretation of terms in everyday life. He experimented with various different methods of finding out about this use and interpretation, but empirical semantics remained for him most intrinsically linked with the use of questionnaires. In a 1960 article he enthused that data collected using questionnaires: 'are often apt to reveal or suggest as much to the researcher as do penetrating meditations or introspections based on data found in one's own head or gathered in an informal way' (Naess 1960: 481). Naess explained that it was a misconception to suppose that using a questionnaire to find out how people used a term must mean directly asking people about their use of that term. In fact, relevant evidence was often obtained indirectly, and often served to strengthen or weaken, but never to prove conclusively, an argument that the researcher was developing.

Writing at about the same time on the status of normative judgments in ethics, Naess complained that the issue had too often been discussed by means of *a priori* arguments, and that it was time for some *a posteriori* arguments, possibly supported by empirical research: 'The spirit of research on questions *a posteriori* shows itself in the systematic and careful way in which the researcher prepares himself for disconfirmation due to new observations. These may indeed overturn his *ad hoc* conclusions, but this does not impair his joy of *a posteriori* research. It is an essential part of the game' (Naess 1959: 32). Naess's pronouncements about data and methodology mirror issues that continue to be highly significant in linguistics. His remarks were not intentionally addressed at linguists, but he was saying things that might be recognized and applauded by researchers working in many present-day fields of the discipline.

7
Interpretation and Preciseness

Arne Naess had a great deal to say about how philosophers ought to study language. He illustrated his claims with empirical investigations conducted over a period of 30 years. For the most part, these investigations were negative or at least open-ended in their conclusions. Naess demonstrated that philosophers had been wrong or over hasty in their pronouncements about ordinary uses of language, and argued that words were often more fluid in their meanings, and more apt to variation depending on context and circumstance, than philosophers had allowed. The chief positive thesis on language that he developed during this time was concerned with the twin concepts of interpretation and preciseness. The publication story of this thesis is complex and sprawling. The limited material resources and the political repercussions in Norway in the years immediately following the Second World War meant that academic publishing was not a high priority. Naess's work *Interpretation and Preciseness* appeared piecemeal in cheaply bound mimeographed volumes between 1947 and 1951. The work was subsequently edited together and published as a single volume by the University of Oslo press in 1953. Naess also disseminated his ideas by summarizing them in articles and lectures from 1949 onwards.

For all Naess's professed egalitarianism, and his desire to democratize the philosophical discussion of language, some of his statements in relation to interpretation and preciseness have a decidedly prescriptive ring to them. His central conceit can be summarized as follows. Natural language is incorrigibly imprecise. Interpretation is subject to the vagaries of context, speaker and hearer. But degrees of precision and imprecision themselves can be studied and measured. Forms of expression can be ranked as more or less precise than each other in terms of how many different interpretations they are empirically found to allow. In ordinary, everyday and casual uses of language a degree of imprecision presents no real problems, may well go unnoticed and requires no remedial action. In more formal and intricate uses, however, the imprecision inherent in language may be more problematic, and those concerned with using language to present complex arguments should be alert to this. Philosophers, in particular, must police their own language and be ready to substitute more precise alternatives for formulations that might be open to unwanted interpretations. They must be prepared to subject their language to a process that Naess described as 'precisation'. However, Naess's various works on the notions of interpretation and preciseness did not consist simply of stark injunctions to philosophers to reform their use of language. Naess's views on precisation were only one consequence of his empirical studies of interpretation, which had implications for a number of the philosophically most salient topics of the time, including the nature of meaning, the possibility of synonymity and the viability of a distinction between the analytic and the synthetic.

The development of Naess's ideas on interpretation and preciseness is intimately bound up with his life story, both intellectual and personal. His work on truth during the 1930s had been enough to convince him that words, even those that have been subjected to the most thorough of philosophical discussions, were far from fixed or settled in their usage. Interpretation in context depended on a host of factors specific to the situation and might also vary in nature and in sophistication depending on the identities of the speaker and the interpreter. Naess's work on truth had also strengthened his conviction that elite and academically privileged voices had weight in philosophical discussions largely because of the prestige associated with their position; ordinary people without philosophical training often had equally sophisticated things to say about concepts such as truth, and deserved an equal hearing. When he was appointed to the chair of philosophy in Oslo in 1939, external events almost immediately forced him into a more immediate engagement with his views on intellectual freedom and his opposition to fixed dogmas. German forces invaded Norway in April 1940, resulting in a five-year occupation. Naess was appalled by Nazism, but also dismayed by the imprecise and unfocused ways in which some of his fellow Norwegians expressed in private their objections to it. He felt compelled to more active opposition and joined the resistance movement, establishing and passing on information about the intentions and targets of the occupying forces. Immediately after the war he was involved in the programme to identify collaborators who had tortured and murdered members of the resistance movement, and confront them with the families of their victims.

During the later1940s, Naess's particular combination of linguistic, sociological and political expertise brought him to the attention of UNESCO, then intent on establishing agreement on the nature and scope of the concept of 'democracy'. In 1948–9, Naess led the UNESCO investigation into democratic ideology. Naess himself later claimed that the broad-ranging approach that he took to the term 'democracy' led directly to the project's termination. He argued that both Western and Soviet interpretations of democracy were particular precisations of the term, each with a long and distinguished tradition behind it. In the late 1940s such broad-minded semantics was not permissible; 'UNESCO had to be very cautious because of the cold war, and "hot" issues had to be avoided. If not, certain nations would threaten to leave the institution' (Naess 1980: 161). Despite the withdrawal of UNESCO funding, Naess continued to work for some years more on the nature of democracy. In particular he developed an interest in the practical analysis of political texts. This work was cited with approval in at least one textbook on language and ideology in the 1970s (Drucker 1974: 70).

One of the things that Naess found most striking during his work on the UNESCO project was the degree of imprecision with which even salient and ideologically loaded words such as 'democracy', were used. He observed practical problems that seemed to arise directly from this, and these in turn heightened his interest in the notions of clarity and preciseness in relation to philosophical study and uses of language. He developed the idea of precisation as a necessary tool in philosophical discussion, and also considered the relevance of 'definiteness of intention'. In effect, he argued that communicative intentions of speakers and writers were not uniform and were not constant. They varied between individuals and between different contexts or styles of language use, ranging from the ideally very definite and clear-cut in philosophical debate to the vague or almost non-existent in some everyday casual exchanges.

Philosophical scrutiny of precision in the use of language, even a prescriptive attention to the degree of preciseness appropriate to philosophical discussion, was not unique to Naess. Such preoccupations had been around for centuries, and can be found in the works of major philosophers from a variety of traditions. What was new in Naess's work was the dogged empirical investigation of degrees of preciseness in language using the sociological techniques he had developed during his work on truth, together with an attempt at a formal definition of how different expressions in a language may be related in terms of preciseness. Previous philosophical treatments of the subject were largely impressionistic and generalizing. Naess himself suggested a classical pedigree for the notion of definiteness of intention in the work of Sextus Empiricus (Naess 1968b: 10). In more recent philosophy, Locke had included in *An Essay Concerning Human Understanding* a chapter titled 'Of the abuse of words', complaining of careless uses of language that caused unnecessary confusion and made communication harder than it need be. People used words 'without much troubling their heads to examine what are the precise *ideas* they stand for' (Locke 1690, Book III, Chapter X: 274, original emphasis). There was no point in trying to reform all the languages of the world, Locke conceded, and indeed this form of communication seemed to serve perfectly adequately for the purposes of the market place and of gossip. But 'those *who* pretend *seriously* to *search after* or maintain *truth*, should think themselves obliged to study how they might deliver themselves without obscurity, doubtfulness, or equivocation' (Locke 1690, Book III, Chapter XI: 280, original emphasis). At much the same time the Port Royale grammarians had been concerned with the importance of the clarity of terms to philosophy. They produced a descriptive grammar with the aim of promoting better understanding of language and therefore clearer use of it in argument and reasoning (Arnauld and Lancelot 1660).

In the twentieth century, philosophers were divided along predictable lines in their reactions to impreciseness in natural language, seeing it either as an incorrigible flaw or an interesting and suggestive essential property. Bertrand Russell commented in his introduction to Wittgenstein's *Tractatus* that 'In practice, language is always more or less vague, so that what we assert is never quite precise' (Russell 1922: x). For Russell this introduced the need for a logically perfect language. Wittgenstein himself moved away from this severe position as he began to celebrate the philosophical importance of natural language. Michael Forster has linked Naess's ideas on precisation to the later Wittgenstein. He outlines Wittgenstein's views on the 'vagueness or fluidity' of a family of concepts in their ordinary use and adds: 'Empirical studies strongly support the view that the ordinary use of concepts from this family is in important respect indeterminate and inconsistent', footnoting *Interpretation and Preciseness* (Forster 2004: 139).

Naess's contemporaries in Oxford were also apparently aware of the imprecision rampant in the use of language. Grover Maxwell and Herbert Feigl pointed out in 1961, without reference to Naess, that even ordinary language philosophy, with its insistence on the efficacy and sophistication of everyday language, nevertheless acknowledged that this language was sometimes in need of reform for the purposes of scientific or philosophical discussion. Certainly Austin's readiness to adopt technical and specialized terms to explain some of the more rarefied aspects of speech act theory would seem to bear out this claim. But Maxwell and Feigl went further than this: 'we strongly suspect that many cases of putative ordinary-usage analysis are, in fact, disguised reformations' (Maxwell and Feigl 1961: 489).

In *Interpretation and Preciseness*, Naess confronted his readership with a dense collection of definitions and abbreviations, together with a host of questionnaires and statistical findings. He began with a number of versions of the types of questionnaire that could be used to elicit judgments about synonymity, the topic he had been investigating since his early work on truth. One typical such questionnaire involved the researcher presenting a subject with a text that contained a particular formulation (T). After the subject had read and considered the text, the researcher was to ask: 'Suppose the formulation U (here, U is mentioned) had occurred in the text instead of T, and in T's place. Would U have expressed the same proposition to you as T did when you read T?' (Naess 1947/51, vol 1: 10). Curiously, Naess admitted in a footnote that the term 'proposition' might be too sophisticated for use in such a questionnaire, and in any case was perhaps not a very good translation of the Norwegian term 'påstand'; 'assertion' might be better. In other types of questionnaires, subjects were asked about the sets of conditions that would confirm or disconfirm either T or U. Synonymity was then to be defined in terms of the degree of overlap between the confirmation and disconfirmation of T and U.

This notion of 'degree' was perhaps the most significant aspect of Naess's account. Synonymity was relative. That is, Naess found no empirical support for absolute or stable synonymity. Any description of two expressions as synonymous must always make reference to individual speakers and contexts. And in many cases a pair of expressions was best described as being either more or less synonymous than another pair of expressions, rather than being judged in isolation. This comparison depended on the size and extent of the consent about synonymity relative to groups of subjects and situations of use:

If T_0 and T_1 is [sic] synonymous within the group of persons P_1, and within the group of situations S_1, whereas U_0 and U_1 is synonymous within a group of persons P_2 and a group of situations S_2, none of which are totally included in P_1 or S_1, but at least one of which includes at least one of the groups P_1 or S_1, then it is said that the relation of synonymity between U_0 and U_1 extends further that that between T_0 and T_1.

(Naess 1947/51, vol. 1: 18)

Interpretation and Preciseness also introduced 'definiteness of intention', although this was something that Naess developed in more detail in later publications. The concept remained ambiguous, or perhaps indiscriminate, between producers and receivers of language. Most of the empirical tests that Naess conducted in an attempt to establish definitenesses of intention in individual circumstances involved interrogating subjects about their understanding of a text they had just heard or read. But the morals he drew from these were largely to do with the strictures that should be placed on those constructing texts, at least those with serious philosophical intent. Definiteness of intention concerned the extent to which someone had considered the different available interpretations of a text and made a choice as to which of these they either intended to convey or had decided to interpret. It necessarily had much in common with preciseness. The degree of definiteness could vary between individuals and between situations, ranging from the very specific to the very vague. In some everyday situations, such as casual conversation, a very low degree of definiteness of intention might cause no real problems of communication, and might pass more or less unnoticed, while in philosophical discussion it could be very damaging.

Naess described his initial investigations of definiteness of intention in brief and informal terms in *Interpretation and Preciseness*. But in later work he recalled more about how he and his fellow researchers proceeded in this area, and gave a fuller account of the type of empirical work undertaken. One such account is particularly arresting, both because of the scenario described, and because of the morals Naess drew from it.

> The experimenter announced a lecture to an association of students of physics, and about 250 gathered in an auditorium. After talking for about twenty minutes the lecturer said: 'The earth is surrounded by a gravitational field' in a rather natural context, but without particular stress. This was a signal to a mob of assistants to invade the gathering with copies of a questionnaire which were handed to the students. The basic question read: 'How did you interpret the utterance "The earth is

surrounded by a gravitational field?"' 'Do any of the following sentences convey to you what the utterance conveyed to you?'

Two classes of answers are of particular interest, the 'I do not know'-answers and the 'no discrimination' answers. They reveal the limits of the definiteness of interpretation among hearers.

(Naess 1981: 143–4)

Naess found the cases in which the students were at a loss for an answer about how they had interpreted a sentence they had just heard, or had to admit that they could not discriminate between two possible interpretations, to be the most interesting. Such cases revealed how frequently it was possible for interpreters to be attentive to what they were hearing and be satisfied that they had understood, and yet be able to identify no clear definiteness of intention at all. Definiteness of intention increased on a continuum from this low point; as with questions of synonymity, it was a matter of degree. Definiteness of intention varied in terms of individuals. Naess's formal definition in *Interpretation and Preciseness* is worded as follows:

> The definiteness of intention of a person P_1 as interpreter of a formulation T_0 in a situation S, is greater in relation to a given reference class $T_1 - T_n$, than the definiteness of intention of P_2 as interpreter of T_0 in S in relation to that reference class, if and only if P_1 does not fail to discriminate between any possibilities between which P_2 discriminates, and in addition to this discriminates in relation to at least one more possibility.
>
> (Naess 1947/51, vol. 1: 52–3)

Like definiteness of intention, and also like synonymy, preciseness was for Naess a relative term and a matter of degree. It reflected the fact that a range of interpretations were always available for any text or expression. Whereas degrees of definiteness of intention relied on the psychological or the cognitive state of individuals, preciseness was dependent on the form of expression used, although always relative to producer, receiver and context. Naess linked his definition of preciseness explicitly to that of synonymity in a 1949 summary of his work in this area:

> If two sentences T and U are synonymous (equipollent) for at least some persons in some situations, T will be said to be a possible interpretation of U and U a possible interpretation of T. If all interpretations

of T are also interpretations of U, whereas some interpretations of U are not interpretations of T for some persons in some situations, we say that T is more precise than U for those persons in those situations.
(Naess 1949: 227)

On this account, 'more precise than' sounds as if it would have a lot in common with 'less ambiguous than', but Naess argued that his version of preciseness was much more specific than usual philosophical uses of 'ambiguity'. He pointed out that 'more precise than' was itself a technical term, connected to 'more precise than' in vernacular usage but with some important differences.

Naess was keen to emphasize and defend his empirical methods in *Interpretation and Preciseness*. He did so by dwelling on the shortcomings of philosophical judgments about meaning and truth that relied on intuition, an approach that was tied up, for Naess, with the belief that language contained a set of dependable laws from which meaning could reliably be established. The twin reliance on linguistic laws and intuition were what had led many philosophers into the error of unempirical pronouncements about language and meaning. Naess took issue with G. E. Moore, for instance, who had made reference to 'correct English usage', on the grounds that this was not empirically meaningful. On the contrary, in his own work Naess pledged that 'stress is laid upon observations of usage and the uncertainties as regards the outcome of such observations. What does "correct usage" mean operationally?' (Naess 1947/51, vol. 1: 5–6).

Naess devoted a three-page digression to a humorous dialogue between A (enraged reader), B (patient reader) and N (author) on the subject of intuition and the need to supplement it with empirical findings. The enraged reader urged the case for accepting intuitive evidence for what it would mean to describe two expressions as synonymous, even synonymous between different speakers. The patient reader drew attention to the danger of relying on 'feelings' that we know what we and others mean by an expression. Rather, the readers should both hope for 'an account of empirical work which makes it possible to see the concepts in use, and to make a first hand decision on their relative fruitfulness', a hope that the author promised to fulfil (Naess 1947/51, vol. 2: 34). Later, Naess explicitly criticized wrong assumptions about usage, which came about because 'hypotheses about usage outside the exact sciences and the science of law, mostly tend to be based on arm chair methods involving questionnaires put forth and answered by the same person' (Naess 1947/51, vol. 2: 14).

Naess's own response to this problem was of course mainly to insist that the questionnaires should be answered by people other than those who had designed them. The best way for the philosophical researcher to proceed was to ask non-philosophical subjects about their usage and their interpretation. But he also introduced some other techniques for empirical research. These concerned consulting written texts produced previous to the experimental study and for other purposes, in order to find out about how terms had been used. The final volume of *Interpretation and Preciseness* is devoted to what Naess called 'occurrence analysis'. Much of what he said by way of introducing this could in fact be seen as undermining his own work with questionnaires. He stressed that people were not always able to offer viable definitions of usage; it would be better to observe how people use expression than to ask them how they do it. He acknowledged that his questionnaire technique would have to be regarded as unsatisfactory if there were a viable alternative method by which meanings could be revealed by observation of use. As things stood, however, 'The non-existence of a method by which meanings can be "seen" by observation of use is one of the strong reasons not to abandon the synonymity questionnaire' (Naess 1947/51, vol. 6: 2). It seems that Naess might have been prepared to replace his questionnaire techniques with the observation and analysis of collections of texts if he had been confident that such a procedure could be conducted with suitable rigour.

Naess contended that no such rigorous procedure had been developed. As some preliminaries towards a possible procedure, he proposed tools such as card indexes to record instances of usage for easy reference, and numbered lists of occurrences of the word under investigation. He suggested identifying and investigating the other words with which a target word typically occurred. For instance, a study of the use of the word 'people' may become relevant to a description of the word 'democracy', once a link was established between the two words by means of an occurrence sentence in which 'democracy' was defined in relation to 'people'. He also dwelt on the problems associated with insufficient data to confirm particular hypotheses. It was difficult to conduct occurrence analyses on a large enough scale to procure adequate evidence, but Naess suggested that the combination of the methods of occurrence analysis and questionnaire might go some way to avoiding the worst consequences of this problem. Often in occurrence analysis of single texts:

> There is insufficient material to confirm or disconfirm strongly any hypothesis of interest. One way out of the difficulty is to create

a supplementary text of high relevancy. This can be done by questionnaire methods. The questions can be formed in such a way that answers are apt to throw light on just those hypotheses which are tentatively formed on the basis of occurrence analysis. Generally, however, it is convenient to use questionnaires at first, and then go into occurrence analysis, or to mix both methods during all the stages of the investigation.

(Naess 1947/51, vol. 6: 52)

As had been the case with Naess's earlier monograph on his research into 'truth', contemporary reviews of *Interpretation and Preciseness* were far from complimentary. Carl Hempel had earlier identified problems for the inductive method that saw verification replaced by confirmation. Responding to the 1949 summary of Naess's work, Hempel had serious reservations about his empirical methodology. His questionnaires were 'formulated, at least partly, in terms which are abstract and vague and may well be understood in different ways' by different subjects. Hempel noted that Naess acknowledged that synonymity was relative to various parameters, including situation of use, but 'there is no clear indication of what the range of permissible values for the situation variables is to be; and this indefiniteness is likely to deprive the resulting concepts of the required scientific preciseness'. Hempel also pointed out that Naess's philosophy depended on a system of concepts, such as synonymity and preciseness, that he first defined and then sought to connect (Hempel 1950: 154). Benson Mates, who had himself called for empiricism in the study of synonymity, was kinder, although he too was troubled by Naess's methodology. Naess's questionnaires were certainly open to criticism, and his process of occurrence analysis was laborious. Nevertheless Mates commented charitably on: 'how easy it is to criticize the empirical procedures utilized by the author, and how difficult to propose any that are better' (Mates 1958b: 553).

Despite the reservations of its critics, *Interpretation and Preciseness* was firmly established as a central text in Norwegian philosophy for many years, and all students taking courses in philosophy at the University of Oslo took an exam on the concepts it covered. In the mid-1960s Naess brought out what was in effect a textbook on his own work, the English title of which was *Communication and Argument*. Predictably enough, this is in many ways an easier read than *Interpretation and Preciseness*. The main definitions of synonymity and preciseness are introduced, but without the full range of questionnaires and experimental support, and without the bewildering array of abbreviations and symbolisms that make the earlier book such hard going. The focus of the textbook is different too. It is less concerned with the details of different types of relationships between expressions, and more engaged with the practical applications of Naess's philosophy. In fact, the book's subtitle is 'elements of applied semantics', and it is striking to find 'applied' where, given the context of Naess's work as a whole, 'empirical' might be expected. His textbook drew heavily on his earlier empirical work, but he was more concerned this time with what he saw as the desirable applications of that work within philosophy itself.

It was the practical aspects of communication, then, that concerned Naess most centrally in *Communication and Argument*. He applied his notion of precisation in what almost amounted to a handbook of argumentation for his students. His main theme is predictable enough. There was a functional divide between philosophical and everyday uses of language that made a high degree of preciseness and definiteness of intention imperative in the former while it might be unnecessary or even undesirable in the latter. In fact the process of precisation itself could help to distinguish between thoughtful and superficial uses of expressions: 'Mindless chatter cannot be precizated. The attempt to render an expression precise may therefore be a way of finding out whether we mean anything at all when we use it' (Naess 1966: 53).

Naess's stated desire to eliminate from serious discussion all expressions that might be liable to misinterpretation is in some ways reminiscent of his former mentor Carnap. Like other members of the Vienna Circle, Carnap had urged the need to neaten up language, if necessary translating everyday into more formal expressions, before it could be deemed good enough for the purposes of philosophy. Carnap recognized a philosophical imperative to distinguish between genuine expressions of science and philosophy on the one hand, and mere everyday imprecision on the other, in which he included metaphysics and philosophical pseudo-problems. There are certainly overtones of logical positivism in the following remark from Naess, in a section concerned with distinguishing between relevant arguments and forms of persuasion: 'One of the least debatable principles of the scientific approach is to realize as consistently as possible the distinction referred to in the heading of this section. The distinction has not always been respected' (Naess 1966: 134). He went on to complain about, for instance, sixteenth- and seventeenth-century philosophers who mixed their philosophy with religious statements, or even used such statements as their premises.

However, Naess continued to differ from Carnap and from the other members of the Vienna Circle, in that his views on the appropriate distinctions between the scientific and the everyday were based on empirical research into usage of and attitudes to language. Like Austin, but unlike present day linguists, his basic drive in studying language was the desire for it to serve philosophy. Like Austin he argued that philosophers would be ill-advised to ignore ordinary language, and that words vary in meaning depending on context. But unlike Austin he argued that philosophical usage must necessarily be different from the everyday, because of the different demands placed on it. He did not of course go as far as Neurath, who proposed that children should be taught to speak only scientific language, but he did argue that a process of precisation was necessary for some forms of discourse. Decisions about this were to be entirely pragmatic. As he wrote in a slightly later commentary on the language of science and philosophy: 'Economy of thought requires that we work with a definiteness of intention commensurate with the requirements of the task or the problem confronting us at any time' (Naess 1970b: 112).

Naess's attitude to the role of precisation in rigorous philosophical discussion was equivocal. On the face of it, his account should straightforwardly have implied that the higher the degree of preciseness the better the philosophical discussion. But he admitted that he frequently found more depth and interest in philosophers who were often less than precise. He commented in an interview that 'To be a great philosopher seems to imply that you think precisely, but do not explain all the consequences of your ideas. That's what others will do if they have been inspired' (Rothenberg 1993: 98). This view even seems to have slightly tempered his admiration for Carnap: 'Carnap's philosophical style, at its best, prevents his formulations from being interpreted in widely different directions. The limitation of his thought is therefore unusually clear' (Naess 1970a: 337–8). Almost, inevitably, Naess's own work was evaluated in terms of the standards of precision outlined in *Interpretation and Preciseness*. In the 1950s Laura Grimm, formerly apparently an enthusiastic member of the Oslo School, turned the methodology of precisation on *'Truth' as Conceived by Those Who Are Not Professional Philosophers*, in particular, and found it severely wanting (Grimm 1955).

Arguably the main contribution to the philosophy of language in *Communication and Argument* is to be found in the short and underdeveloped chapter on analytic and synthetic sentences. Here Naess turned the armoury of his notion of preciseness, and by extension the body of empirical investigations on which it was based, on this venerable issue. Given his insistence that interpretation was always relative to individuals and situations, it is not surprising that he was wary of the distinction. Unlike Quine, however, he did not reject it altogether. He saw the term 'analytic' as applicable not to particular sentences, only ever to particular types of uses of sentences in particular contexts. Naess argued that the very notion of analyticity depended on particular rules of usage. The type of rules that Naess was envisaging here was the type that might be fixed in advance for a particular context or text, as when someone offers a definition of certain key terms. There was no room in his account of language, he did not even mention as a possibility, the existence of more general rules of meaning independent of any particular context of use.

In effect, Naess argued that different contextually dependent degrees of precisation could mean that what was apparently one and the same sentence was sometimes analytic and sometimes synthetic. Rules of usage are dependent on context, and 'An expression can be analytic in relation to some rules but synthetic in relation to others' (Naess 1966: 75). He continued this definition with an example: 'The Middle Ages ended before 1550' is analytic in a context where the rule of usage is that 'The Middle Ages' means the same as 'the period from 500 to 1500'. It is synthetic in a context where the rule is that 'The Middle Ages' means the same as 'that time in European history when Catholicism was the only form of faith'.

For Naess, the distinction between analytic and synthetic was viable but unstable; it could only ever be decided on a case-by-case, context-by-context basis. His implicit disagreement on this matter with logical positivism was of course entirely consistent with his general philosophy of language. Philosophers such as Carnap drew on an assumption that the meanings of words were fixed and could be established *a priori* in order to distinguish between sentences that were inherently analytic and those that were inherently synthetic, a distinction that was necessary to the whole logical positivist enterprise. Naess dismissed such assumptions about language as incorrigibly unempirical. For him all statements about meaning must be based on empirical evidence of use and understanding, and such evidence pointed to the fact that meanings varied depending on people, situations and purposes. Hence decisions between analytic and synthetic, to the extent that they were viable, could only be made with careful reference to these factors.

Naess's account of meaning as contingent and context-dependent had implications for the nature of philosophical and scientific discussion. His insistence that the distinction between analytic and synthetic was dependent on context, in part, explains his distrust of any notion of absolute truth or certain knowledge. The truth status of any statement must always be provisional, relative to definiteness of intention and to specific context. By 1970 he was writing that '*All non-contradictory fundamental* (philosophical, metaphysical) positions (systems, points of view) *have the same non-zero status of validity* (are equivalid, are acceptable at one time)' (Naess 1970b: 111, original emphasis). It was not, he argued, that there could not be an ultimate truth of any matter, just that it was not practical ever to expect to reach certainty about it. A decade later, he expressed himself reluctant to use the term 'meaning' at all: 'In E[mpirical] S[emantics] that term is avoided through use of the synonymity terminology' (Naess 1981: 147). So Naess's work on synonymity, which arose from his early studies of truth and was developed in the course of the work described in *Interpretation and Preciseness*, became the alternative that he preferred to the empirically unacceptable term 'meaning'. This point was given fuller expression in a summary of Naess's work by Naess and Ingemund Gullvåg, first published in 1996: 'Arne Naess developed a theory of ambiguity and interpretation as pragmatic concepts, a theory that does not presuppose a concept of "sense" or "meaning" but only concepts of "synonymity" (meaning the same as) and "non-synonymity", with substitutability in actual use as a criterion of synonymity' (Naess and Gullvåg 1996: 58).

There is of course something familiar about the claim that philosophers should avoid the term 'meaning' in favour of considering when expressions are more or less similar in their applications. And Naess was not the first or only philosopher to question the existence of a single phenomenon of synonymity. The philosophers who had become uneasy about the distinction between analytic and synthetic were expressing similar concerns. In 1953, Quine suggested that 'Quite possibly the ultimately fruitful notion of synonymy will be one of degree: not the dyadic relation of *a* as synonymous with *b*, but the tetradic relation of *a* as more synonymous with *b* than *c* with *d*' (Quine 1953a: 63). In the same year Nelson Goodman commented that 'The extreme difficulty of finding in practice any two terms that surely have exactly the same meaning opens the way to acceptance of the view that there are no absolute synonyms but only terms that have a greater or lesser degree, or one or another kind, of likeness of meaning' (Goodman 1953: 92).

Naess continued to distinguish himself from these other philosophers by his insistence on empirical foundations and justification for such claims. In a contribution to the debate over synonymity in the mid-1950s, he argued in defence of *Interpretation and Preciseness* that the use of questionnaires to investigate a category such as synonymity did not require a unitary definition of the category: 'It is our sense that the great range of phenomena more or less vaguely and ambiguously referred to by the term "synonymity" is such that there is no reason to expect that an [sic] single, carefully introduced concept could somehow be made to cover *the* essential features of these phenomena' (Naess 1956/8: 472–3, original emphasis). His work was not, in fact, presupposing a concept of synonymity, as Mates and others had claimed; it was based on the belief that a large number of concepts dealing with slight differences in meaning were required. He maintained that the construction of any such concepts must be based on empirical observation.

It is not clear, however, that much productive interpretative work was actually completed in this way. Siri Blom, herself a member of the Oslo School, considered using Naess's method in her study of the meaning of 'probability' but seems to have run up against the problems inherent in a study of meaning that refrains from presupposing any categories. Her chosen method entailed defining the relevant expression without preconceived ideas that might impose limits on what the researcher might find in the data: 'However, we found it difficult to produce interesting interpretations of the occurrence sentences without having definite hypotheses of usage to guide the search for variations in meaning' (Blom 1955: 77). She chose instead to group occurrences of 'probability' according to three predecided alternative interpretations, deciding in each case which was the most plausible. Others contemporaries were more outspoken in their comments on the potential usefulness of Naess's techniques. Campbell Crockett referred to his 'clumsy empirical techniques', and questioned the appropriateness and reliability of his methods: '*Some* of the techniques developed by Naess rely upon statistical surveys, and it is not at all clear that the description of a stock use of an expression is assisted by counting the noses of those who employ it in this way' (Crockett 1959: 109, original emphasis).

Much of Naess's philosophical career was spent in defending what Crockett dismissed as nose-counting. For Naess, knowledge of language did not have any special status that made it immune from evidence. Like any other type of knowledge, it required a firm empirical basis, and the only type of evidence that made any sense in relation to language was evidence about usage. As a means of obtaining such evidence, the questionnaire method was undoubtedly flawed, but was pragmatically expedient because of the lack of a viable alternative. Naess did worry about the possible gap, pointed out by many of his critics, between what people say they do and what they actually do. His problem was that spontaneous occurrences or interpretations of particular key terms were hard to come by and difficult to analyse. In *Interpretation and Preciseness* he explained why occurrence analysis, although potentially the most valuable source of empirical evidence, could not in practice be used as a sole or main source of data. Writing at much the same time, he admitted that although 'the direct investigation of usage of "true" etc. has been planned by us', the plans had never been carried through. Naess cited the sheer methodological difficulties of such an enterprise (Naess 1953: 35).

When advancing his views on the proper conduct of language study, Naess more than once drew an analogy with botany, exactly the analogy that had so pleased Austin. Unlike Austin, Naess was himself a keen amateur botanist. He urged that trying to work from introspection would be unacceptable in this field, and should straightforwardly be viewed as equally unacceptable in the study of language. As early as *'Truth'as Conceived by Those Who Are Not Professional Philosophers* he insisted that: 'Meditations and deductions from general principles will not do – just as little in this field of research as in botany' (Naess 1938: 153). More than 40 years later he returned to this analogy, when arguing for empirical evidence and theoretical interpretation as complementary tools in relation to argumentation analysis: 'A pronounced empirical approach such as the one I am advocating does not exclude theory-construction. Botany is empirical yet contains, and also presupposes, theory-construction. Debates, perhaps even more than flowers, inspire deep reflection!' (Naess 1982a: 11).

There is much that separates Naess and Austin, but this shared analogy highlights what they had in common. They both argued that philosophers should start with a careful accumulation of data about ordinary usage before attempting to use claims about meaning in the course of their arguments. They differed fundamentally and irreconcilably over the appropriate nature of that data. That is, they differed over what in their analogy were the linguistic equivalents of plant specimens. Austin insisted that his desk-bound intuitive collection of data was objective and empirical because it was collaborative. Naess was confident that his data were both objective and empirical because he collected it from a large number of independent subjects and analysed it statistically. Naess's questionnaires could be recognized as particular versions of the questions the ordinary language philosophers set themselves: questions about what they would say when and what it would mean. Benson Mates's guarded praise for the results of Naess's empirical approach, in fact, contains a thinly veiled comparison with Austin:

> In general, the reviewer believes that very often the same linguistic phenomena which have led certain recent philosophers to surprising

conclusions about ordinary usage can better be explained or described by means of the notions of synonymic alternative, precization, and definiteness of intention. We may grant, for example, that it is possible to say 'He yawned' without intending either 'He yawned voluntarily' or 'He yawned involuntarily'; but this seems to justify a conclusion about the definiteness of intention of the speaker rather than one to the effect that there are yawns which are neither voluntary nor involuntary.

(Mates 1958b: 552)

As well as his dubious claims to objectivity, Austin's perceived elitism was a focus for his critics. He was accused of a form of class and social isolationism; when he was talking about ordinary language he was actually talking about the language of an Oxford common room. Naess's efforts with questionnaires, on the other hand, were designed to find out what people said about their language, particularly people who were not professional philosophers. In 1960 he explicitly cautioned against using professionals as subjects, although at this point not drawing any particular parallels with ordinary language philosophy; professional and experts 'tend to refuse answering isolated questions and insist upon reformulating, modifying and expanding the formulations of the questionnaire in a way that make *comparison* with other respondents very difficult' (Naess 1960: 482, original emphasis). In *Communication and Argument*, in connection with judgments about synonymity, he gave a related warning: 'we all too commonly and rashly presume that what applies in our own case, or in that of some limited group, is also true generally' (Naess 1966: 21). Nevertheless, for all Naess's professed distrust of philosophers' statements about what ordinary people say, he was not averse to making up dialogues just as a philosopher of ordinary language might. For instance, discussing the way in which ordinary people use 'real' in what might be described as a metaphysical sense, he offered the following: 'A: To me Mr. B does not appear *real*. C: Yes, there is something lacking in him. To me he is less real than any other I know' (Naess 1992: 332).

Naess commented directly on the differences between his work and Austin's. In 1961 he expressed concern that 'so-called empirical trends' in twentieth-century philosophy actually relied either on formal methods or on intuition: 'With the ordinary language movement at Oxford one has, so far, paid little attention to intersubjective methods for testing hypotheses about functions or jobs of language, and to the special tasks of scientific discourse' (Naess 1961a: 178). In a slightly longer commentary a few years later, Naess was somewhat kinder and even expressed reluctant admiration for Austin's patience, hard work and dedication to finding out the facts. He also offered a partial defence of ordinary language philosophy against the accusations levelled for instance by Gellner that it was an inherently conservative approach. Naess noted that 'Austin, like many other linguistic philosophers, was not himself a conservative and was indeed fervently interested in social and political reforms' (Naess 1968a: 160). He then went on to praise Austin's work on performatives as a valuable contribution to the philosophy of language.

The ordinary language philosophers, however, were generally wary or openly hostile towards what Naess was doing. Austin's apologist J. O. Urmson, in his commentary on Austin's method, argued that 'The device of a statistical survey of "what people would say" by means of a questionnaire is no substitute for the group, (1) because there cannot be the necessary detail in the questionnaire, (2) because the untrained answerers can so easily make mistakes, (3) because we are raising questions where unanimity is both desirable and obtainable' (Urmson et al. 1965: 80).

Urmson's third point highlights a major difference between the two approaches. Austin and his colleagues were struck by the frequency with which they reached consensus about use and interpretation, and convinced that this showed they were really finding out the facts about ordinary language. For Naess unanimity was neither desirable nor obtainable. His focuses were the diverse uses to which language was put, the ways in which meaning and interpretation varied with context, and how these factors exposed the myth of independent language that could be described and analysed in isolation from individual occurrences of use. Despite apparent similarities and communalities of interest, there was really no possible common meeting ground between Oslo philosophy and ordinary language philosophy. This point is borne out by one of Geoffrey Warnock's recollections of Austin:

> I remember that he once came back from America – I think in 1956 – a good deal perturbed by what he thought to be the increasing prestige there of Arne Naess. This must have been because he thought he saw the right *purpose* – a more empirical, 'objective' way of doing philosophy, offering the hope of getting things actually settled by patient industry – in danger of being compromised by what he took to be radically wrong *methods*. 'It's infiltrating from the West', he said, shaking his head.
>
> (Warnock 1973: 43)

Austin and Naess did meet and discuss their differences face-to-face. Again, Geoffrey Warnock summarized the event, or at least Austin's role in it. During a discussion with Naess in Berkeley in 1958 Austin spoke in favour of systematic cooperation in philosophy, but 'was careful to distinguish the programme he had in mind from the kind of Gallup-poll, empirical team work which Naess believed in, and which Austin regarded as, in principle, misguided' (Warnock 1963: 14).

One particular instance of the differences in methodology and assumptions between Oslo philosophy and ordinary language philosophy is provided by a comparison between the work of Naess and Grice, although caution has to be exercised in taking Grice straightforwardly as a representative of ordinary language philosophy, for reasons outlined in the Chapter 5. The comparison is suggested by the fact that they both wrote on the interpretation of natural language 'or'. In doing so they each used very different methods of study and, perhaps as a result, reached very different conclusions. The major question about natural language 'or', which had confronted philosophers for centuries, was the extent to which its meaning could be equated to logical disjunction. Logical disjunction, represented symbolically by '$\vee$' was generally accepted to be inclusive in nature. That is, a disjunctive proposition was true if either one or both of its disjuncts were true. The status of exclusive disjunction, in which truth of the proposition as a whole depended on just one but not both of the disjuncts being true, was a matter of some controversy, but it was generally not taken to be the primary logical meaning. Now it is apparent that natural language 'or' can have both an inclusive and an exclusive interpretation. It is exclusive when used to offer a simple choice or to set out two distinct alternatives: 'You can have wine or beer with your meal', 'The philosopher is in his armchair or in his laboratory'. There are also inclusive uses of 'or', in cases where the context makes clear that both disjuncts are compatible and possible: 'Visitors qualify for reduced entry if they are over 65 or have mobility problems', 'You can apply for an Irish passport if you have an Irish parent or an Irish spouse'. In 1952 P. F. Strawson published a text book on logic that included a summary of the current received wisdom about both the uncertain meaning of 'or' and the relationship between it and logical disjunction. Strawson drew attention to the commonly acknowledged fact that 'in certain verbal contexts, "either ... or ..." plainly carries the implication "and not both ... and ...", whereas in other contexts, it does not. These are sometimes spoken as, respectively, the exclusive and inclusive senses of "or"; and, plainly, if we are to identify "$\vee$" with either, it must be the latter'

(Strawson 1952: 92). The common understanding among logicians was that while inclusive disjunction gave the true or correct meaning of 'or', the word was generally used and understood in ordinary language as equivalent with exclusive disjunction.

Naess published an article in 1961 that reported on a particular investigation into the interpretation of natural language 'or'. Predictably enough, he castigated logicians for their glib assumption that 'or' was used in ordinary language for the concept of exclusive disjunction. He lamented that formal logic had become detached from how people actually thought, perceived and acted. He called for attention from logicians to the understanding and use of logical terms, which for Naess meant attention to the behaviour of people with respect to these terms. He considered how different styles of questionnaire might encourage subjects to think in various ways about the distinction between inclusive and exclusive 'or'.

Naess presented questionnaires to 350 American college students who had no formal training in logic and compiled a table of results showing the percentage of students who chose exclusive and inclusive interpretations for the different questions. He described a number of such questions; the following are typical: (1) A has made a bet with B that 'Jack is qualified to receive a fellowship in this department'. Fellowships are open to those who are competent in Greek or in Latin. If Jack is competent in both Latin and Greek, would you consider that A won the bet? (2) A has made a bet with B that 'Jack is married to Joan or he is married to Phyllis'. If Jack is married to both Joan and Phyllis, would you consider that A won the bet?

Naess discovered that there was in general wide consensus among his subjects about the interpretation of each example, but that the interpretation depended strongly on the subject matter of the example and the verbal context given. For instance, his subjects overwhelmingly offered an inclusive interpretation in the case of (1) and an exclusive interpretation in the case of (2). Contrary to the unempirical prediction made by most philosophers, he argued, there was no discernible default preference for exclusive readings. Naess concluded his article with the revelation that he had in fact approached 'a small number' of professional logicians, asking them to predict how his questionnaires would most likely be answered by those without any training in logic. His intention was to find out whether those who practised logic had thought about how people actually reacted to such expressions. 'The straggling answers confirmed the impression that it is difficult and hazardous for professionals to pronounce on how non-professionals reason and how they use the logical connectives without having performed series of experiments' (Naess 1961c: 60). It was only with reference to such experiments that theoreticians could hope to find an appropriate terminology for their discussions.

Grice discussed 'or' during his William James lectures. He did not devote a specific lecture or even a clearly demarcated part of a lecture to the term, and he hinted at possible accounts rather than offering a definitive version. What is sometimes now described as the 'Gricean' account of disjunction owes much to later interpretations and expansions of his ideas. Nevertheless, a discernible solution to the problem of natural language 'or' emerged from the lectures, as part of his wider concern with the apparent discrepancies between natural language terms and their supposed logical equivalents. One of the motivating forces behind his theory of conversation was to show that such discrepancies were indeed only apparent. Traditional logic successfully explained the semantics of ordinary language expressions. Divergences from logical meaning could be explained by general principles of language use rather than by specific linguistic differences; they occurred at the level of 'what is implicated' rather than at the level of 'what is said'.

For Grice, these differences between logic and interpretation could be explained by means of generalized conversational implicatures based on the maxims of cooperation. In effect, the semantic meaning of 'or', that is 'what is said' when it is used, could indeed be logical inclusive disjunction. The fact that in many contexts hearers reached an exclusive interpretation was due to a default implicature that both disjuncts were not true, based on expectations of quantity. Grice noted that using 'or' in a statement was inherently uninformative: '"A or B" is characteristically employed to give a partial answer to some "W"-question, to which each disjunct if assertible, would give a fuller, more specific, more satisfactory answer' (Grice 1967: 68). He went no further with this analysis, but we can assume by extension that a speaker in a position to offer the more informative statement 'p and q' would be expected to do so. The use of 'p or q' therefore gives rise to an implicature that the speaker is not in a position to make a stronger statement of 'p', of 'q' or indeed of 'p and q'.

Grice was much less preoccupied with questions of data and methodology than Naess. Without either acknowledgment or justification he pursued a recognizably 'ordinary language' approach, appealing to his audience's intuitive knowledge of how they would interpret particular expressions in specified contexts. He did offer some specific examples, for instance 'the prize is either in the attic or in the garden', but the most likely interpretations of these were presumed rather than researched. Naess's empirical work, prior to the William James lectures but presumably unknown to Grice, sheds interesting light on Grice's example. Certainly, it seems uncontroversial that an exclusive interpretation would be overwhelmingly most likely in this case. But Naess's work suggests that this should be considered in relation to the subject matter of the disjunction itself. As in most normal interpretations of Naess's Joan and Phyllis example, the two disjuncts are mutually incompatible; a single prize cannot simultaneously exist in both the attic and the garden.

Although he argued for logic to be based on a whole-scale reanalysis of how people actually behave in relation to particular words, Naess himself does not seem to have extended his study to any other natural language expressions, and his rallying cry has had no impact on the work of logicians. Grice's account of 'or' was one aspect of his programme to reassert the centrality of traditional logic to natural language semantics, and to explain the very general principles that distinguished meaning from meaning in use. This programme has of course had a huge impact on linguistic study. His interpretation of 'or' has formed part of the subsequent development of his ideas by others to include the notion of 'scalar implicatures'. Scalar implicatures are generalized conversational implicatures and as such arise by default. They draw on the maxims of quantity to ensure that the utterance of a weaker item on a semantic scale will implicate the negation of a stronger one; 'or' will implicate 'not and', giving the exclusive interpretation (see, in particular, Horn 1989).

It is striking, however, that Naess's short and apparently isolated study of 'or' has resonances in more recent developments in linguistics. For instance, relevance theorists have rejected the notion of generalized conversational implicature, and hence of scalar implicature, in favour of a model in which an underspecified semantic form is enriched in context until the hearer is confident that an adequately relevant interpretation has been reached (Sperber and Wilson 1995 and, for a more detailed discussion of scalars in particular, Carston 1998). On a relevance theoretic account, 'or' might be contextually enriched to either an exclusive or an inclusive interpretation, depending entirely on the specifics of the context. Naess would not of course have agreed with the positing of semantic form, however underspecified; for him any talk of meaning independent of or prior to context was illegitimate. But the equal availability of inclusive and exclusive readings, and the lack of any marked alternative between the two, are properties of the account of 'or' shared by Naess and by relevance theory.

There are also communalities between Naess's work on 'or' and some recent work in experimental pragmatics. This has in effect reproduced his experiments in more sophisticated form and produced some remarkably similar findings. Gennaro Chierchia and his fellow researchers reached the conclusion that test subjects either produce or fail to produce the interpretations predicted as scalar implicatures depending entirely on the specific properties of the example under scrutiny (Chierchia et al. 2004: 299). Ira Noveck departed even further from Grice's apparent predictions, arguing that the supposed default implicature does not in fact form part of the most ready interpretation. The exclusive interpretation of 'or' was not produced quickest by his test subjects (Noveck 2004: 319). Naess's general philosophy of language would not sit easily with the theoretical orientations of either of these two studies. Chierchia et al. find in their experimental work, support for the 'Semantic Core Model', in which 'semantic and pragmatic processing takes place in tandem' (Chierchia et al. 2004: 284). In turn, Noveck argues that his findings support a relevance theoretic framework. These recent experimental studies may not share much theoretical common ground with Naess, but like his experiments their findings challenge the idea that one of the possible interpretations of 'or' is independently more likely to occur.

The relevance of such findings to an assessment of the Gricean account of 'or' is not a straightforward matter, for reasons rehearsed in Chapter 5 in relation to possible experimental tests for pragmatic theories. The extent to which these findings challenge Grice is dependent on the extent to which Grice is read as predicting and explaining contextualized interpretation, as opposed to offering a formal model of the relationship between logic and language. Recent experimental studies certainly chime in interesting ways with what Naess was saying in the 1950s and early 1960s, but in the case of Grice it is difficult to draw any exact morals.

Despite the similarities in his experimental findings, Naess's perspective on language was very different from that of present day experimental pragmatics. Naess allowed no linguistic system underlying individual instances of use, a fact that distinguishes his philosophy of language from the semantic core model, from relevance theory and indeed from many of the major trends in later twentieth-century linguistics. Hans Skjervheim commented that 'The general view upon language which is the working presupposition of *Interpretation and Preciseness* is just the opposite of the fundamental principles of structuralist linguistics. Naess argues that only speech occurrences have a real existence; language is a rational reconstruction based on speech occurrences, thus it is a fictitious entity' (Skjervheim 1982: 129). Skjervheim went on to criticize Naess for failing seriously to engage with linguists, or to confront his views on the empirical study of language with the views and methodologies of linguistics.

Naess himself seems to have been aware of the disparity between his work and that of linguists and to have steered away from linguistics as a result. Replying to Skjervheim's criticism he explained that fairly early in his career he established that there was little common ground between his work and that of contemporary linguists: 'my kind of detailed empirical studies of terms such as "true", "it is the case", "certain", "democracy" could scarcely contribute to structural linguistics. Strictly speaking there was, however, no such interesting *opposition* as suggested by Skjervheim. Opposition of interest, yes, opposition of theory, no. In discussion with Noam Chomski (sic.) about 1955, we shared the same kind of conclusion' (Naess 1982b: 147). Tantalizingly, Naess did not elaborate on the nature of these shared conclusions. Given the discrepancies between the approaches to language of Naess and of Chomsky, summarized by Skjervheim, it is difficult to imagine that they can have agreed on more than a superficial level.

However, some more recent trends in linguistics have developed similar concerns about the notion of an autonomous language system. Ordinary language philosophy, perhaps largely because of its reliance on the dubiously empirical notion of core meaning, has appealed to pragmaticists. Naess's work, which dispenses with this, might have more in common with recent trends in for instance sociolinguistics and corpus linguistics, a possibility that will be considered in the next chapter. Commenting on empirical semantics in 1968, Jan Berg could have been describing what was about to happen in linguistics. He noted that traditionally in philosophy concepts such as synonymy were discussed in relation to formal languages without any reference to language users. 'In *empirical semantics*, however, which is the main concern of Naess and his school, even the *persons* who use the language and the *situations* in which the language is used are taken into account throughout' (Berg 1968: 228, original emphasis). Writing after such developments in linguistics had been put in motion, Richard Hirsch is one of the few present-day linguists to refer to Naess. Considering Naess's work in relation to cognitive semantics, he comments that it can be seen 'as a forerunner and complement to current developments in Anglo-American linguistic semantic analysis' (Hirsch 1997: 61). Hirsch is particularly struck by Naess's idea that semantic content is not stable or certain but depends on context. He analyses conversational data to offer support for Naess's hypothesis.

Austin and Naess each harboured ambitions for his particular empirical methodology as the basis of a future science of language. These ambitions were not fulfilled, perhaps in part because their methodologies were both superseded by technological advances and the new equipment and methods that these made available for the empirical study of language. The next chapter will be concerned with the ways in which the debate over the nature of empiricism in language study has been played out in linguistics, in particular in relation to the results of these technological advances. In this context, the relative merits of intuited, elicited and collected data are a major focus of discussion. One striking feature of these discussions is that they cover ground very similar to that covered by debates in philosophy in the middle part of the twentieth century. Even linguists who have been keen explicitly to distance themselves from any theoretical stance towards the study of language have philosophical forebears that take us full circle to Vienna.

8
Empiricism in Linguistics

The previous five chapters have traced the impact of the Vienna Circle on the study of language. The approaches discussed were in many ways very different from each other, but they shared both an underlying dissatisfaction with some aspects of what the Vienna Circle had said about language and an impetus to study it in a more genuinely and justifiably empirical manner. According to the usual, questionable divisions between academic subjects, they all belong to the field of philosophy. During the twentieth and into the twenty-first centuries, many accounts of how language should be studied have of course been developed in the emergent field of linguistics.

Linguistics has been influenced indirectly by the Vienna Circle by means of the responses of linguists to these various threads in the philosophy of language. For instance, pragmatics was founded, at least in part, as a result of ordinary language philosophy, and transformational generative linguistics developed against the background of the mid-twentieth-century debate about the nature of scientific method and its relationship to the study of language. But the Vienna Circle also had a more direct influence on linguistics. Perhaps surprisingly, given the somewhat dismissive attitude of philosophers such as Schlick and Carnap to natural language, their work was read with approval by some of the pioneers of what is recognizable as modern linguistics. Rather than sharing the worry of philosophers such as Quine, Austin and Naess that the work of the Vienna Circle was unempirical, these linguists strove to match in their study of language what they saw as the rigorous standards of empiricism it had set; linguistics was to be a properly scientific enterprise. Later developments in linguistics have variously acknowledged, rejected or ignored these positivist foundations, and the question of whether or not linguistics is a science has become controversial, but with a few notable exceptions linguists have stuck with the conviction that their discipline is best when it is empirical. The big question has been what is to count as empirical in relation to the study of language.

The proper character of empiricism in linguistics has been open to question because there is no consensus about what essentially constitutes the subject under investigation. The question of the nature of language is itself one of the most significant facing linguists, although answers to that question are often implicit in linguistic studies rather than explicitly argued. Linguists working in different branches of the discipline variously conceptualize language as a form of behaviour, a mental state, a practical means of communication or a form of social interaction and display, among other possibilities. The nature of the subject matter in any area of study of course determines what count as the appropriate data to examine. A linguist who views language as a mental state will inevitably seek out different types of data for analysis from a linguist who views language as a form of social interaction. An empirical study depends on some suitable method for manipulating and interpreting the data; if the nature of the data is in dispute so too is the appropriate form of empirical study.

In the history of linguistics over the past half-century or more, these issues have perhaps most frequently been aired in a debate about the status and value of linguistic intuitions. This debate has been protracted, at times heated and on occasions conducted without reference to the larger questions about the ontology of language of which it is a consequence. It echoes the major points of conflict between J. L. Austin and Arne Naess: both committed to empiricism in language study, both adamant that ordinary ways of using and understanding language must be a major focus of inquiry, but irreconcilably opposed on the question of what sources of information to consult. In more recent manifestations, the debate has largely been played out between linguists in fields such as sociolinguistics and particularly corpus linguists, on the one hand, and formal linguists in the Chomskyan tradition, on the other hand. It will be a major theme of this chapter.

Language had of course been a focus of study in its own right long before the time of the Vienna Circle. When Ferdinand de Saussure outlined 'the science that has been developed around the facts of language' in the early years of the twentieth century he drew on a long and established tradition (Saussure 1916: 1). The renaissance of positivism was manifest in linguistics in the form of the American interpretation of structuralism that developed during the 1920s and 30s, particularly in the work of Leonard Bloomfield. Bloomfield explicitly advocated an inductive methodology in the study of language. He envisioned linguistics as an objective, descriptive and independent discipline. These ideals are manifest in his seminal work *Language*, first published in 1933. There he famously stipulated that 'The only useful generalizations about language are inductive generalizations. ... when we have adequate data about many languages, we shall have to return to the problem of general grammar and to explain these similarities and divergences, but this study, when it comes, will not be speculative but inductive' (Bloomfield 1933: 20). The accumulation of data, and the patterns and regularities apparent in this, were to be the sole driving forces in the study of language.

Bloomfield also described the appropriate subject matter for the linguist and therefore the nature of the relevant data. He specified that, in describing and analysing any instance of language, that is any act of speech, the linguist must take account of 'A. Practical events preceding the act of speech. B. Speech. C. Practical events following the act of speech' (Bloomfield 1933: 23). According to Bloomfield, only objectively observable phenomena were to be described. The preceding practical events were relevant because they prompted or triggered the speech event. The following events were relevant because they gave evidence of the practical effects of the speech event. No further concept of 'meaning' was permitted, certainly no notion of 'intention' or 'thought'. The speech event itself was described in deliberately physicalist, objective vocabulary; the speaker 'makes a noise with her larynx, tongue, and lips' (Bloomfield 1933: 22).

Bloomfield made no explicit references to logical positivism or to the Vienna Circle in *Language*. His inductive and scientific approach has, however, been linked to developments in contemporary philosophy by a number of commentators. For instance, Frederick Newmeyer has argued that 'The predominance of the Bloomfieldian wing of American structural linguistics was a function of the wide appeal of empiricist philosophy in the American intellectual community in the 1930s and 1940s' (Newmeyer 1986: 5). Newmeyer links the later decline in Bloomfieldian linguistics to the perceived failure of empiricism after the work of, for instance, Hempel.

One article, published soon after *Language*, shows clearly the link between Bloomfield's work and logical positivism. Bloomfield, a professor of German, had read articles from the Vienna Circle long before they appeared in English translation, and before they were described to an English-speaking audience by A. J. Ayer. He did not acknowledge a direct influence; in fact he was keen to emphasize that the Vienna Circle had been working in complete isolation from contemporary American philosophers and linguists, but reaching much the same conclusions. In particular, philosophers such as Carnap and Neurath had claimed that scientifically meaningful statements must be about physical processes, not abstractions. A proper consequence of this view, Bloomfield argued, was that linguists could legitimately deal only with noises, not with any unverifiable concept of 'ideas': 'If we are right, then the term "idea" is simply a traditional obscure synonym for "speech-form", and it will appear that what we now call "mental" events are in part private and unimportant events of physiology and in part social events (responses which in their turn act as stimuli upon other persons or upon the responder himself), namely speech acts' (Bloomfield 1936: 95). Bloomfield likened his own rigorous empiricism, and resulting refusal to allow any posited mental states into his account of language, to the antispeculative, antimetaphysical stance of the Vienna Circle.

The scientific nature of linguistics continued to be a major concern for what have become known as the 'Post-Bloomfieldians' in mid-twentieth-century American linguistics, particularly for Zellig Harris. In Harris's work two terms that were to become significant in linguistics made their first appearance, although the terms had rather different meanings for Harris from those they were eventually to acquire. Harris introduced the terms 'discourse analysis' and 'transformation'. He used the first of these in relation to his conviction that linguistic analysis should take account of whole texts rather than isolated sentences. Only then could linguistics claim true scientific credentials because: 'Language does not occur in stray words or sentences, but in connected discourse' (Harris 1952: 3). Harris's method was to attempt to establish hidden communalities of distribution between elements in an extended text, and he introduced the notion of 'transformation' as a way of exemplifying the actual similarities between apparently disparate sentences within a text.

Harris's method of analysing texts had little in common with present-day discourse analysis; Malcolm Coulthard has suggested that, despite the promising choice of title for his activity, Harris's work in this area is 'disappointing' (Coulthard 1985: 3). Nevertheless, Harris was a pioneer of the idea that the linguist's data should be a body of texts, which he labelled a 'corpus'. He even urged that a corpus should ideally be a 'sample' of a language, although acknowledging this to be a problematic term: 'How large or variegated a corpus must be in order to qualify as a sample of the language, is a statistical problem; it depends on the language and on the relations which are being investigated' (Harris 1961: 13). Writing with C. F. Voegelin he also urged that, in investigating spoken discourse, linguists should use a 'combination of eliciting and text recording' (Voegelin and Harris 1951: 322). They pointed out that this task was made easier and more reliable by the recent advent of magnetic recording. It is striking that Harris and Voegelin published this aspiration for empirical language study in 1951 and therefore in a time at which Austin was still very much active with his own methodologies, in fact during the heyday of his Saturday mornings and his linguistic botanizing. The technology for the more systematic collection of spoken language data was available to Austin and his colleagues, but they simply had their own way of doing things.

Noam Chomsky was a disillusioned nineteen-year old on the point of dropping out of the University of Pennsylvania when he met Zellig Harris. Under Harris's influence he changed his plans, stayed on at the university, and studied linguistics. Chomsky clearly differed significantly from his mentor in his own subsequent work, but he agreed with him on the essentially scientific nature of linguistic research, and he kept the notion of linguistic transformations, although in Chomsky's work these became elaborate operations on individual sentences, mediating between the deep and surface structures. Probably his main point of departure from Harris was in terms of data. For Chomsky it was the sentence rather than the text that provided the highest level for linguistic analysis, and the sentences to be analysed were best obtained not by seeking out occurrences but by introspection and judgment, possibly on the part of linguists themselves. Chomsky championed the use of intuitive data, arguing that the supposed prize of objectivity was not perhaps so important to the scientific understanding of a subject as was genuine insight, which could be offered by 'the enormous mass of unquestionable data' offered by speaker intuition (Chomsky 1965: 20).

For Chomsky, structural linguistics in the Bloomfieldian tradition did not, and could not, take account of the speaker's mental state or of creativity in language. These were the true location and the true measure of human language, so only data drawn from the mind could serve as appropriate evidence. While maintaining that his style of linguistics was the only empirical way of proceeding, he conceded that the evidence provided by introspective data was indirect. The linguist's chief goal was to find out not about intuitive grammaticality judgments themselves, but about the underlying mental structures that made them possible. The use of indirect evidence was inevitable; mental structures themselves were inaccessible to objective scrutiny. Furthermore, they were not available even for direct introspection. Language was generated by a system of rules and principles but, 'Our perfect knowledge of the language we speak gives us no privileged access to these principles; we cannot hope to determine them by introspection or reflection, "from within", as it were' (Chomsky 1980: 231). Linguists must exercise caution even in the credibility afforded to individual judgments: 'In general, informant judgments do not reflect the structure of the language directly; judgments of acceptability, for example, may fail to provide direct evidence as to grammatical status because of the intrusion of numerous other factors' (Chomsky 1986: 36).

One of Chomsky's most famous focusses of interest, the innately endowed universal grammar underlying all human languages, is even less directly available for inspection. Speakers' grammaticality judgments may give indirect and imperfect evidence about their linguistic knowledge but this knowledge in turn, the 'steady state' achieved by the adult speaker, can then be used to infer properties of the 'initial state' of the new-born mind (Chomsky 1986: 24). Chomsky has remained adamant that this too is an empirical issue. For instance, in a televised debate with Michel Foucault in the early 1970s, he commented that 'A person who is interested in studying languages is faced with a very definite empirical problem', and went on to describe the 'reasonably clear and well-defined scientific problem, namely that of accounting for the gap between the really quite small quantity of data, small and rather degenerate in quality, that's presented to the child, and the highly articulated, highly systematic, profoundly organized resulting knowledge that he somehow derives from these data' (Chomsky and Foucault 1974: 136).

When Chomsky first advanced his ideas on linguistic methodology, ordinary language philosophy, also reliant on intuitive data, was still flourishing. However, Chomsky's enthusiasm for the isolated intuitions of the individual researcher was unpalatable to many ordinary language philosophers. Some even suggested that linguists in Chomsky's tradition should emulate Austin by working collaboratively. Urmson picked up on what he saw as the fallibility of individual intuition as a weakness of Chomsky's method, in contrast to Austin's. He commented on Chomsky's judgment that 'Read you a book on modern music?' is not a grammatical sentence of English, suggesting the following dialogue: A. 'Read me a book on modern music.' B. 'Read you a book on modern music? Not for all the gold in Fort Knox!'. Urmson suggested that in contrast with this hasty generalization by Chomsky, a number of researchers working together provided their own sample: 'Chomsky should have been working in a group' (Urmson et al. 1965: 80).

158 *Language and Empiricism*

Not all early responses to what Chomsky was doing were so critical of his methodology. Jerrold Katz and Jerry Fodor supported Chomskyan linguistics as truly empirical and truly scientific. In contrast, logical positivism was unempirical because it ignored the facts of natural language and ordinary language philosophy was unscientific because of its excessive reliance on the mere stating of intuitions. It was not, they urged, that intuition had no place in the study of language; indeed it was the central source of data on which any account of language must be based. But that data must be used in the service of a systematic theoretical account, rather than being assumed to supply the account by itself: 'Intuition in its proper role is indispensable to the study of language, but misused it vitiates such a study' (Katz and Fodor 1962: 219).

Chomsky's contemporaries may have been divided over the merits of his reliance on intuition, but commentators on both sides generally shared the assumption that empiricism was an appropriate and laudable goal for language study; it was simply a matter of determining how empiricism could best be achieved. This assumption has survived in most present-day linguistics. However, some linguists have argued against Chomsky, not on the grounds that he was failing in his aspiration to empiricism in linguistics, but that the aspiration was wrongheaded from the start. From the mid-1970s onwards a small number of linguists have gone against the mainstream in suggesting that linguistics simply is not an empirical subject, and should not be described or judged in the same terms as an empirical science.

Roger Lass urged that it was wrong to make claims about empiricism for branches of study where that method was not appropriate: 'I think that the word *empirical* has become so prestigious that it has blinded linguists to the respectability of non-empirical theories: even to the point where they use the term in contexts where in any strict sense it is not applicable' (Lass 1976: 217). Lass suggested that many linguistic theories were not falsifiable, because experiments or tests relevant to their predictions were simply not possible. But he also argued that theories of this type had a valid justification, and he cited Popper in this cause. Popper allowed that some theories that could be neither demonstrated nor refuted were nevertheless 'rationally arguable'.

Jerrold Katz had clearly changed his mind in the 20years since his collaborative article with Jerry Fodor. He argued in the early 1980s that linguistics could never be an empirical discipline because its subject matter was an abstract object. Unlike Chomsky, he argued that language existed independent of the minds of its speakers: 'There is a distinction between the speaker's knowledge of a language and the language itself'

(Katz 1981: 9). The second of these was the proper subject of linguistics. The first, which was Chomsky's actual concern, was a matter for empirical psychology. The subject matter of linguistics might be unrelated to the subjectivity of speakers, but nevertheless, 'statements about the grammatical structures of sentences are no more *empirical* than statements about numbers' (Katz 1981: 23, original emphasis). Linguistics should be an *a priori* discipline, like mathematics.

At much the same time, Esa Itkonen made similar claims for the *a priori* status of linguistics, likening it to philosophical logic. Itkonen allowed that linguistic knowledge was an appropriate subject matter for the linguist, but for him this distanced linguistics from the empirical sciences: 'The philosophical tradition which claims that methods of natural science, ultimately methods of causal analysis, must be applicable in all sciences, is identifiable as (*neo-)positivism*. Logic and philosophy are prime exceptions to the positivistic program, and ... grammar too is an exception to it' (Itkonen 1980: 363).

Jon Ringen also claimed that linguistic facts were no more empirical than philosophical ones, and should not be treated as such. Like Itkonen, he differed from Katz in seeing language as a mental structure rather than an abstract object, and argued on this basis that Chomsky's claims to empiricism were wrong-headed. Linguistic facts of the type used in Chomskyan linguistics 'may be predicted and explained by linguistic theories, but description of such facts are not descriptions of events or states of affairs which are observable in Popper's sense' (Ringen 1980: 112). Ringen compared linguistics with logic and formal analytic philosophy: 'Investigators in these disciplines characteristically reject the suggestion that verification of their factual claims requires anything like informant surveys' (Ringen 1980: 124–5). Interestingly, in a footnote to this point he drew on the example of the generally harsh responses from philosophers to Naess's investigations, particularly into the concept of 'truth'. For Ringen, contemporary linguistic theory had a lot in common with logic and formal analytic philosophy, and like these disciplines it could afford to eschew the usual trappings of empirical research.

Not all linguists who have appealed to Popperian falsification against Chomsky have turned it on his claims to empiricism. Philip Carr has described linguistics as justifiably and appropriately empirical, but at the expense of Chomsky's claim that language, as a type of knowledge, exists exclusively in the mind of the native speaker. For Carr, language is indeed a type of knowledge, but it is knowledge of a mind-external, objective reality. This is what makes hypotheses of what he calls 'autonomous linguistics' (AL) falsifiable and therefore empirical in the Popperian tradition: 'It seems to me that a clear case can be made for saying that linguistic hypotheses in AL are testable against data consisting of sets of well-formed and/or ill-formed expressions, and may be falsified by them' (Carr 1990: 30). In this way, native speaker judgments about expressions offer valid empirical evidence concerning the nature of a language that has a reality external to the individual speaker, not because it has any spatio-temporal existence, but because it is a public object.

For many other linguists, Chomsky's aspiration to empiricism was correct but his method of going to work was simply wrong-headed. Many commentators, particularly from the 1970s onwards, took issue with Chomsky's reliance on intuitive data, and on his insistence that the proper focus of linguistics was the abstract system of grammar, which could be investigated in isolations from variables of context (for an overview of some of these responses, see Chapman 2006: 54–61). At the vanguard of these objectors to Chomsky's reductive approach to linguistic reality were many of those working in sociolinguistics. This is hardly surprising, given the very different assumptions and aspirations on which sociolinguistics is based, and there was a tendency among early sociolinguists to define themselves in opposition to mainstream, that was Chomskyan, linguistics. But it would be far too simplistic to see the discipline as arising simply out of a collective horror at what Chomsky was doing. Sociolinguistics had its own pedigree. It drew on the same structuralist tradition as Chomsky, emphasizing different aspects of this tradition. It also had roots in sociology, which had emerged in the nineteenth century as an attempt to study society using the methods of natural science. As early as 1935, J. R. Firth commented that 'sociological linguistics is the great field for future research' (Firth 1935: 27). It took a good three decades for sociolinguistics to emerge as a recognizable discipline, but work of the type envisaged by Firth had been conducted in the meantime. In the opening editorial statement of *Language in Society,* launched in 1972, Dell Hymes commented that 'if the term "sociolinguistics" is new, the notion of a study of language concerned with its role in social life is not' (Hymes 1972: 2).

From the start, sociolinguistics has defined itself in terms of this emphasis on language as one of the forms of behaviour that makes up human social life. As such, language must be studied in conjunction with as much as its context as possible. Any reductive attempts to isolate and study only the linguistic elements of a situation would necessarily miss many significant patterns and regularities, and many connections between linguistic practice and social structure. As such, sociolinguistics has necessarily always prized the collection and analysis of language data from subjects and informants, rather than introspection on the part of the researcher. It is chiefly in this area that the distance between sociolinguistics and 'mainstream' linguistics has been emphasized. In his 1974 introduction to sociolinguistics Dell Hymes complained that 'From its beginnings early in this century, modern linguistics has slighted the study of the use of language', and proposed that sociolinguists would need to redress this imbalance (Hymes 1974: 130). Sociolinguists' methods in doing so have been in many ways remarkably similar to those that earned Naess such censure from the philosophical community in the 1930s, although they have been more explicitly justified, better developed and more rigorous. Naess was developing his research methods, particularly his use of the extended questionnaire, at much the same time as Firth made his optimistic prediction for the sociological study of language. Almost 40 years later, Joshua Fishman identified the methodologies of the new discipline of 'sociology of language' as being 'participant observation, survey methods, experimental designs and depth interviews' (Fishman 1971: 6).

William Labov developed and refined many of the methods of data collection and analysis now most closely associated with sociolinguistics, and employed them in a number of celebrated studies. He has also produced a number of theoretically informed and strikingly conciliatory writings on methodology itself. He has remained explicit in his view that linguistics should be conducted as a science, citing Popper as his model (Labov 1972: 99). Predictably for a sociolinguist, he has worked mainly with collected and elicited data. But he is more eclectic than the 'sociolinguistic' label might suggest; for instance concluding a paper on linguistic methodology with the claim that 'Data from a variety of distinct sources and methods, properly interpreted, can be used to converge on right answers to hard questions' (Labov 1972: 119).

In reaching this conclusion, Labov has drawn attention to the different weaknesses in the various methods available to linguists. These weaknesses were in no case sufficient for the methodology in question to be abandoned, and were inherent in the task of studying language. But they meant that linguists must be cautious about overreliance on data from any one source. Introspective data had their value and their place in linguistics, but must be treated with caution because they were 'poorly controlled', in a scientific sense (Labov 1975: 101). Experiments to elicit responses from subjects could be more carefully controlled, and Labov has made extensive use of these in his work. He has urged caution here too, however. He has drawn attention to a number of concrete examples where he has identified a mismatch between what subjects self-consciously claim they do and their actual linguistic behaviour (see, for instance, Labov 1996). He has therefore urged observation of actual use as an essential tool for the linguist, although one that is best supplemented by data from introspection and from the reports of informants.

Other linguists interested in language in its social context have also found reason to maintain the practice of eliciting data from informants, and of balancing these with data from other sources. Asking native speakers to make judgments about the acceptability and applicability of sample sentences, and to comment on their own linguistic practice, has provided a particularly important source of information for researchers studying a languages of which they are not native speakers. In a recent article on what she calls 'semantic fieldwork', Lisa Mathewson advocates elicitation as a complement to text analysis: 'A texts-only approach relies on the assumption that we are capable of extracting all relevant information about a language merely from a set of texts', an assumption that Mathewson claims is misguided and ignores the complexity of linguistic knowledge (Matthewson 2004: 376). Some linguists have combined the methodologies of tape recording usage, intuition and elicitation to provide the data for their studies. For instance, Penelope Brown and Stephen Levinson make clear in *Politeness*, a book with allegiances to both sociolinguistics and pragmatics, that they have drawn on all these sources (Brown and Levinson 1987: 59).

Elsewhere, any sampling of data that removes it from its original context, or draws on responses to hypothetical questions, has been criticized. Integrationism, the approach developed since the early 1980s by a number of linguists but principally by Roy Harris, is based on an insistence that linguistic signs cannot be studied or described in isolation. They cannot be said to have any significance apart from actual instances of use. A study of the significance of any linguistic sign must, and can only, make reference to details of the situations that prompt it to be uttered and the effects it has in those situations. As Harris himself has explained: 'the integrationist views the communication process as one which requires a continuous creation of signs (and thus of signification)' (Harris 1996b: 154). Most mainstream linguistics is incorrigibly 'segregationist', in that it depends on the assumption that linguistic elements can be isolated from a total piece of behaviour and can coherently be discussed without reference to context.

The style of empiricism embraced by integrationism draws on the notion of language as an irreducible part of some forms of human behaviour, and it might therefore appear to have particular affinities with the work of Quine. Perhaps surprisingly Harris rejects such an impressive potential forebear. He might be expected to be enthusiastic about Quine's refusal to accept any concept of meaning that is detached from empirical details of usage, and particularly about the corollary of this that translation is indeterminate and that there is no objectively available mental reality behind linguistic usage for the linguist to study. But Harris argues that Quine's position, like that of his opponents', presupposes: 'that there is indeed a conceptual content to be identified – correctly or incorrectly – in verbal communication' (Harris 1996b: 233). For Harris, the central debate in which Quine has been involved is ultimately a debate about whether context-free meaning can be translated determinately: 'Since integrationist theory finds no place for context-free meanings anyway, the debate about their determinacy or indeterminacy is a matter of tilting against windmills' (ibid.). Quine insisted that, while it might be possible to be right or wrong about stimulus meanings, linguists can never establish accurately the truth of an analytical hypothesis about a word's meaning precisely because there is no such meaning to be accurate about. Nevertheless, this assessment causes Harris to distance integrationism from Quine's work.

Harris is no more complementary about Austin. In common with many of Austin's contemporary critics, he targets his reliance on core linguistic meaning. Austin's insistence on considering the different things that people did with language in context might have been revolutionary, but his actual account was built on an orthodox segregationist foundation: 'in developing his very untraditional theories of illocutionary force and performative acts, Austin took care not to disturb the old metalinguistic foundations on which those theories were built' (Harris 1996a: 180). Unusually among linguists, Harris mentions Naess, but here again his attitude is hostile. Like Quine, Naess might be thought to appeal to integrationists. He rejected the idea of autonomous, independent meaning, and insisted that the significance of any expression was always tied to context and to the specifics of speaker and interpreter. However, Harris dismisses Naess's empirical methodology with this terse statement: 'Juggling with the various theoretical possibilities in this way is a typically segregationist manoeuvre, adapted from the natural sciences' (Harris 1996b: 157). He is unimpressed by Naess's practice of experimenting by changing some variables while keeping others constant, which entailed viewing 'speaker', 'hearer', 'expression' and 'situation' as discreet elements in a speech event. To the integrationist, this is unacceptable because it is contrary to the view of human communication as an essentially unitary, indivisible process.

One of the major developments in linguistics in recent decades, the one that is perhaps most significant to the debate about empiricism in language study and has certainly had the most impact on discussion of what count as linguistic data, is the rise of corpus linguistics. The large-scale storage and sorting of bodies of texts in electronic form has of course been dependent on technological capabilities, and the story of corpus linguistics can be very crudely summarized as a steady growth in the size of corpora and the sophistication with which they can be indexed and analysed. With the increase in the corpus data available, many linguists have sensed an increase in the legitimacy of claims to empiricism, or even the only hope for a valid claim to empiricism in linguistics. Geoffrey Sampson, for instance, has hailed the bringing together of the corpus and the computer as the development that has made possible 'the new empirical linguistics' (Sampson 2001: 6).

Concerted attempts to amass and analyse texts in order to find out about the language predate electronic corpus linguistics. This was what Naess was doing in his forays into 'occurrence analysis'. Corpus linguists point to other forebears, whose intentions were often educational rather than philosophical, and who often handled impressive amounts of data. In the mid-1940s Edward Thorndike and Irving Lorge produced a wordbook for teachers that was based on word counts of some 14 million words, all drawn from written texts such as magazines. They comment in their preface that: 'It will be easy for future workers to extend and amend this book by adding counts of 2 ¼, or 4 ½, or 6 ¾, or 9 million words of any sort' (Thorndike and Lorge 1944: v). In his *The Structure of English* Charles Fries described how, having previously used letters as his main source of data, from 1946 onwards he was able to record and transcribe conversations in American English. Fries argued that recent advances in technology left 'little excuse' for linguistic studies not based on actual instances of communication. Even a native speaker could not rely solely on intuition: 'He has a much more satisfactory base from which to proceed with linguistic analysis if he has a large body of mechanically recorded language which he can hear repeated over and over, and which he can approach with more objectivity than he can that which he furnishes from himself as informant' (Fries 1957: 4n.). Fries's corpus was just 250,000 words, but he was very confident about its adequacy: 'I have assumed that fifty hours of very diverse conversations by some three hundred different speakers would cover the basic matters of English structure' (Fries 1957: x).

Questions of the possibility of a corpus being 'representative' of a language and of the desirable size for this to be achieved were more widely discussed as corpus studies became computerized. Throughout, the justification, indeed the boast of corpus linguistics, has been much the same as that set out by Fries; by studying large collections of what people have actually written or spoken, the linguist has access to the most reliable data about the language. Tony McEnery and Andrew Wilson have described corpus linguistics as 'the study of language based on examples of "real life" language use' (McEnery and Wilson 1996: 1). Christiane Fellbaum emphasizes the genuinely 'everyday' nature of corpus data: 'Corpora are based on naturally occurring texts or spoken languages, which are created everyday by non-expert language users' (Fellbaum et al. 2004: 32). This spontaneous or 'real world' nature of corpus data continues to be celebrated by corpus linguists, as it was by Fries, at the expense of linguistics that is based on data drawn from intuition. Such data are often described using the pejorative term 'invented examples'. Early in the 1990s, John Sinclair claimed that 'In time, it will be realized that there is just no reason or motivation to invent an example when one is knee-deep in actual instances' (Sinclair 1991: 5).

This belief in the supremacy of corpus data is underpinned by an assumption, which is not always explicitly acknowledged, that language consists primarily in the observable speech and writing that people produce for communicative purposes. Studying these phenomena simply is studying language. The Chomskyan would argue that intuited data are just as 'real' as recorded data, if not more so, because they give the best possible access to the mental structure that constitutes language. For the corpus linguist it is the verbal output rather than the mental structure that is the appropriate focus of study. Graeme Kennedy has claimed that 'It is now possible for researchers with access to a personal computer and off-the-shelf software to do linguistic analysis using a corpus, and to discover facts about a language which have never been noticed or written about previously' (Kennedy 1998: 3). The unwritten assumption here is that, for the corpus linguist, facts about the corpus data are 'facts about the language'.

There is no clear consensus among corpus linguists about the methods by which interrogation of the data leads to facts about the language. Michael Stubbs has argued reasonably that 'The methods are clearly broadly inductive, in the rough sense that observing large amounts of data leads to the proposal of significant patterns and generalisations' (Stubbs 2006: 17). Some corpus linguists, however, seem to favour the falsification model of scientific discovery. Geoffrey Sampson cites

Popper in this context. He is keen to claim the same empirical credentials for linguistics, if it is conducted using corpus methods, as for the natural sciences. Of the current state of linguistics he concludes ruefully that 'Although there have been changes over thirty years, the virtues of empirical scientific method evidently remain less thoroughly accepted in linguistics than in other scientific disciplines' (Sampson 2005: 34). John Sinclair does not mention falsification explicitly in this passage from a 1990 article, but he comes close to the mysticism concerning the genesis of hypotheses of which some members of the Vienna Circle accused Popper:

> If we are going to take advantage of the computer's ability to test hypotheses over large stretches of text, there is a price to pay, but the opportunity is worth paying for. The price is the requirement of precision of statement, which will add pressure to move linguistics towards scientific rigour; the opportunity is the freedom to speculate and get fairly quick feedback from the computers about the accuracy and potential of the speculations. Far from restricting the theorist, the computers will actually encourage hunch-playing and speculation at the creative stage. The wealth of data and the ease of access will however encourage the compilation of statements which are firmly compatible with the data.
>
> (Sinclair 2004: 16)

Reaching consensus, or even formulating a precise statement of positioning in relation to earlier debates on scientific methodology and validity may not be of primary concern to the majority of corpus linguists. But corpus linguistics has followed, even if it has not directly drawn on, some notable philosophical attempts at avowedly empirical studies of language. Of all the branches and fields of linguistics that have developed over the last half-century, it is corpus linguistics that promises to offer the most, and might perhaps benefit the most, in the context of a discussion of the philosophies of Austin and Naess. Other branches may have more obvious continuities with their work. Pragmatics explicitly traces its descent from Austin's ordinary language philosophy, and shares his conviction in the adequacy of data drawn from intuition. Sociolinguistics has similar emphases and has developed similar methodologies to those of Naess's empirical semantics. But the aspirations and assumptions of corpus linguistics find particular resonances in what Austin and Naess were separately saying about language and empiricism in the middle part of the twentieth century.

It is invidious to make too much of how particular thinkers 'would have' reacted to subsequent developments in the field, or what direction their own work might have taken if it had been continued longer. Both Austin and Naess had ceased their active engagement with the study of language before technology made anything like a recognizably modern form of corpus linguistics possible. Both philosophers were also ambitious for something further; in different ways each saw the empirical study of language as a necessary staging post towards philosophical discovery rather than an end in its own right. It would therefore be rash to hail corpus linguistics as the science of language to which either one or the other aspired. But it is fairly safe to say that there are aspects of the discipline that echo what they were each trying to do. For instance, corpus linguistics emphasizes the importance of paying attention to many instances of how a word is used, and of considering the other words and the types of grammatical structures with which it predominantly occurs. This approach to language study would seem to chime with Austin's preoccupations, particularly his emphasis on meticulously analysing the use of a word before advancing to more speculative pronouncements. Corpus linguistics's carefully designed methods of sampling, sorting and analysing statistically seem to offer something of what Naess was searching for in his series of elaborate and complex research methodologies.

It is perhaps surprising that corpus linguists have drawn on neither Austin nor Naess as philosophical forebears. If Austin is mentioned at all, it is for his insights into speech acts, and the resultant understanding in linguistics that discussions of meaning must take account of function. Corpus linguists sometimes cite Wittgenstein with approval (for instance Stubbs 2001). It is true that the slogan associated with his later work, 'meaning is use', accords well with the corpus semanticist's claim that any account of meaning must be based on the analysis of a large number of instances of use (see, for instance, the essays in Barnbrook et al. 2004). But even in his later work Wittgenstein had nothing to say about how his position on meaning might impact on its study, and he certainly never attempted any large-scale analysis of the use of a word. Austin and Naess, on the other hand, each developed his own methodology, however flawed, for the study of meaning. As a result of these studies they each said things about meaning that would not sound out of place in recent work from corpus linguistics, although this recent work is generally informed by more systematic and more carefully described research.

Austin challenged logical positivism on the grounds that words did not have fixed meanings but rather that analysis of use would reveal that they often had a complex web of applications. The word 'real' covers a number of ways in which a speaker might want to exclude a notion of 'not real'. The word 'head' is applied to a wide range of phenomena. These claims, and the reliance on data of usage to back them up, prefigure concordance findings about meaning and usage. Some of the passages from Austin's writings that are most significant in the light of the development of corpus linguistics, however, are those where he discussed the ways in which words typically co-occurred. For instance, as early as 1946 he made the following comments about the ways in which a particular word tended to be used, and the type of association it tended to carry with it: '"Symptoms", a term transferred from medical usage, tends to be used only, or primarily, in cases where that of which there are symptoms is something undesirable (of incipient disease rather than of returning health, of despair rather than of hope, of grief rather than of joy): and hence it is more colourful than "signs" or "indications"' (Austin 1946: 73).

Austin here made observations, drawn presumably from his own peculiar mix of reference books and intuition, about the other words, and the types of other words, with which 'symptoms' most usually occurred. He was commenting on what corpus linguists would call the 'collocations' of 'symptoms'. Work on collocations was pioneered by John Sinclair, who saw it as an important feature of language that had been revealed by corpus linguistics. According to Sinclair, the words that co-occur in the general context of some particular word are constrained by far greater patterning and regularity than might be apparent without the evidence of the large number of occurrences available in a corpus: 'On some occasions, words appear to be chosen as pairs or groups and these are not necessarily adjacent' (Sinclair 1991: 115). He argues that collocation has a profound effect on meaning, but that it has been overlooked in traditional and recent language study because of the emphasis on syntax and structure.

Austin's comments about the 'colourful' nature of 'symptoms' is a striking forerunner of a refinement of the notion of collocation, due to John Sinclair and Bill Louw, known as 'semantic prosody'. This is the tone or colouring of meaning that a word takes on as a result of the types of words with which it generally collocates. Semantic prosodies are generally characterized as falling either into the category 'good' or 'positive', or into the category 'bad' or 'negative'. Austin's identification of the 'undesirable' properties associated with 'symptoms' could be re-expressed as an insight that it has negative prosody. Interestingly, Louw has specifically categorized semantic prosodies as inaccessible to intuition: 'They are essentially a phenomenon that has been only revealed computationally, and whose extent and development can only be properly traced by computation methods' (Louw 1993: 159).

Dictionaries that are based on corpus data generally include information about collocational relationships and semantic prosodies. It is argued that a true picture of the meaning of a word can be obtained only with reference to information about the contexts in which it typically appears, that is the co-occurrence relationships it typically enters into, as revealed by corpus analyses (Clear 1993: 291, Summers 1996: 262). It is striking that some of Austin's contemporaries, particularly his detractors, likened what he was doing to lexicography. Quine commented on Austin's technique of introspective inquiry that 'Despite its philosophical antecedents, it is an inquiry whose affinities in linguistics are not in theoretical linguistics; they are in lexicography' (Urmson et al. 1965: 86). Ernest Gellner made much of this comparison in his sustained attack on Austin's philosophy, describing the activity of ordinary language philosophy as 'impressionistic lexicography' (Gellner 1959: 295–6). The practical implications of Austin's method, which his contemporary detractors saw as occasion for criticism and even mockery, are analogous to one of the applications for which corpus linguistics is most celebrated.

Austin's insights were of course not backed up by the systematic examination of data that corpus linguistics allows, although they could perhaps provide starting points for such examinations: the basis for the 'hunch-playing' that Sinclair sees as indispensable to corpus linguistics. Michael Stubbs has linked semantic prosody to illocutionary force, since both are concerned with reasons for speaking. He has suggested that what speech act theory has lacked has been backing from access to systematic data of language use, and argued that 'It is only corpora which can provide data for studying prosodies from the bottom up, and therefore show how we could do real "ordinary language philosophy"' (Stubbs 2006: 26). Austin might have agreed. If Urmson's report is to be believed, Austin would not necessarily have been averse to the rigours of corpus linguistics just because it was different from his own practice. Describing Austin's research method, Urmson commented that the technique was justified by its success: 'if another technique proved more successful it would be better. In deserting Austin's technique for this we would not be abandoning one theory of the nature of philosophy for another, but doing something more like substituting the camera for the human eye in determining the winners of horse races'

(Urmson et al. 1965: 77). Urmson's discussion of Austin's method predates the emergence of corpus linguistics in its modern form, but it is tempting to compare the difference between the human eye and the camera to that between the researcher's intuitions and concordance results.

Nevertheless, the very fact that Austin was making observations about language in the 1940s that prefigured the discovery of collocation and semantic prosody might be seen as some challenge to the claims of corpus linguistics, or at least the claims that were repeated in the early days of the discipline when many heralded corpus data as the only legitimate basis for statements about the language. Some more recent work in the field displays a softening of this attitude, or a new interest in the need to balance corpus methods with more subjective approaches. For instance, Sam Whitsitt has cautioned his fellow corpus linguists against 'being too empirical' (Whitsitt 2005: 294); corpus linguists need to be prepared to make judgments about what to investigate and how, based initially on intuition. Tony McEnery and others have commented that, compared to linguistics based on intuition, 'the corpus-based approach can offer the linguist improved reliability because it does not go to the extreme of rejecting intuition while attaching importance to empirical data' (McEnery et al. 2006: 7).

Naess was always wary of intuitive elements in the study of language. Talking in the early 1990s, he remembered how in his philosophy of language he had maintained that descriptions of usage should be based on a large body of occurrences that could collectively lend support to a particular hypothesis. Contrasting himself with the Vienna Circle, he explained that he advocated using statistics to establish: 'Not the truth, but a very good hypothesis about how certain terms are used, rules that we as users of ordinary language don't know anything about, even though we use the words all day long.' (Rothenberg 1993: 27). These claims of revealing unknown facts about language, or at least probabilistic statements about usage, are remarkably similar to things said by present-day corpus linguists. For instance, Michael Stubbs has argued that 'A major part of the patterning revealed by concordances is the extent of phraseology, which is not obvious to speakers, and has indeed been ignored by many linguists. ... These probabilistic semantic patterns (collocations, colligations, etc.) revealed across many speakers' usage in corpora are not within the control of individual speakers' (Stubbs 2001: 153).

Naess's continued insistence on seeking evidence from attested linguistic use and his optimism for the possibilities of such an approach mean that many passages in his works read as if they might almost have been written by a corpus linguist. In 1960, he enthused that

> If carried out with an eager and open mind, painstaking empirical research leads us into vast unchartered regions of facts and relations. The more one penetrates into the thickness of such regions, the more one is fascinated. One is – often against ones will – drawn further and further into the study of details and intricate structures revealed by the data found or collected.
>
> (Naess 1960: 481)

As a result of his reliance on 'data found or collected', Naess called into question distinctions found in theoretical discussions of language, such as the distinction between literal and metaphorical meaning. Like a corpus linguist, he demanded that any such distinction must have a basis in what could be observed in the behaviour of language users. In 1971 he took part with A. J. Ayer in one of a series of philosophical debates broadcast on Dutch television. During the course of this debate Naess, who was by then wholeheartedly involved in deep ecology, advanced the thesis that 'all living beings are ultimately one'. There ensued a heated, but inconclusive, debate about the viability of this statement. Ayer proffered an account on which it might be scientifically valid – in effect that all life forms are made up of atoms – but resisted the implicit claim that this led to ethical commitments. Naess argued for a more fluid interpretation of the statement. It was neither a description nor a norm, but an intuitively accepted utterance. For Ayer, perhaps betraying his continued allegiance to logical positivism, the utterance in question was simply false; Naess must be speaking metaphorically. Naess's response to this is particularly telling: 'First of all, there is no definite literal sense of an utterance like this in relation to its metaphorical sense. You have to analyse it from a great many points of view. Its so-called literal meaning is hardly exemplified in any available text; what is the literal sense of the identity of all living beings?' (Ayer and Naess 1974: 33). Naess's professed bafflement concerning Ayer's notion of 'literal meaning' was based on his belief that the expression in question would not be used with this particular meaning in any text that might be subjected to occurrence analysis.

Naess was convinced that analysis of available texts, or of people's answers to questions about meaning, showed not just that there was no viable distinction between the literal and the metaphorical, but further that meaning was never fixed or determinate; it varied almost without limit depending on situation, speaker and hearer. In *Interpretation and Preciseness* he noted that 'A great deal of plausible interpretations of the words isolated from the sentence are not plausible in that particular context defined by the sentence. There may further be plausible interpretations of the words as occurring in the sentence, which are not plausible if considered in isolation' (Naess 1947/51, vol 1: 32). Claims about the dependency of meaning on context are commonplace in corpus linguistics. Wolfgang Teubert has listed as one of his 'theses' for the current state of the discipline:

> There is no true and no fixed meaning. Everyone can paraphrase a unit of meaning however they like, therefore the meaning of any lexical item type is always provisional. The next paraphrase may already lead to a revision. The members of the discourse community will continue to negotiate, among themselves, what a unit of meaning means. They may agree or not: the issue is not truth, but acceptance.
> (Teubert 2005: 6–7)

Naess's conviction that his empirical work revealed that meaning was never fixed led him to reject the notion of synonymity, and hence of analyticity, at least as exact concepts. Analysis of use always revealed differences in degrees of preciseness between apparently synonymous terms. Corpus linguistics has also concerned itself with how apparent synonyms are in fact distinguished by usage. Tony McEnery and others have recently drawn attention to cases in which 'Corpora have been used to detect subtle semantic distinctions in near synonyms' (McEnery et al. 2006: 103).

There is some evidence that in recent years the positions taken by linguists in different subdisciplines have become less entrenched. There is less of a tendency for each branch to insist that it must be right to the exclusion of all others, and that there must be a single viable methodology best suited to studying language. That is, more voices are joining Labov in the case he has been making for some decades for different linguistic methodologies to be seen as complementary rather than competing, offering insights into different aspects of the complex subject matter. Charles Meyer has offered the following optimistic overview of relations between corpus and generative linguists, although his praise for the latter is decidedly measured:

> The division and divisiveness that has characterized the relationship between the corpus linguist and the generative grammarian rests

on a false assumption: that all corpus linguists are descriptivists, interested only in counting and categorizing constructions occurring in a corpus, and that all generative grammarians are theoreticians unconcerned with the data on which their theories are based. Many corpus linguists are actively engaged in issues of language theory, and many generative grammarians have shown an increasing concern for the data on which their theories are based, even though data collection remains at best a marginal concern in modern generative theory.

(Meyer 2002: 1)

More generally, there is a growing awareness among linguists that different approaches to the subject have different things to offer, but may also lead to different types of findings. Rudolf Botha has argued against 'the idea that a linguist's ontology has no significant consequences for the content of his/her formal linguistic theory and associated grammars' (Botha 1992: 250). Martina Penke and Anette Rosenbach, making a distinction between the broad categories of formal and functional linguists, have commented: 'Both ask different questions, accordingly different types of empirical evidence dominate in these approaches, and evidence is used in different ways. However, it is important to keep in mind that all types of evidence may – in principle – be relevant for both linguistic orientations. No type of evidence is *per se* better or worse than another' (Penke and Rosenbach 2004: 514). Alison Sealey and Bob Carter argue that different people with different purposes and interests 'might hold very different concepts of "language" without any one of these being "wrong"' (Sealey and Carter 2004: 62).

H. G. Widdowson has challenged corpus linguistics on similar grounds: not that it is completely wrong or misdirected, but rather that it cannot properly be claimed to describe language as a whole. Corpus analysis reveals only what he calls the 'textual traces' of the processes involved in language production (Widdowson 2000: 7). It cannot account for the full social and discoursal context in which language is produced, nor can it represent the individual speaker's awareness of the language. Summarizing corpus linguistics and critical discourse analysis he comments that 'All enquiry is partial, and each partiality has things of interest to reveal. Both kinds of text description that I have been discussing are of enormous interest precisely because their findings are partial and conditional on a particular perspective' (Widdowson 2001: 23).

Widdowson's comments are relevant to the full range of linguistic approaches, not just the two he singles out for scrutiny. No single approach can or should be expected to say everything that needs to be said about language. The success of one approach cannot be said to make others inviable. Nor is it possible coherently to compare different approaches in terms of degrees of empiricism. The debate that raged during the middle part of the twentieth century in relation to scientific method demonstrates that what is empirical is far from straightforward and can never be treated as a given. What counts as empirical is ultimately a social construction, or at least a construction of the particular research culture in which the individual is working. The tradition of taking a sociological approach to describing scientific study that runs from Neurath through Kuhn and Feyerabend, might provide a useful framework here. Empiricism continues to be defined not by something that is determinate and external to the work conducted in its name, but by the local and socially constructed norms within which that work is carried out. This general feature of empiricism, common to all areas of study, is compounded in the case of linguistics by the fundamental differences of opinion over what is the true nature of the subject matter, and therefore the most appropriate form of data. This is best viewed not as a flaw in the discipline or as a problem that needs to be resolved. Human language is not one-dimensional and it is not easily delineated; facts reflected by the discipline in which it is studied.

References

Arnauld, Antoine and Claude Lancelot (1660) *A General and Rational Grammar*, France. Menston: The Scolar Press (1968).
Austerlitz, Robert (ed.) (1975) *The Scope of American Linguistics*, Lisse: The Peter de Ridder Press.
Austin, J. L. (1940) 'The meaning of a word', in J. L. Austin (1961): 23–43.
—— (1946) 'Other minds', *Proceedings of the Aristotelian Society*, reprinted in J. L. Austin (1961): 44–84.
—— (1950) 'Truth', *Proceedings of the Aristotelian Society*, reprinted in J. L. Austin (1961): 85–101.
—— (1952) 'How to talk, some simple ways', *Proceedings of the Aristotelian Society*, reprinted in J. L. Austin (1961): 181–200.
—— (1954) 'Unfair to facts', in J. L. Austin (1961): 102–22.
—— (1956a) 'A plea for excuses', *Proceedings of the Aristotelian Society*, reprinted in J. L. Austin (1961): 123–52.
—— (1956b) 'Ifs and cans', *Proceedings of the British Academy*, reprinted in J. L. Austin (1961): 153–80.
—— (1961) *Philosophical Papers*, Oxford: Clarendon Press.
—— (1962a) *Sense and Sensibilia*, Oxford: Clarendon Press.
—— (1962b) *How to do Things with Words*, Oxford: Clarendon Press.
Ayer A.J. (1940) *Foundations of Empirical Knowledge*, London: Macmillan (1964).
—— (1946) *Language Truth and Logic*, 2nd edn, Harmondsworth: Pelican (1971). [1st edn London 1936].
—— (1959) 'Editor's Introduction', in A. J. Ayer (ed.) (1959): 3–28.
—— (ed.) (1959) *Logical Positivism*, Glencoe, Ill.: The Free Press.
—— (1987) 'Reflections on *Language, Truth and Logic*', in Barry Gower (ed.), 23–34.
Ayer, A. J. and Arne Naess (1974) 'The glass is on the table: an empiricist versus a total view', in Fons Elders (ed.): 13–68.
Bach, Kent (2001) 'You don't say?', *Synthese*, 128: 15–44.
—— (2006) 'Speech acts and pragmatism' in Michael Devitt and Richard Hanley (eds): 147–67.
Baker, Mona Gill Francis and Elena Tognini-Bonelli (eds) (1993) *Text and Technology*, Amsterdam: John Benjamins.
Barnbrook, Geoff, Pernilla Danielsson and Michaela Mahlberg (eds) (2004) *Meaningful Texts*, London: Continuum.
Berg, Jan (1968) 'Remarks on empirical semantics', *Inquiry*, 11: 227–42.
Bergmann (1938) 'Letter to Otto Neurath', in Friedrich Stadler (ed.) (1993): 193–208.
Berkeley, George (1710) *Principles of Human Knowledge*, Dublin. Harmondsworth: Penguin (1988).
Bernicot, Josie and Virginie Laval (2004) 'Speech acts in children: the example of promises', in Dan Sperber and Ira Noveck (eds): 207–27.
Bezuidenhout, Anne and J. Cooper Cutting (2002) 'Literal meaning, minimal propositions, and pragmatic processing', *Journal of Pragmatics*, 34: 433–56.

Black, Max (1963) 'Austin on performatives', *Philosophy*, reprinted in K. T. Fann (ed.) (1969): 401–11.
Blom, Siri (1955) 'Concerning a controversy on the meaning of "*probability*"', *Theoria*, XXI: 65–98.
Bloomfield, Leonard (1933) *Language*, USA. London: Allen and Unwin (1935).
—— (1936) 'Language or ideas?', *Language*, 12: 89–95.
Blumberg, Albert and Herbert Feigl (1931) 'Logical positivism', *The Journal of Philosophy*, 28: 281–96.
Borg, Emma (2004) *Minimal Semantics*, Oxford: Clarendon Press.
Botha Rudolf (1992) *Twentieth Century Conceptions of Language*, Oxford: Blackwell.
Brown, Penelope and Stephen Levinson (1987) *Politeness*, Cambridge: Cambridge University Press.
Canfield, John and Keith Lehrer (1961) 'A note on prediction and deduction', *Philosophy of Science*, 28: 204–8.
Cappelen, Herman and Ernest Lepore (2005) *Insensitive Semantics: A Defense of Semantic Minimalism and Speech Act Pluralism*, Oxford: Blackwell.
Carnap, Rudolf (1932) 'The elimination of metaphysics through logical analysis of language', in A. J. Ayer (1959) 60–81.
—— (1936) 'Testability and meaning I', *Philosophy of Science*, 3: 419–71.
—— (1937a) 'Testability and meaning II', *Philosophy of Science*, 4: 1–40.
—— (1937b) *The Logical Syntax of Language*, London: Routledge and Kegan Paul.
—— (1946) *Introduction to Semantics*, Cambridge: Harvard University Press.
—— (1963) 'Intellectual autobiography', in Paul Schilpp (ed.): 3–84.
Carnap, Rudolf, Hans Hahn and Otto Neurath (1929) 'The scientific conception of the world. The Vienna Circle', Vienna. Reprinted in Sahotra Sarkar (ed.) (1996) *The Emergence of Logical Empiricism*, New York: Garland Publishing: 321–40.
Carr, Philip (1990) *Linguistic Realities*, Cambridge: Cambridge University Press.
Carston, Robyn (1998) 'Informativeness, relevance, and scalar implicature', in Robyn Carston and Seiji Uchida (eds) *Relevance Theory: Applications and Implications*, Amsterdam: John Benjamins: 179–236.
—— (2002) *Thoughts and Utterances: The Pragmatics of Explicit Communication*, Oxford: Blackwell.
Cavell, Stanley (1958) 'Must we mean what we say?', *Inquiry*, 1: 172–212.
Chapman, Siobhan (2005) *Paul Grice: Philosopher and Linguist*, Basingstoke: Palgrave Macmillan.
—— (2006) *Thinking about Language*, Basingstoke: Palgrave Macmillan.
Chierchia, Gennaro, Maria Teresa Guasti, Andrea Gualmini, Luisa Meroni, Stephen Crain and Francesca Foppolo (2004) 'Semantic and pragmatic competence in children's and adults' comprehension of *or*', in Ira Noveck and Dan Sperber (eds): 283–300.
Chomsky, Noam (1957) *Syntactic Structures*, The Hague: Mouton.
—— (1965) *Aspects of the Theory of Syntax*, Cambridge, Mass.: The M.I.T. Press.
—— (1969) 'Quine's empirical assumptions', in Donald Davidson and Jakko Hintikka (eds) *Words and Objections*, Dordrecht: D. Reidel: 53–68.
—— (1972) 'Some empirical issues in the theory of transformational grammar', in Stanley Peters (ed.) *Goals of Linguistic Theory*, Englewood Cliffs, NJ: Prentice-Hall: 63–127.
—— (1975) 'Questions of form and interpretation', in Robert Austerlitz (ed.): 159–96.

—— (1976) *Reflections on Language*, London: Temple Smith.
—— (1980) *Rules and Representations*, Oxford: Blackwell.
—— (1986) *Knowledge of Language*, New York: Praeger.
—— (2000) *New Horizons in the Study of Language and Mind*, Cambridge: Cambridge University Press.
Chomsky, Noam and Michel Foucault (1974) 'Human nature: justice versus power', in Fons Elders (ed.): 135–97.
Clear, Jeremy (1993) 'From Firth principles: computational tools for the study of collocation', in Mona Baker, Gill Francis and Elena Tognini-Bonelli (eds): 271–92.
Cobitz, J. L. (1950) 'The appeal to ordinary language', *Analysis*, 11: 9–11.
Coffa, José (1968) 'Deductive predictions', *Philosophy of Science*, 35: 279–83.
Cohen, Jonathan (1964) 'Do illocutionary forces exist?', *Philosophical Quarterly*, reprinted in K. T. Fann (ed.) (1969) 420–44.
Coulthard, Malcolm (1985) *An Introduction to Discourse Analysis*, 2nd edn, London: Longman [1st edn 1977].
Creath, Richard (1991) 'Every dogma has its day', *Erkenntnis*, 35: 347–89.
Crockett, Campbell (1959) 'An attack upon revelation in semantics', *The Journal of Philosophy*, 56: 103–11.
Dascal, Marcelo (1994) 'Speech act theory and Gricean pragmatics: some differences of detail that make a difference', in Savas Tsohatzidis (ed.): 323–34.
Devitt, Michael and Richard Hanley (eds) (2006) *The Blackwell Guide to the Philosophy of Language*, Oxford: Blackwell.
Drucker, H. M. (1974) *The Political Uses of Ideology*, Basingstoke: Macmillan.
Dummett, Michael (1973) *Frege: Philosophy of Language*, London: Duckworth.
—— (1976) 'What is a theory of meaning?', in Michael Dummett (1993): 34–93.
—— (1979) 'What does the appeal to use do for the theory of meaning?', in Michael Dummett (1993): 106–16.
—— (1993) *The Seas of Language*, Oxford: Clarendon Press.
Edmonds, David and John Eidinow (2001) *Wittgenstein's Poker*, London: Faber and Faber.
Elders, Fons (ed.) (1974) *Reflexive Water: The Basic Concerns of Mankind*, London: Souvenir Press.
Fairclough, Norman (1989) *Language and Power*, Harlow: Longman.
Fann, K. T. (ed.) (1969) *Symposium on J. L. Austin*, London: Routledge.
Fellbaum, Christiane with Lauren Delfs, Susanne Wolff and Martha Palmer (2004) 'Word meaning in dictionaries, corpora and the speaker's mind', in Geoff Barnbrook, Pernilla Danielsson and Michaela Mahlberg (eds): 31–8.
Feyerabend, Paul (1975) *Against Method*, London: Verso (1978).
Firth, J. R. (1935) 'The technique of semantics', in J. R. Firth (1957) *Papers in Linguistics 1934–51*, Oxford: Oxford University Press: 7–33.
Fishman, Joshua (1971) 'A sociology of language', in Joshua Fishman (1972) *Language in Sociocultural Change*, Stanford: Stanford University Press: 1–15.
Flew, Anthony (1953) 'Introduction', in Anthony Flew (ed.) (1953): 1–10
—— (ed.) (1953) *Logic and Language (Second Series)*, Oxford: Blackwell.
Fodor, Jerry (1964) 'On knowing what we would say', *The Philosophical Review*, 73: 198–212.
Fodor, Jerry and Jerrold Katz (1963) 'The availability of what we say', *The Philosophical Review*, 72: 57–71.

References

Fodor, Jerry and Ernie Lepore (2006) 'Analyticity again', in Michael Devitt and Richard Hanley (eds): 114–30.
Forster, Michael (2004) *Wittgenstein on the Arbitrariness of Grammar*, Princeton: Princeton University Press.
Frege, Gottlob (1892) 'On sense and meaning', in Peter Geach and Max Black (eds) (1980) *Translations from the Philosophical Writings of Gottlob Frege*, Oxford: Blackwell. [1st edn 1952]: 56–78.
Fries, Charles (1957) *The Structure of English*, London: Longman.
Furberg, Mats (1969) 'Meaning and illocutionary force', in K. T. Fann (ed.): 445–67.
Galison, Peter (1993) 'The cultural meaning of *Aufbau*', in Friedrich Stadler (ed.): 75–93.
Gellner, Ernest (1959) *Words and Things*, London: Victor Gollancz. Harmondsworth: Penguin (1968).
Gibbon, Margaret (1999) *Feminist Perspectives on Language*, London: Longman.
Gibbs, Raymond (2004) 'Psycholinguistic experiments and linguistic-pragmatics', in Ira Noveck and Dan Sperber (eds): 50–71.
Glucksberg, Sam (2004) 'On the automaticity of pragmatic processes: a modular proposal', in Ira Noveck and Dan Sperber (eds): 72–93.
Gödel, Kurt (1931) *On Formally Undecidable Propositions of Principia Mathematics and Related Systems*, Germany. Edinburgh and London: Oliver and Boyd [B. Meltzer, trans.] (1962).
Goodman, Nelson (1953) 'On some differences about meaning', *Analysis*, 13: 90–6.
Gower, Barry (ed.) (1987) *Logical Positivism in Perspective*, London: Croom Helm.
Graham, Keith (1977) *J. L. Austin: A Critique of Ordinary Language Philosophy*, Brighton: Harvester.
Grice, Paul (1967) 'Indicative conditionals', in Paul Grice (1989): 58–85.
—— (1975) 'Logic and conversation' in Peter Cole and J. L. Morgan (eds) *Syntax and Semantics 3: Speech Acts*, New York: Academic Press. Reprinted in Paul Grice (1989): 22–40.
—— (1986) 'Reply to Richards', in Richard Grandy and Richard Warner (eds) *Philosophical Grounds of Rationality*, Oxford: Clarendon Press: 45–106.
—— (1989) *Studies in the Way of Words*, Harvard: Harvard University Press.
Grice, Paul and Peter Strawson (1956) 'In defence of a dogma', *The Philosophical Review*. Reprinted in Paul Grice (1989): 196–212.
Grimm, Laura (1955) 'On the application of the concept of precisation', *Synthese*, 9: 104–20.
Gullvåg, Ingemund (1982) 'Naess's early philosophy of science and philosophy', in Ingemund Gullvåg and Jon Wetlesen (eds): 22–55.
Gullvåg, Ingemund and Jon Wetlesen (eds) (1982) *In Sceptical Wonder*, Oslo: Universitetsforlaget.
Haggstrom, Warren (1952) 'On careful reasoning in ordinary language', *Analysis*, 12: 82–5.
Hampshire, Stuart (1960) 'J. L. Austin, 1911–1960', *Proceedings of the Aristotelian Society*, in K. T. Fann (ed.) (1969): 33–48.
Handley, Simon and Aidan Feeney (2004) 'Reasoning and pragmatics: the case of *even-if*', in Ira Noveck and Dan Sperber (eds): 228–53.
Hare, R. M. (1957) 'Are discoveries about the uses of words empirical?', *The Journal of Philosophy*, 54: 741–50.

Harris, Roy (1996a) *The Language Connection*, Bristol: Thoemmes Press.
—— (1996b) *Signs, Language and Communication*, London: Routledge.
Harris, Zellig (1952) 'Discourse analysis', *Language*, 28: 1–30.
—— (1961) *Structural Linguistics*, Chicago: The University of Chicago Press [first published as *Methods in Structural Linguistics*, 1951].
Hart, H. L. A. (1958) 'Legal responsibility and excuses', in H. L. A. Hart (1968) *Punishment and Responsibility*, Oxford: Clarendon Press: 28–53.
Hempel, Carl (1945) 'Studies in the logic of confirmation (I)', *Mind*, 54: 1–26.
—— (1950) 'Review of *Toward a Theory of Interpretation and Preciseness* by Arne Naess', *The Journal of Symbolic Logic*, 15: 154.
—— (1963) 'Implications of Carnap's work for the philosophy of science', in Paul Schilpp (ed.): 685–709.
—— (1993) 'Empiricism in the Vienna Circle and in the Berlin Society for Scientific Philosophy. Recollections and Reflections', in Friedrich Stadler (ed.) (1993): 1–9.
Henle, Paul (1957) 'Do we discover our uses of words?', *The Journal of Philosophy*, 54: 750–8.
Hintikka, Jakko (1993) 'Ludwig's apple tree: on the philosophical relations between Wittgenstein and the Vienna Circle', in Friedrich Stadler (ed.): 27–45.
Hirsch, Richard (1997) 'Semantic content and depth of intention: a study in cognitive semantics', in Wolf-Andreas Liebert, Gisela Redeker and Linda Waugh (eds) *Discourse and Perspective in Cognitive Linguistics*, Amsterdam: John Benjamins: 61–83.
Holton, Gerald (1993) 'From the Vienna Circle to Harvard Square: the Americanization of a European world conception', in Friedrich Stadler (ed.): 47–73.
Honey, John (1997) *Language is Power*, London: Faber and Faber.
Horn, Laurence (1989) *A Natural History of Negation*, Chicago: University of Chicago Press.
Hymes, Dell (1972) 'Editorial introduction', *Language in Society*, 1: 1–14.
—— (1974) *Foundations in Sociolinguistics*, Philadelphia: University of Pennsylvania Press.
Isaacs, Nathan (1960) 'What do linguistic philosophers assume?', *Proceedings of the Aristotelian Society*, 40: 211–30.
Itkonen, Esa (1980) 'Qualitative vs. quantitative analysis in linguistics', in Thomas Perry (ed.): 334–66.
—— (1983) *Causality in Linguistic Theory*, London: Croom Helm.
Kant, Immanuel (1781) *Critique of Pure Reason*, Germany. London: Macmillan [Norman Kemp Smith, trans.], (1929).
Kasher, Asa (ed.) (1976) Language in Focus: Foundations, Methods and Systems, Dordrecht: D. Reidel Publishing Company.
Katz, Jerrold (1977) *Propositional Structure and Illocutionary Force*, Hassocks: The Harvester Press.
—— (1981) *Language and Other Abstract Objects*, Oxford: Blackwell.
Katz, Jerrold and Jerry Fodor (1962) 'What's wrong with the philosophy of language?', *Inquiry*, 5: 197–237.
Kennedy, Graeme (1998) *An Introduction to Corpus Linguistics*, London: Addison Wesley Longman.

Korner, S. (1957) 'Some remarks on philosophical analysis', *The Journal of Philosophy*, 54: 758–66.
Kraft, Victor (1953) *The Vienna Circle* [Arthur Pap, trans.], New York: Philosophical Library.
Kuhn, Thomas (1962) *The Structure of Scientific Revolutions*. Chicago: University of Chicago Press.
—— (1970) 'Logic of discovery or psychology of research?', in Imre Lakatos and Alan Musgrave (eds): 1–23.
Labov, William (1972) 'Some principles of linguistic methodology', *Language in Society*, 1: 97–120.
—— (1975) 'Empirical foundations of linguistic theory', in Robert Austerlitz (ed.): 77–133.
—— (1996) 'When intuitions fail', in L. McNair, K. Singer, L. Dolbrin and M. Aucon (eds) *Papers from the Parasession on Theory and Data in Linguistics, Chicago Linguistics Society*, 32: 77–106.
Lakatos, Imre (1970) 'Falsification and the methodology of scientific research programmes', in Imre Lakatos and Alan Musgrave (eds): 91–196.
Lakatos, Imre and Alan Musgrave (eds) (1970) *Criticism and the Growth of Knowledge*, Cambridge: Cambridge University Press.
Lass, Roger (1976) *English Phonology and Phonological Theory*, Cambridge: Cambridge University Press.
Leech, Geoffrey (1983) *Principles of Pragmatics*, Harlow: Longman.
Levinson, Stephen (1983) *Pragmatics*, Cambridge: Cambridge University Press.
Levinson, Stephen (2000) *Presumptive Meanings*, Cambridge, MA: The MIT Press.
Lewis, C. I. (1934) 'Experience and meaning', *The Philosophical Review*, 43: 125–46.
Locke, John (1690) *An Essay Concerning Human Understanding*, London: Everyman (1993).
Louw, William (1993) 'Irony in the text of insincerity in the writer? The diagnostic potential of semantic prosodies', in Mona Baker, Gill Francis and Elena Tognini-Bonelli (eds): 152–76.
Mates, Benson (1950) 'Synonymity', *University of California Publications in Philosophy*, 25: 201–26.
—— (1958a) 'On the verification of statements about ordinary language', *Inquiry*, 1: 161–71
—— (1958b) 'Review of *Interpretation and Preciseness* by Arne Naess', *The Philosophical Review*, 67: 546–53.
Matthewson, Lisa (2004) 'On the methodology of semantic fieldwork', *International Journal of Applied Linguistics*, 70: 369–415.
Maxwell, Grover and Herbert Feigl (1961) 'Why ordinary language needs reforming', *The Journal of Philosophy*, 58: 488–98.
McCawley, James (1981) *Everything that Linguists have Always Wanted to Know about Logic*, Oxford: Blackwell.
McEnery, Tony and Andrew Wilson (1996) *Corpus Linguistics*, Edinburgh: Edinburgh University Press.
McEnery, Tony, Richard Xiao and Yukio Tono (2006) *Corpus-Based Language Studies*, London: Routledge.
McGee, Vann (2006) 'Truth', in Michael Devitt and Richard Hanley (eds): 392–410.
Mehta, Ved (1963) *Fly and the Fly-Bottle*, London: Weidenfeld and Nicolson.
Meyer, Charles (2002) *English Corpus Linguistics*, Cambridge: University of Cambridge Press.

Miller, Alexander (2006) 'Meaning scepticism', in Michael Devitt and Richard Hanley (eds): 91–113.
Moore, Jared (1939) Review of *'Truth' as Conceived by Those Who Are Not Professional Philosophers* by Arne Ness, *The American Journal of Psychology*, 52: 489–90.
Mundle, C. W. K. (1979) *A Critique of Linguistic Philosophy*, 2nd edn, London: Glover and Blair. [1st edn 1970].
Naess, Arne (1937/8) 'Invitation to Oslo', *Erkenntnis*, 7: 384.
—— (1938) *'Truth' as Conceived by Those Who Are Not Professional Philosophers*, Oslo: Jacob Dybwad.
—— (1947/51) *Interpretation and Preciseness*, vols 1–6, Oslo: Universitetets Studentkontor.
—— (1949) 'Toward a theory of interpretation and preciseness', *Theoria*, 15: 220–41.
—— (1953) *An Empirical Study of the Expressions 'True', 'Perfectly Certain' and 'Extremely Probable'*, Oslo: Jacob Dybwad.
—— (1956) 'Synonymity and empirical research', *Methodos*, VIII: 3–22.
—— (1956/8) 'Logical equivalence, intentional isomorphism and synonymity as studied by questionnaires', *Synthese*, 10: 471–9.
—— (1957) 'Synonymity as revealed by intuition', *The Philosophical Review*, 66: 87–93.
—— (1958) 'Editorial statement', *Inquiry*, 1: 1–6.
—— (1959) 'Do we know that basic norms cannot be true or false?', *Theoria*, XXV: 31–53.
—— (1960) 'Typology of questionnaires adopted to the study of expressions with closely related meanings', *Synthese*, 12: 481–94.
—— (1961a) 'The inquiring mind', *Inquiry*, 4: 162–89.
—— (1961b) 'Can knowledge be reached?', *Inquiry*, 4: 219–27.
—— (1961c) 'A study of "or"', *Synthese*, 13: 49–60.
—— (1966) *Communication and Argument*, Oslo: Universitetsforlaget.
—— (1968a) *Four Modern Philosophers*, Chicago: University of Chicago Press [first published in Norwegian in 1965].
—— (1968b) *Scepticism*, London: Routledge and Kegan Paul.
—— (1970a) 'Rudolf Carnap 1891–1970', *Inquiry*, 13: 337–8.
—— (1970b) 'A plea for pluralism in philosophy and physics', in W. Yourgrau and A. D. Breck, *Physics, Logic and History*, New York: Plenum Publishers. Reprinted in *The Trumpeter*, 21 (2005): 110–18.
—— (1980) 'Norway I', in John Burr (ed.) *Handbook of World Philosophy: Contemporary Developments Since 1945*, London: Aldwych Press: 159–64.
—— (1981) 'The empirical semantics of key terms, phrases and sentences', in Stig Kanger and Sven Öhman (eds) *Philosophy and Grammar*, Dordrecht: D. Reidel Publishing Company: 135–54.
—— (1982a) 'A necessary component of logic: empirical argumentation analysis', in E. M. Barth and J. L. Martens (eds) *Argumentation: Approaches to Theory Formation*, Amsterdam: John Benjamins: 9–22.
—— (1982b) 'Pluralism in cultural anthropology', in Ingemund Gullvåg and Jon Wetlesen (eds): 147–54.
—— (1992) 'Ayer on metaphysics, a critical commentary by a kind of metaphysician', in Lewis Edwin Hahn (ed.) *The Philosophy of A. J. Ayer*, La Salle, Illinois: Open Court: 329–40.
—— (1993) 'Logical empiricism and the uniqueness of the Schlick seminar: a personal experience with consequences', in Friedrich Stadler (ed.): 11–25.

Naess, Arne and Ingemund Gullvåg (1996) 'Vagueness and ambiguity', in Marcelo Dascal, D. Gerhardus, K. Lorenz and G. Meggle (eds) *Philosophy of Language: An International Handbook of Contemporary Research*, vol. 2, Berlin and New York: Walter de Gruyter. Reprinted in *The Trumpeter*, 22 (2006): 56–74.

Nagel, Ernest (1939) Review of *'Truth' as Conceived by Those Who Are Not Professional Philosophers* by Arne Ness, *The Journal of Philosophy*, 36: 78–80.

Neurath, Otto (1932) 'Protocol statements', in Otto Neurath (1983) *Philosophical Papers 1913–1946*, Dordrecht: D. Reidel Publishing Company: 91–9.

New, C. G. (1966) 'A plea for linguistics', *Mind*. Reprinted in K. T. Fann (ed.) (1969): 148–65.

Newmeyer, Frederick (1986) *Linguistic Theory in America*, 2nd edition, New York: Academic Press [1st edn 1980].

Noveck, Ira (2004) 'Pragmatic inferences related to logical terms' in Ira Noveck and Dan Sperber (eds): 301–21.

Noveck, Ira and Dan Sperber (eds) (2004) *Experimental Pragmatics*, Basingstoke: Palgrave Macmillan.

Penke, Martina and Anette Rosenbach (2004) 'What counts as evidence in linguistics?' *Studies in Language*, 28: 480–526.

Perry, Thomas (ed.) (1980) *Evidence and Argumentation in Linguistics*, New York: Walter de Gruyter.

Popper, Karl (1935) *The Logic of Scientific Discovery*, Vienna. London: Routledge (2002).

—— (1963) 'The demarcation between science and metaphysics', in Paul Schilpp (ed.): 183–226.

—— (1976) *Unended Quest*, La Salle, Illinois: Open Court.

Popper, Karl and John Eccles (1974) 'Falsifiability and freedom', in Fons Elders (ed.): 71–131.

Quine, W. V. O. (1943) 'Notes on existence and necessity', *The Journal of Philosophy*, 40: 113–27.

—— (1951) 'Two dogmas of empiricism' in W. V. O. Quine (1953b): 20–4.

—— (1953a) 'The problem of meaning in linguistics', in W. V. O. Quine: 47–64.

—— (1953b) *From a Logical Point of View*, Harvard: Harvard University Press.

—— (1960) *Word and Object*, Cambridge, Mass.: The M.I.T. Press.

—— (1963) 'Carnap and logical truth', in Paul Schilpp (ed.): 385–406.

—— (1970a) 'Methodological reflections on current linguistic theory', *Synthese*, 21: 386–98.

—— (1970b) 'On the reasons for indeterminacy of translation', *The Journal of Philosophy*, 67: 178–83.

—— (1973) *The Roots of Reference*, La Salle, Illinois: Open Court.

—— (1974) 'On Popper's negative methodology', in Paul Arthur Schilpp (ed.) *The Philosophy of Karl Popper*, La Salle, Illinois: Open Court: 218–20.

—— (1975) 'Mind and verbal dispositions', in Samuel Guttenplan (ed.) *Mind and Language*, Oxford: Clarendon Press: 83–95.

Radford, Andrew (1981) *Transformational Syntax*, Cambridge: Cambridge University Press.

Recanati, François (1994) 'Contextualism and anti-contextualism in the philosophy of language', in Savas Tsohatzidis (ed.): 156–66.

—— (2004) *Literal Meaning*, Cambridge: Cambridge University Press.

Ringen, Jon (1980) 'Linguistics facts', in Thomas Perry (ed.): 97–132.
Rogers, Ben (2000) *A. J. Ayer, A Life*, London: Vintage.
Rothenberg, David (1993) *Is it Painful to Think? Conversations with Arne Naess*, Minneapolis: University of Minnesota Press.
Russell, Bertrand (1912) *The Problems of Philosophy*, Oxford: Oxford University Press (1967).
—— (1922) 'Introduction' in Ludwig Wittgenstein: ix–xxii.
—— (1924) 'Logical atomism', in A. J. Ayer (ed.) (1959): 31–50.
—— (1956) 'The cult of "common usage"', in Robert Egner and Lester Denonn (eds) (1961) *The Basic Writings of Bertrand Russell*, London and New York: Routledge: 135–41.
—— (1957) 'Mr Strawson on referring', *Mind*, 66: 385–9.
Russell, Bertrand and Alfred Whitehead (1910) *Principia Mathematica*, Cambridge: Cambridge University Press.
Ryle, Gilbert (1951) 'Ludwig Wittgenstein' *Analysis*, 12: 1–9.
—— (1956) 'Introduction', in Gilbert Ryle (ed.) *The Revolution in Philosophy*, London: Macmillan: 1–11.
Sampson, Geoffrey (2001) *Empirical Linguistics*, London: Continuum.
—— (2005) 'Quantifying the shift towards empirical methods', *International Journal of Corpus Linguistics*, 10: 15–36.
Saussure, Ferdinand de (1916) *Course in General Linguistics*, France. London: Peter Owen [Wade Baskin, trans.], (1960).
Schilpp, Paul (ed.) (1963) *The Philosophy of Rudolf Carnap*, La Salle, Illinois: Open Court.
Schlick, Moritz (1930) 'The turning point in philosophy', in A. J. Ayer (ed.) (1959): 53–9.
—— (1932) 'Positivism and realism', in A. J. Ayer (ed.) (1959): 82–107.
—— (1936) 'Meaning and verification', *The Philosophical Review*, 45: 339–69.
Sealey, Alison and Bob Carter (2004) *Applied Linguistics as Social Science*, London: Continuum.
Searle, John (1969) *Speech Acts*, Cambridge: Cambridge University Press.
—— (1975) 'Speech acts and recent linguistics', *Annals of the New York Academy of Science*, reprinted in John Searle (1979): 162–79.
—— (1978) 'Literal meaning', *Erkenntnis*, reprinted in John Searle (1979): 117–36.
—— (1979) *Expression and Meaning*, Cambridge: Cambridge University Press.
Sinclair, John (1991) *Corpus, Concordance, Collocation*, Oxford: Oxford University Press.
—— (2004) *Trust the Text*, London: Routledge.
Skjervheim, Hans (1982) 'Structuralism, Empiricism and Intentionalism', in Ingemund Gullvåg and Jon Wetlesen (eds): 129–46.
Smith, Barry (1987) 'Austrian origins of logical positivism', in Barry Gower (ed.): 35–68.
Sperber, Dan and Ira Noveck (2004) 'Introduction', in Ira Noveck and Dan Sperber (eds): 1–22.
Sperber, Dan and Deirdre Wilson (1995) *Relevance*, 2nd edn, Oxford: Blackwell [1st edn 1986].
Stadler, Friedrich (ed.) (1993) *Scientific Philosophy: Origins and Developments*, Dordrecht: Kluwer Academic Publishers.

Sterrett, Susan (2006) *Wittgenstein Flies a Kite*, New York: Pi Press.
Storheim, Eivind (1959) Review of Arne Naess *Wie fördert man heute die empirische Bewegung? Eine Auseinandersetzung mit dem Empirismus von Otto Neurath und Rudolph Carnap*, *Theoria*, XXV: 187–91.
Strawson, Peter (1950) 'On referring', *Mind*, 59: 320–44.
—— (1952) *Introduction to Logical Theory*, London: Methuen.
—— (1964) 'Intention and convention in speech acts', *Philosophical Review*, reprinted in K. T. Fann (ed.) (1969): 380–400.
—— (1998) 'Intellectual autobiography', in Lewis Edwin Hahn (ed.) *The Philosophy of P. F. Strawson*, Chicago and La Salle: Open Court.
Stubbs, Michael (2001) 'Text, corpora and the problems of interpretation: a response to Widdowson', *Applied Linguistics*, 22: 149–72.
—— (2006) 'Corpus analysis: the state of the art and three types of unanswered questions', in Geoffrey Thompson and Susan Hunston (eds) *System and Corpus: Exploring Connections*, London: Equinox: 15–36.
Summers, Della (1996) 'Computer lexicography: the importance of representativeness in relation to frequency', in Jenny Thomas and Mick Short (eds) *Using Corpora for Language Research*, London: Longman: 260–6.
Tarski, Alfred (1933) 'The concept of truth in formalized languages', Poland. Reprinted in Alfred Tarski (1956) *Logic, Semantics, Metamathematics*, Oxford: Clarendon Press: 152–78. [J. H. Woodger, trans.].
—— (1944) 'The semantic conception of truth and the foundations of semantics', *Philosophy and Phenomenological Research*, 4: 341–74.
Tennessen, Herman (1965) 'Ordinary language *in memoriam*', *Inquiry*, 8: 225–48.
Teubert, Wolfgang (2005) 'My version of corpus linguistics', *International Journal of Corpus Linguistics*, 10: 1–13.
Thompson, J. R. (2007) 'Still relevant: H. P. Grice's legacy in psycholinguistics and the philosophy of language', *Teorema*, XXVI: 77–109.
Thorndike, Edward and Irving Lorge (1944) *The Teacher's Word Book of 30,000 Words*, New York: Teachers College, Columbia University.
Tsohatzidis, Savas (ed.) (1994) *Foundations of Speech Act Theory*, London: Routledge.
Urmson, J. O. (1967) 'Austin's philosophy', in K. T. Fann (ed.) (1969): 22–32.
Urmson, J. O., W. V. O. Quine and Stuart Hampshire (1965) 'A symposium on Austin's method', 62nd annual meeting of the American Philosophical Association, Eastern Division, in K. T. Fann (ed.) (1969): 76–97.
Voegelin, C. F. and Zellig Harris (1951) 'Methods for determining intelligibility among dialects of natural languages', *Proceedings of the American Philosophical Society*, 95: 322–9.
Waismann, Friedrich (1945) 'Verifiability', *Proceedings of the Aristotelian Society Supplementary Volumes*, reprinted in Anthony Flew (ed.) (1953): 117–44.
Warnock, G. J. (1958) *English Philosophy since 1900*, London: Oxford University Press.
—— (1963) 'John Langshaw Austin, a biographical sketch', *Proceedings of the British Academy*, reprinted in K. T. Fann (ed.) (1969): 3–21.
—— (1973) 'Saturday mornings', in Isaiah Berlin (ed.) *Essays on J. L. Austin*, Oxford: Oxford University Press: 31–45.
—— (1989) *J. L. Austin*, London: Routledge.

White, Morton (1950) *John Dewey: Philosopher of Science and Freedom*, New York: The Dial Press.
Whitsitt, Sam (2005) 'A critique of the concept of semantic prosody', *International Journal of Corpus Linguistics*, 10: 283–305.
Widdowson, H. G. (2000) 'On the limitations of linguistics applied', *Applied Linguistics*, 21: 3–25.
Wittgenstein, Ludwig (1922) *Tractatus Logico-Philosophicus*, Germany. London: Routledge and Kegan Paul [trans. D. F. Pears and B. F. McGuinness], (1961).
Yourgrau, Palle (2005) *A World Without Time*, London: Allen Lane.

Index

adequacy, *see* Chomsky, Noam
analytic/synthetic distinction
  Austin on, 72–3, 75
  Grice and Strawson on, 85–6
  Kant on, 11–12, 14
  logical positivism and, 15, 51–2, 55, 139
  Naess on, 138–9, 172
  Quine on, 51–5, 57, 59, 72
Aristotle, 3, 21
Arnauld, Antoine and Claude Lancelot, 130
Austin, J. L., 1, 14, 48, 66
  and analytic sentences, 72–3
  attitude to ordinary language, 71, 74–6, 77, 82, 131
  criticisms of, 80–5, 87, 106, 143, 163, 169
  and the descriptive fallacy, 73–4, 91, 97
  How to Do Things with Words, 91–5
  philosophical method of, 3, 5, 69, 74, 76–8, 86, 92, 97, 109, 156, 169–70
  'A plea for excuses', 75–6, 77–8, 82, 85
  reaction to logical positivism 68–71, 88, 94, 167–8
  relevance to linguistics, 2, 5, 6, 69, 89, 153, 166–70
  response to Naess, 109, 144–5
  Sense and Sensibilia, 71–2
  'Truth', 73, 76
  see also speech acts; ordinary language philosophy; Naess, Arne (comparison with Austin).
Ayer, A. J., 8, 14, 15, 24, 28, 71, 109, 171
  Language, Truth and Logic, 10, 25–6, 69–70

Bach, Kent, 101, 104
behaviourism
  Naess and, 112
  Quine and, 58–9, 61–2
Berg, Jan, 150
Bergmann, Gustav, 26, 27
Berkeley, George, 7
Bernicot, Josie and Virginie Laval, 103
Bezuidenhout, Anne and J. Cooper Cutting, 104
Black, Max, 95
Blom, Siri, 141
Bloomfield, Leonard, 44–5
  response to logical positivism, 154–5
Blumberg, Albert and Herbert Feigl, 14
Borg, Emma, 104
Botha, Rudolf, 173
Brown, Penelope and Stephen Levinson, 162

Canfield, John and Keith Lehrer, 42
Cappelen, Herman and Ernest Lepore, 42, 104
Carnap, Rudolf, 15, 19–20, 23–4, 26, 30, 32–3, 35–6, 39, 73
  academic background, 9, 13
  relationship with Naess, 109, 111, 120–1, 138
  relationship with Quine, 49, 53
  views on language, 9, 18, 20, 53, 74, 99–100, 137
Carr, Philip, 159–60
Carston, Robyn, 104, 148
Cavell, Stanley, 81
Chapman, Siobhan, 68, 97, 160
Chierchia, Gennaro, 149
Chomsky, Noam,
  and adequacy, 65, 66
  debate with Quine, 5, 46–8, 62–6, 87
  and empiricism, 45–8, 63, 102
  and innateness, 45, 157
  and mentalism, 5

and methodology in linguistics, 44–8, 62–6, 106, 156–7
responses to, 157–60
Syntactic Structures, 45
and transformational-generative grammar, 45, 47, 66, 106, 152
and Universal Grammar, 65, 66
Clear, Jeremy, 169
Cobitz, J. L., 84
Coffa, José, 42
cognitive semantics, 150
Cohen, Jonathan, 95–6
collocation, *see* corpus linguistics
confirmation, principle of, *see* verification, principle of
Congress on Unified Science, 20, 113, 120–1, 122
conversation, theory of, 86, 97–101, 104, 106, 107
and conversational implicature, 5, 98, 147, 148
corpus linguistics, 6
collocation in, 168–9, 170
and data, 153, 165, 169
development of, 164–5
and methodology, 165–6
and philosophy, 3, 89, 109, 150, 166–72
relationship to mainstream linguistics, 170, 172–3
responses to, 172–3
semantic prosody in, 168–9, 170
correspondence theory, 21, 22, 113, 117
Coulthard, Malcolm, 155
Creath, Richard, 53
Crockett, Campbell, 141

Dascal, Marcelo, 94, 100
deductive method, 4, 40–1, 45–7, 63
definiteness of intention, *see* Naess, Arne
descriptive fallacy, *see* Austin, J. L.
discourse analysis, 155
disjunction, 111, 145–9
Drucker, H. M., 129
Dummett, Michael, 13, 56, 100

Edmonds, David and John Eidinow, 8
empirical semantics, 1, 108, 122, 123, 125, 126, 140, 150, 166
empiricism
of the Enlightenment, 3, 11
in linguistics, 5–6, 45–8, 66, 67, 81, 153, 156–60, 174
and ordinary language philosophy, 79, 80–1, 87, 89, 94, 107
and scientific method, 10, 38–42
social construction of, 6, 174
of the Vienna Circle, 10–12, 29, 50
Erkenntnis, 20, 23, 69
experimental pragmatics, 101, 103–4, 149

Fairclough, Norman, 66
falsifiability, criterion of, 4, 38–42
and linguistics, 4, 28–9, 103, 160, 165–6
problems for, 42–4
Fellbaum, Christiane, 165
Feyerabend, Paul, 44, 174
Firth, J. R., 160
Fishman, Joshua, 161
Flew, Anthony, 25
Fodor, Jerry, 80
and Ernie Lepore, 56–7
and Jerrold Katz, 80–1
Forster, Michael, 130
Frege, Gottlob, 7, 12–13, 52, 73
Fries, Charles, 164–5
Furberg, Mats, 96

Galison, Peter, 19
Gallup Poll, 113, 145
Gellner, Ernest, 81, 84, 94, 144, 169
Gibbon, Margaret, 66
Gibbs, Raymond, 103
Glucksberg, Sam, 103
Gödel, Kurt, 30
Goodman, Nelson, 52, 140
Graham, Keith, 83–4

Grice, Paul, 5, 70, 85–6
 on logic, 97–8, 147–8, 149
 and ordinary language philosophy, 7, 86, 89–90, 97, 99, 106, 145, 147
 William James lectures on 'Logic and Conversation', 98–100, 147
 see also conversation, theory of; neo- Gricean theory
Grimm, Laura, 138
Gullvåg, Ingemund, 123, 140

Haggstrom, Warren, 84
Hahn, Hans, 9, 18, 26, 30
Hampshire, Stuart, 79
Handley, Simon and Aidan Feeney, 102
Hare, R. M., 84
Harris, Roy, 162–4
Harris, Zellig, 155–6
 and C. F. Voegelin, 156
Hart, H. L. A., 84
Hempel, Carl, 37–8, 42, 55–6, 63, 136, 154
Henle, Paul, 84
Hintikka, Jakko, 17
Hirsch, Richard, 150–1
holistic account of knowledge, 32, 50–61
Holton, Gerald, 56
Honey, John, 66
Horn, Laurence, 99, 104, 148
Hume, David, 33
Hymes, Dell, 160, 161

implicature, *see* conversation, theory of
indeterminacy of translation, *see* Quine, W. V. O.
inductive method, 4, 33–8, 40, 49, 63, 136
 in linguistics, 45, 154, 165–6
Inquiry, 125
integrationism, 162–3
Isaacs, Nathan, 83
Itkonen, Esa, 102, 159

Kant, Immanuel, 11, 55
Katz, Jerrold, 97, 100, 106, 158–9
 and Jerry Fodor, 158
Kennedy, Graeme, 165

Korner, S., 84
Kraft, Victor, 8
Kuhn, Thomas, 42–4, 47–8, 54, 118, 174

Labov, William, 161–2, 172
Lakatos, Imre, 43
Lass, Roger, 158
Leech, Geoffrey, 66
Levinson, Stephen, 99, 104, 162
Lewis, C. I., 31
linguistics, 6–7, 149–51, 172–4
 Chomskyan, 4, 44–8, 66, 105–6, 150, 153–60, 173
 and data, 1, 6, 67, 126, 151, 153–66, 174
 and logical positivism, 1, 9–10, 152–3
 as a science, 4, 28–9, 44–5, 152–4, 156, 158–9, 166
 the subject matter of, 1, 6, 29, 153, 174
 see also cognitive semantics; corpus linguistics; discourse analysis; experimental pragmatics; integrationism; pragmatics; sociolinguistics
literal meaning, 5, 89, 90, 95–6, 98, 99, 102–4, 106–7, 171
Locke, John, 7, 11, 130
logic, 12–14, 16–17, 159
 and natural language, 9, 15–16, 99, 111, 145–6
 see also disjunction
logical positivism, 1, 14, 25–6, 27, 29, 49–50, 55, 68–9, 117, 139
 development of, 19
 and religion, 24
 see also verification, Vienna Circle
Louw, Bill, 168–9

Mates, Benson, 81, 100
 response to Naess, 124, 136, 142–3
mathematics, 9, 12–14, 29–30, 159
Mathewson, Lisa, 162
Maxwell, Grover and Herbert Feigl, 130–1
McCawley, James, 99

McEnery, Tony, 170, 172
  and Andrew Wilson, 165
McGee, Vann, 21
Mehta, Ved, 88
mentalism, *see* Chomsky, Noam
metaphor, 99, 103, 171
metaphysics, 16, 17, 19, 21, 23, 36
Meyer, Charles, 172–3
Miller, Alexander, 56
modernism, 19
Moore, G. E., 68, 134
  see also Russell, Bertrand (*Principia Mathematica*)
Moore, Jared, 119
Mundle, C. W. K., 81–2

Nagel, Ernest, 119
Naess, Arne, 1, 48, 66
  on the analyticity/synthetic distinction, 128, 138–9, 172
  attitude to natural language, 110, 127–8, 138
  comparison with Austin, 5, 108–9, 123, 138, 142–3, 151
  Communication and Argument, 136–9, 143
  criticisms of, 119–20, 136, 141, 144–5, 159, 163–4
  and deep ecology, 108, 109, 125, 171
  on definiteness of intention, 129, 132–3, 137, 140
  on 'democracy', 129, 135
  Interpretation and Preciseness, 127, 131–6, 138, 140, 141–2, 172
  life, 108–10, 120, 128–9
  on logic, 111, 146–7
  on precisation, 128, 130, 137, 138, 139
  relationship with Carnap, 111, 120–1, 138
  relevance to linguistics, 1, 6, 109, 126, 148–51, 153, 161, 166–7, 170–2
  response to logical positivism, 107, 111–12, 137, 139
  response to ordinary language philosophy, 143
  use of occurrence analysis by, 135–6, 142, 171
  use of questionnaires by, 109, 113, 115, 118, 119–20, 121, 122, 125, 126, 130, 132–3, 135–6, 141, 142–3, 146–7
  on synonymity, 122, 123–5, 128, 130–1, 140–1, 172
  "Truth" as Conceived by Those Who Are Not Professional Philosophers, 114–20, 138, 142
neo-Gricean theory, 104
Neurath, Otto, 9, 18, 21, 26–7, 31–3, 43, 50, 54, 111, 113, 118, 138, 174
New, C. G., 81
Newmeyer, Frederick, 154
Noveck, Ira, 103, 149
  and Dan Sperber, 101

ordinary language philosophy, 1, 7, 67, 131, 142, 145, 150, 169
  and Chomskyan linguistics, 157–8
  criticisms of, 80–5, 107, 143–4
  development of, 15, 68–71
  and general philosophy, 85–6
  and the slogan 'meaning is use', 94, 100–1
  see also Austin, J. L.; speech acts; conversation, theory of
Oslo school of philosophy, 2, 67, 107, 122, 125, 126, 141, 145
Oxford philosophy, *see* ordinary language philosophy

Penke, Martina and Anette Rosenbach, 173
performatives, *see* speech acts
Popper, Karl, 4, 28, 36, 49, 63–4, 109, 111, 113, 120
  cited by linguists, 46, 103, 158, 159, 160, 161, 166
  The Logic of Scientific Discovery, 38–42
  and the Vienna Circle, 38–9
pragmatics, 3
  and Chomskyan linguistics, 105–7
  and empiricism, 87, 90, 102–4
  and ordinary language philosophy, 5, 69, 89–90, 101, 152, 166
  see also experimental pragmatics

precisation, *see* Naess, Arne
protocol statements, 31–3, 50

Quine, W. V. O., 4–5, 48
  and analytic sentences, 51–5, 59, 72, 86
  debate with Chomsky, 5, 46–8, 62–6, 87, 125
  and holism, 50–61
  and indeterminacy of translation, 57–62, 65, 163
  relationship with Carnap, 49, 51–2, 54, 55
  response to Naess, 109, 125
  response to ordinary language philosophy, 82, 92, 169
  and scientific method, 63–6
  'Two dogmas of empiricism', 50–7
  and the Vienna Circle, 49, 51, 55–6, 63, 112
  see also behaviourism, synonymity

Radford, Andrew, 47
realism, 17–18, 31
Recanati, François, 105
Reichenbach, Hans, 20
relevance theory, 104, 148, 149
Ringen, Jon, 159
Rogers, Ben, 26
Russell, Bertrand, 14, 15–16, 17–18, 34–5, 74, 130
  attitude to ordinary language philosophy, 75–6, 83, 84–5
  Principia Mathematica (with Alfred Whitehead), 2, 12, 13–14, 16, 30, 73
Ryle, Gilbert, 2, 3, 25, 68, 84–5

Sampson, Geoffrey, 164, 165–5
Saussure, Ferdinand de, 153
Schlick, Moritz, 8, 14, 15, 18, 20, 23, 24, 25, 26, 33, 36, 39, 50
scientific paradigms, *see* Kuhn, Thomas
Sealey, Alison and Bob Carter, 173
Searle, John, 96, 100, 101–2, 104–5, 106
semantic prosody, *see* corpus linguistics

sense data, 17, 31, 70–1, 75
Sextus Empiricus, 130
Sinclair, John, 165, 166, 168, 169
Skjervheim, Hans, 149–50
Smith, Barry, 8, 24
sociolinguistics, 1, 3, 6, 109, 150, 153, 160–2, 166
sociology, 9, 31–2, 84, 112, 114, 118, 160
speech acts, 2, 5, 69, 86, 101, 106, 107
  development of the theory of, 89, 90–1
  and illocution, 93, 94–6, 169
  and locution, 93, 94–6, 104, 106
  and performatives, 91–2
  and perlocution, 93, 94
  primary and secondary, 96
  reactions to the theory of, 94–6, 103
Sperber, Dan and Deidre Wilson, 104, 148
  see also relevance theory
Sterrett, Susan, 16
Storheim, Eivind, 111–12
Strawson, P. F., 7, 70, 85–6, 95, 145–6
Stubbs, Michael, 165, 167, 169, 170
Summers, Della, 169
synonymity
  in corpus linguistics, 172
  Grice and Strawson on, 86
  Naess on, 122, 123–5, 130–1, 136, 140–1
  Quine on, 52, 56–7, 59, 124–5, 140

Tarski, Alfred, 20–3, 52, 73, 113
  response to Naess, 109, 121–2
Tennessen, Herman, 84
Teubert, Wolfgang, 172
Thompson, J. R., 105
Thorndike, Edward and Irving Lorge, 164
The Times, 74, 84–5
transformational-generative grammar, *see* Chomsky, Noam

UNESCO, 129
Universal Grammar, *see* Chomsky, Noam
Urmson, J. O., 78–9, 88–9, 144, 157, 169–70

verification, principle of, 3, 10, 15, 23, 26, 28, 31, 51
　replaced by confirmation, principle of, 35–8, 136
Vienna, 8, 15, 19, 24, 26
Vienna Circle, 1, 3, 14–15, 17, 20–4, 110–11
　history of, 8–9, 26–7
　manifesto of, 7, 18–19
　responses to, 2, 3–4, 25, 27, 28–39, 49, 50, 152, 154–5
　see also logical positivism; verification, principle of

Waismann, Friedrich, 9, 15, 26, 42
Warnock, Geoffrey, 79, 88, 144–5
White, Morton, 52, 55
Whitsitt, Sam, 170
Widdowson, H. G., 173
Wittgenstein, Ludwig, 14, 36
　later work, 15, 68, 101, 130, 167
　Tractatus Logico-Philosophicus, 15–18, 21, 34

Yourgrau, Palle, 30